ECONOMICS
from the Heart

Paul Samuelson

ECONOMICS
from the Heart
A SAMUELSON SAMPLER

Edited and with Introductory Remarks
and Notes by Maryann O. Keating

HARCOURT BRACE JOVANOVICH, PUBLISHERS
San Diego   New York   London

Newsweek columns copyright Newsweek, Inc., 1967, 1968, 1969, 1971, 1972, 1973,
1974, 1975, 1976, 1977, 1978, 1979, 1980, 1981. Reprinted with permission.

Library of Congress Cataloging in Publication **Data**
Samuelson, Paul Anthony, 1915–
Economics from the heart.
1. Economics—Addresses, essays, lectures.
I. Keating, Maryann O. II. Title.
HB171.S259 1983   330   82-23318
ISBN 0-15-627551-1 (pbk.)

Designed by Nancy Dale Muldoon

Printed in the United States of America

B C D E F G H I J

CONTENTS

PREFACE

WHEN Thomas Horton proposed to publish companion volumes containing the economic columns of Professor Milton Friedman and of mine, I had to agree that this might serve a useful educational purpose. Professor Friedman is an able scholar and a forceful spokesman for the libertarian form of conservative economics. He is also an old friend. Yet my liberal mind is not persuaded by a considerable number of conservative arguments. And I had to agree that learners of economics of all political leanings—right, center, left and new left—might be expected to get a better-rounded view of the debate if exposed to more than one of its sides.

Still, I hesitated to agree to this publication. These analyses of the passing economic scene were *deliberately* written so as not to present a debater's view. Conversion of the reader was furthest from my mind. Instead of trying to press reality into the distorting confines of simple sermons, I wanted to bring out the interesting variety of economic problems.

I've never believed in Economics in One Lesson. And that is why I hesitated. But in the end I acquiesced. With this proviso—no afterthoughts, no prettying up forecasts after the fact, no tampering with commas. Indeed, the publisher agreed to take full responsibility in choosing which of my many contemporary writings to include in the present volume. I take responsibility for the birth of these brain children, but not for their reincarnation in present form.

Economics used to be a dry subject that told you what you couldn't do. From a scholar's viewpoint that was never very good political economy in the first place. Readers of this generation are luckier than we used to be in my time. *You* can go beyond the quantity of economic life to its quality—beyond gross national product to net economic welfare. You can examine unflinchingly the flaws in the system as well as its merits. You can discover where conventional wisdoms need to be junked and, best of all, where new research can add to our knowledge.

I hope these writings add to your interest and enjoyment in political economy.

Paul A. Samuelson
Massachusetts Institute of Technology

INTRODUCTORY REMARKS

PAUL A. Samuelson, one of the world's most respected economists, is Institute Professor of Economics at Massachusetts Institute of Technology. Early in his career he wrote *Foundations of Economic Analysis,* which uses the power of mathematics to focus and refine economic understanding. *Economics,* written by Samuelson and now in its eleventh edition, is the most successful and influential economics text of our time. In 1970, he received the Nobel Prize in Economics for his contribution to theory. In addition, for fifteen years he wrote a regular column for *Newsweek.* Approximately half of those columns are reproduced in their entirety is this selection.

In each of these articles, it is as if the reader were taking a short walk with Samuelson. Sometimes the pace is brisk, and at other times merely a stroll. Sometimes the reader is led around the block so quickly that he or she is breathless or confused at having re-entered through another door.

Besides encouraging the publisher to produce this Samuelson sampler, my role in selecting and introducing the articles has been an exercise in sympathy with the author, discrimination and moral and cultural reflection. The true owners of these works are the public, which will appropriate them for its own use. I urge each reader to take advantage of and profit from Samuelson's wisdom.

Maryann O. Keating
South Bend, Indiana

ECONOMICS
from the Heart

Chapter 1

REALISTIC HOPES CONCERNING ECONOMICS AND DEMOCRACY

HOW is Samuelson different from all other economists? How does he think economists should approach their subject matter? What, according to Samuelson, is the appropriate economic role of government? What are the limitations of economic analysis? How are human beings motivated? This selection of readings, written between 1969 and 1981, provides clues to Samuelson's thinking with respect to these significant economic problems.

Nowhere in these articles does Samuelson reject the notion of the rational self-interested individual. However, he seems to be reminding himself, his colleagues and readers that, at times, human beings act in a different fashion. He allows for a modicum of reciprocal altruism as well as a social contract. Furthermore, he rejects economic determinism. He sees no economic gain underlying all sociological, governmental and religious behavior.

Production trends, relative shares of profits and wages, inflation and per capita living standards are the appropriate concerns of the economist.

According to Samuelson, there is a randomness to the economic system; one does not always receive what one contributes. Some individuals and groups are lucky, and others are not. Given that reductions in inequality of condition and opportunity necessitate government involvement in the economy, Samuelson emphasizes the need for efficient rather than limited government. He considers himself to be a liberal, defined as one concerned with improvements in living standards and reductions in inequality.

Unlike many economists, Samuelson accepts the fact that in a democracy, public choice, rather than theory or ideology, will determine economic policy. It might even be correct to say that he values above all a free democratic society, but at the same time never doubts market efficiency. He understands the political risk of the affluent minority in a democratic society, but suggests that they are well compensated. Besides, the mobility of the rich enables them to cut their losses. Unfortunately, according to Samuelson, Reagan's federalism will encourage the rich to vote with their feet, resulting in geographical separation of rich and poor. However, the disproportionate influence of the rich in a democracy is mitigated somewhat by the persuasive power of intellectuals who argue in favor of reason, merit, equality and justice.

American political parties are oriented according to religion, race, region, class and, to a large extent, economic interest. But the middle classes are shiftable, and neither political party has a monopoly on American ideology. Samuelson is unabashedly in favor of a mixed system using both the market and government to solve economic problems. He tirelessly cautions politicians that the center way may be the hard way but that it is the only way. No matter how well intentioned, extremist economic policy is inimical to democracy and, hence, to politicians.

Continuity within change or gradualist shifts as needed to the left or right characterize Samuelson's policy proposals. The clock cannot and should not be turned back. In other words, it is necessary to accept changes, however personally undesirable, that result from majority rule in a constitutional framework. Furthermore, the passage of time determines changes over which a particular society may exercise little control. The relative economic and, hence, political position of the United States has changed since World War II, and policy must take this into consideration.

A one-to-one correspondence between economic well-being and political stability does not prevail. Progress does not silence discontent. Samuelson, throughout these articles, fears political instability in the face of economic downturn. Rather than a concern with too much government, the fragility of democracy is contrasted with anarchy and authoritarianism. The strength of the market is never doubted.

CHRISTMAS ECONOMICS
December 30, 1974

"THERE is no free lunch." How often we hear that tired substitute for thought, that fractional truth which is a fractional untruth.

My whole life has been one long free lunch—and not just in the first year of life. I have always been overpaid to do that which I would pay to do. But I am simply one of the lucky ones, you say? That's precisely my point.

Our virtues, like our faults, are in the stars we never made. We see it in every family: one child has dyslexia, another total recall; one is born, as William James put it, with a bottle of champagne to his credit, another chronically owing a night's sleep. What, after all, did the sister of Helen of Troy look like? All such gifts are the gifts of the gods.

So it is with nations. A 5-foot-10 American citizen with a certified IQ of 101 is paid eight times what his fellow man in Central America gets. He is paid one and a half times as much as his fellow person in the United States even if she has one-third more IQ. He is paid three times the real income of that great-grandfather who boasted of the same 101 IQ and had to work much harder.

Notice that I speak of what one gets "paid," not of what one "earns." Economists, from Madame Pompadour's medical counselor to last June's newly minted Ph.D., have always realized that there is only the most tenuous connection between rewards and deservingness. When Queen Victoria offered Lord Melbourne the Order of the Garter, he said, "What I like about the Order of the Garter is that there is no damned merit about it." A sheik's son on his way to Monte Carlo could say as much.

Community

I have quoted in many editions of my economics textbook wise words of Britain's greatest sociologist (and I mean L. T. Hobhouse and not Herbert Spencer!) to summarize all this:

"The organizer of industry who thinks he has 'made' himself and his business has found a whole social system ready to his hand in skilled workers, machinery, a market, peace and order—a vast apparatus and a pervasive atmosphere, the joint creation of millions of men and scores of generations. Take away the whole social factor and we have not Robinson Crusoe, with his salvage from the wreck and his acquired knowledge, but the native savage living on roots, berries and vermin."

Or, as a native sage has put it:

"Carry the notion of the individual to its limit and you get a monstrosity . . . not Nietzsche's superman, but Wolf Boy."

What has this to do with economics? Just this. Altruism, like vintage burgundy, you might think, is a luxury that can be afforded only by the affluent. And when we reflect on the evolutionary process of natural selection, we can understand why the preference a mother gives to her own infant might have survival value and therefore have survived. But by the same logic we realize that altruistic mother love, like concern to be a good neighbor, also has survival value and is part of nature's grand design.

We, Inc.

Modern industrial societies typically devote a larger fraction of their total resources to government than do subsistence economies. Democracy is the greatest system of mutual reinsurance ever invented. When we see a friend in the line for unemployment compensation, we each say, "There but for the grace of supply and demand go I."

Justice Oliver Wendell Holmes laid down the doctrine "Taxes are what we pay for civilized society." Although he was the one who also said, "Life is painting a picture, not doing a sum," I believe his political arithmetic cannot be faulted. In the case of Justice Holmes this was more than high-sounding rhetoric. For, like the Athenians of old, he left his not inconsiderable estate to the United States people.

When the husband in O. Henry's story pawned his gold watch to buy the tortoise-shell set to comb the beautiful tresses the wife had sacrificed to buy him a watch chain, that was indeed a splendid Christmas Day. But 364 additional such days each year would be too much. Just because government expenditures stem from the highest human motive is no reason for them to be undertaken unadvisedly—or inefficiently. Governments, like Casanova, too often never know when to stop.

Still, we are told, of faith, hope and charity, the greatest of these is charity. And the wisest translate the word as love.

SOCIAL DARWINISM

July 7, 1975

AMERICAN business ideology at the turn of the century embraced a crude notion that might makes right. The fittest survive, and *should* survive. For every survivor, there must be a dozen perishers. But they also serve who only perish, just as they also serve who are the anvil against which the hardest metal is formed.

Fruits of this vulgar Social Darwinism (or, more accurately, Social Spencerism) were such dicta as:

• "The public be damned" (attributed to William Vanderbilt).

- "The poverty of the incapable . . . starvation of the idle and those shoulderings aside of the weak by the strong . . . are the decrees of a large, far-seeing benevolence" (Herbert Spencer).
- The "formula of most schemes of humanitarianism is this: A and B put their heads together to decide what C shall be made to do for D. I call C the Forgotten Man" (William Graham Sumner, decidedly not FDR).
- ". . . the laboring man will be protected and cared for not by the labor agitators, but by the Christian men to whom God in his infinite wisdom has given the control of the property interests of the country . . ." (George F. Baer).

This ideology did not meet its own first test—survival. How could it be sold to the majority of the electorate, since it was they who were billed as patsies in its scenario?

Sociobiology

A new and, I think, more interesting version of Social Darwinism is now being floated. I refer to the attempt to understand the changing behavior and structure of various groups from the standpoint of *selection*. A subject called sociobiology exists by virtue of the Cartesian syllogism "I have a textbook written about me, therefore I am a discipline." The textbook is the handsome new work of Edward O. Wilson, Harvard's authority on insects. I predict it will earn esteem.

The old Social Darwinism had regarded altruism as dysgenic: thus, Josephine Shaw Lowell advised charity givers never to give a basket of food that would last *more than one day* lest they encourage poverty. Not so with the new Social Darwinism, which has rediscovered Prince Kropotkin's *survival value of reciprocal altruism.* According to this, an ant colony could do worse than follow the precepts of Jesus. The sterile ant soldiers, who mobilize to protect the fecund queen, are really acting to perpetuate the genes of their corporation! And so with a mother who starves herself that her child may live and reproduce her genes. Or with a hero who dies in Flanders or Vietnam so that the American stock can multiply.

Survival

As an economist I've long found heuristic worth in Darwin's concept of survival value. I bet on the corporation with quixotic pricing to go to the wall. And if a new energy source is likely to prove viable, e.g., solar or wind, I seek signs that it is making its way in the competitive market.

But economics is a rather safe area. I foresee greater problems for the sociobiologists when they try to tackle problems of race and sex. How do you keep distinct a Shockley from a Wilson? A Hitler from a Huxley?

Consider woman's role. What will happen to a sociobiologist who speculates that women have been bred by the struggle for existence to be immobile in order to better take care of the young?

Or examine the following argument that wishes to be taken seriously. (A) Homosexuality may be *genetically* inheritable in some degree. (B) Homosexuals tend to have fewer offspring. (C) To explain why genes for homosexuality persist, the ingenious sociobiologist may venture the following hypothesis: (D) Homosexuals are well suited to perform certain social roles, and (E) they perhaps are thereby enabled to favor their own nephews, nieces and siblings. Ergo, (F) reciprocal altruism and natural selection solve the puzzle.

Re-examine the above paragraph. Is it not calculated to maximize social controversy? Every link in the syllogism's chain is problematic and provocative. Do the data on twins establish heritability of homosexuality? Do gay people favor kin? Etc., etc. All that we have, or can have, is a mass of speculation, a collection of inconclusive anecdotes designed to touch off social resentments and controversy.

To survive in the jungle of intellectuals, the sociobiologist had best tread softly in the zones of race and sex.

LOVE

December 29, 1969

AN economist writing on love? Next thing you know, plumbers will be penning sonnets on beauty.

Of course, I am speaking of love not in the Greek sense of *eros*, but rather of *agape* (which Webster's Third defines as "spontaneous self-giving love expressed freely without calculation of cost or gain to the giver or merit on the part of the receiver"). But I am not sure that these two can be completely—ahem—divorced: perhaps Soames Forsyte's troubles in bed were not unrelated to his overweening sense of property.

If the first seven editions of my introductory text on economics managed to omit "love" from the index, why cannot the eighth let well enough alone? It is not really that I have suddenly gone soft in the head. Rather it is a case of having, belatedly, come clear in the head: to explain the scientific facts that are out there to be explained, had love never existed we should have had to invent it.

Clearly I contradict what, at the University of Chicago, I was taught was the first and only law of economics: "There is no such thing as a free lunch."

Milk

No free lunch? What nonsense. That is a scientific law with only 4 billion exceptions. If it were true, no member of the human species would survive for even a week!

Freud claimed character is formed in the early years of life. (As father of six I digress to ask why, in that case, the world is not more clearly divided into the hard and easy teethers.) If Freud is right, we were all developed under communism.

For, as Prof. Lyle Owen of the University of Tulsa points out, family life itself is a form of communism with a small *c.* In the home the doctrine prevails, "From each according to his abilities, to each according to his needs." The good parent does not say, "Because Tiny Tim is lame, he shall get the wing. The go-getters may compete for the drumstick."

It is only when we turn ten that Freud's reality principle breaks in, and we are taught in school the parable of Capt. John Smith's Virginia Colony—that he who does not work shall not eat. That simple lesson carries more weight with congressmen than all the proofs of another Smith on the optimality of competitive pricing.

And actually it was at Forsyte's London club that Samuel Butler was heard to say: "The world will always be governed by self-interest. We should not try to stop this; we should try to make the self-interest of cads a little more coincident with that of decent people."

The same point was made more professionally by the late Sir Dennis Robertson of Trinity College, Cambridge. At Columbia's 200th anniversary, he asked, "What is it that economists economize?" *Love,* was his surprising answer. Love is so precious because there is so little of it in the world. And that is why we must make what we do have go a long, long way.

Mammon

The moral is to render unto the market that which the market can handle. Except in time of siege do not squander patriotism and agape on the allocating of beefsteak.

Hard-boiled game theory teaches that Macy's can serve as a check on Gimbels. If G quotes its price above the competitive margin, M will gain by undercutting. And vice versa. In the end of this special game, the consumer gains from the canceling avarice of market competitors.

But game theory also teaches "Prisoner's Dilemma." In this parable, the district attorney approaches each of two prisoners separately, saying: "Whether you confess, I have the evidence to send you both to jail for one year. If you *both* confess, I'll settle for a five-year sentence each. But if *you alone* confess, giving me the evidence to convict your pal, I'll get him a ten-year sentence and let you off with a three-month term."

Reflection yields the solution: "Universal selfishness would make each confess, giving both of them five-year terms. Only love can achieve the best common state of one year when neither tries to gain by telling on the other." Q.E.D.

Another Captain Smith fairy tale? No. Substitute "non-pollute" for "non-confess" and you realize why a 1970 economic treatise has need for love and for common rules of the road that we coercively enforce on ourselves.

The truths of economics cannot be captured in even a hundred laws. But somewhere on the sacred tablets this truth is written: do not render unto the market that which is not the market's.

ADAM SMITH

March 15, 1976

I T is not easy for a person named Smith, Brown or Green to attain undying fame. Still, Giuseppe Verdi has been rising in reputation these last 75 years. And the Scottish botanist, Robert Brown, peering into his microscope, recorded the *perpetuum mobile* of dancing colloidal particles that we call *Brownian motion* and that provided the young Einstein with the first solid proof of the reality of atoms and molecules.

Within the field of economics, a chap named Smith made good. Indeed, it can be said that he made the field of economics. He is its veritable George Washington, its father. He is even its Thomas Jefferson, Benjamin Franklin and Sir Isaac Newton. He was well named Adam.

This week, on March 9, we celebrate the 200th anniversary of *The Wealth of Nations*. Political economy has made more progress since 1876 than in the previous 99 years. But Adam Smith is still a living force. It is his discipline we study, and hope to improve on.

Spirit of the Times

The clichés about Adam Smith turn out on reflection to be largely true. His importance in the history of ideas stems from the fact that he lived at a time when the feudal order, with its multifarious interferences by government in economic life, was passing away; and when a new commercial and manufacturing era was being born. Along with all the other bicentennials being celebrated in this decade, we must not forget the bicentennial of the Industrial Revolution itself.

The economic doctrines of Adam Smith were, in part, a reflection of this *zeitgeist*. But Smith was also a creative thinker in his own right, and it was his formulations of economic theory that helped to shape the new bourgeois order.

Modern advanced treatises on economics bristle with mathematical equations and statistical regressions. Their findings affect statesmen and public opinion only after a trickle-down process.

Not so with *The Wealth of Nations*. It is an attractive chronicle, replete with sage observations and telling historical facts. It can be read. It was widely read. No educated person could not know it, and the development of parliamentary legislation and public opinion cannot be understood without taking into account its influence.

What is pleasing to the million is usually not caviar to the general. Smith is an exception in that he is as important to economists as he is to the public. David Ricardo, a self-made broker, came to the study of economics from a critical reading of *The Wealth of Nations.* Karl Marx devotes much ink to commentary on Smith, owing to him stimulus on the general subject of modern "alienation" under a regime of extreme division of labor.

In-Season Wisdom

As much as Smith is appreciated, I believe him still to be somewhat underrated by professional economics. In Smith, by virtue of the very eclecticism that bores shallow minds, are the roots of the modern theories of general equilibrium. He abandoned a simple and dogmatic labor theory of value to decompose price into its separate wage, interest and profit and land-rent components because the brute facts required him to do so.

There is more to be learned about the laws of motion of capitalism from *The Wealth of Nations* than from *Das Kapital*—namely, the rising trend of real wages these last two centuries; the meanderings of the rate of profit as the net resultant of technical inventions and capital accumulation.

It is fitting, on this festive occasion, to quote from the birthday child:

• It is not from the benevolence of the butcher, the brewer or the baker that we expect our dinner, but from their regard to their self-interest.

• Every individual endeavors to employ his capital so that its produce may be of greatest value. He generally neither intends to promote the public interest, nor knows how much he is promoting it. He intends only his own security, only his own gain. And he is in this led by an *invisible hand* to promote an end which was no part of his intention. By pursuing his own interest he frequently promotes that of society more effectually than when he really intends to promote it.

To know the truth—and the limitations!—of these passages is the *ultima Thule* of economic wisdom.

The Economic Role of Government

SCOREBOARD FOR LIBERALS
June 19, 1978

IF you measure results by elections lost and won, by referenda on tax limitations or bond refusals, a case can be made that we live in a period of reaction.

Sweden, Australia and New Zealand are examples where labor governments have been defeated at the polls. Recently, California voters opted decisively for severe constitutional limitations on the property tax. The progress in Congress of genuine tax reform does not look promising.

My own concern is with improvements in living standards, not with expansion in bureaucrats' power. Reductions in inequality of condition and opportunity matter more than fulfillment of five-year plans or realization of programs for social reconstruction.

From the standpoint of the things that really matter to men of goodwill the picture appears to be a reasonably cheerful one—not all blue skies and sunshine but definitely not a regression to stormy clouds.

Bright Spots

I have been receiving for a dozen years an annual State Department review of what has been happening to world real incomes. These estimates of planetary product, totals and breakdowns by regions and countries, are prepared by Dr. Herbert Block: the story they tell contradicts the headlines and much of the chatter one hears at cocktail parties.

1. Real incomes continued to grow in the 1970s at about a 4 per cent annual rate: generally in excess of population growth, and at a pace considerably better than at the turn of the century when capitalism was allegedly at its high noon.

2. OPEC sheikdoms aside, the developing nations have been growing as well in the mid-1970s as the most affluent nations. The "widening percentage gap" between the former and the latter has not in fact been characteristic of recent times.

3. Comparing rates of progress in the socialist countries of Eastern Europe and Asia with rates elsewhere reveals no need for humanity to sacrifice its freedoms in order to achieve a better loaf of bread or a longer expectancy of life. The U.S.S.R., if anything, shows disappointing technical change and net capital formation; when mainland China passes out of its virtual subsistence stage of development, no one can foretell whether it will be able to do better or worse than Germany, Japan and North America did at such early stages of development. Mixed economies like Austria, Belgium, Israel, Singapore, South Korea—to say nothing of Taiwan and Thailand—have set a record of accomplishment that planned regimes will not find it easy to surpass.

Here at Home

The record shows that within the United States much has been accomplished since the Kennedy-Johnson first attacks on poverty and discrimination. The respected National Bureau of Economic Research has just published a symposium volume, *The Distribution of Economic Well-Being.* The story it tells is, by and large, a heartening one. Here are only a few of its highlights.

Black Americans have been making genuine progress this last decade, although to be sure there are still earning and opportunity differentials that need to be diminished. At first it was black women who seemed to register relative improvements; after 1965, black men also achieved relative gains;

minority youths have yet to get their turn. I find it hopeful that many of these gains have taken place in the South itself.

Just as an enhanced supply of college graduates has undermined their earning and prestige differentials, the explosion of the female labor force at first tended to erode women's wage rates relative to men's. However, there have been appearing some signs since 1965 that sex discrimination may be abating in virulence.

As white males advance in age, their earnings and perquisites continue to rise. Too often, on the other hand, nonwhites and women reach peak earnings by age 30. A nearer approach to parity will be reached when all categories of labor qualify for promotion and raises with experience and age.

Economic historians will look back with amazement from the next century at the slowness of the liberation and antidiscrimination process. As an economist, I must emphasize this: such slow improvements as have taken place did not just happen out of the spontaneous workings of the laissez-faire marketplace alone. New laws and customs played an important role.

There is still work for liberals to do—hard but rewarding work.

NEW YORK DILEMMA

November 10, 1975

THIS is a hard column to write. How easy it would be if one were simpleminded and could baldly assert: "Let New York go down the drain. It couldn't happen to a nicer bunch of fellows anyway. Bankruptcy not only will teach a lesson, punish the guilty and deter those tempted in the future, but it will also be the first step on the road back to fiscal probity."

Likewise, it would be an easy position to hold if one could believe with conviction: "The federal government should take responsibility for the city's present plight. After all, *the crisis has national, not local, causes.* Any Puerto Rican or Southerner can freely move into the city. Any well-heeled person can freely move out to the suburbs, thereby avoiding his share of the irreducible fiscal burden of the less fortunate who are left in the city. Only the federal government has the powers of the purse to take care of the intolerable load now being put on the city and the state . . ."

Neither of these positions is tenable for an intelligent person of goodwill. But where in the wide middle ground between them is the feasible optimum for policy to be found? Here are some tentative economic considerations that may help set bounds on possible policy alternatives.

After Doomsday

Begin by realizing that bankruptcy and default are not unthinkable. Given President Ford's stand, we should figure them to be probable.

But bankruptcy does not begin to solve the problem. It is naïve to think that putting matters into the hands of a judge, or a panel of judges, is tantamount to introducing rationality and austerity into the future handling of New York finances. These days we are straining to a dangerous degree the institution of the judiciary. Just as Congress could not enforce Prohibition, Boston and Louisville judges, for all their sacred black robes, are meeting with real resistance in the area of school integration.

Andrew Jackson, in an unpleasant confrontation with the Supreme Court, said: "John Marshall has made his decision; now let him enforce it." That will be a bad day when, Gandhi-like or IRA-like, the citizenry simply refuses to obey orders of the court.

Default can be a sobering influence at the bargaining table

with public servants: policemen, fire fighters, teachers, sanitation workers. Still, the whole history of unionism has been a history in which unions wield their most specific influence in *determining how industries in decline are accelerated toward their extinction.* Cases in point are the glass blowers, the railroad and mine workers and the Northern textile workers.

Calvin Coolidge reached the White House by being tough with striking policemen. However, with the step-up of violence since 1919, this is not a safe political gambit for one bucking for re-election. Swiss roulette—playing with avalanches—may be more fun than Russian roulette; but both are dangerous, and may become dangerous to innocent bystanders.

I have seen no careful analysis of how much of New York's problem is related to intransigence and inefficiency among its civil-service employees. How much total wage costs can be brought down, in comparison with those in Chicago and Boston, may be known to Secretary Simon and other advocates of a tough policy; but I have seen no cogent discussion of this crucial issue.

The streets of New York cannot be allowed to go the way of the streets of Belfast and Beirut. One way or another, rapproachement will be necessary with those who guard order and provide minimum services.

Before Nirvana

It is too late to say that New York's difficulties must be contained at the Hudson. Already municipal borrowing costs are up everywhere.

Large banks stuck with much city paper may well have their stockholders suffer. Their executives proved to have been particularly negligent or culpable can be made to walk the plank. But it is unthinkable that bank depositors should lose their money. Failure of one or more large banks would be intolerable, with domino effects felt nationally.

Before the full story is told, the federal government will find itself heavily involved in guarantees. Someday we may all read in the history books that William Simon turned out to be one of our most expensive secretaries of the Treasury, in a class with Andrew Mellon.

REPUBLICAN GAME PLANS

February 16, 1981

WILL Rogers used to say: "All I know is what I read in the newspapers."

That won't get you far if you're trying to make sense of what the Reagan program in economics is going to be. Devour the *New York Times* and *Wall Street Journal* and you are still left without a clue as to whether the Reagan deficit will exceed what Carter would have had, and whether inflation will get better or worse in 1981.

John Maynard Keynes used to insist that there are two opinions: public opinion and insider opinion. Maybe so for the Edwardian London society. But as foreign spies have ruefully learned, it is an illusion to think that hidden under the veil of official secrecy there is in Washington a coherent plan that Congress and the Administration will be acting on.

Still, to try to narrow the odds, I decided I'd better get inside the Washington black box. Attending meetings of academic consultants, gossiping with residents of conservative and liberal think tanks, talking with some of the new economic team and checking with staff members of the many Congressional committees, I located no Deep Throat with the definitive game plan. But I found the safari rewarding in clarifying some of the probabilities.

Surface Dreams

Like Freud, begin with conscious desires. Then if the reality principle dictates that these are not all feasible, examine the conscious and unconscious compromises that the conservative elite are prepared to fall back on.

· Ronald Reagan wants to end inflation.

· He aims to balance the budget.

· He believes we need stronger defense.

· The octopus of government has been expanding, limiting the sphere of private liberty and market autonomy. This growth trend must end, and be reversed.

· Taxes must be brought down to spur incentives for capital formation and greater productivity. The pendulum of redistributive taxing has swung too far, and simple fairness requires that the middle classes be allowed to keep a larger share of what they've earned.

Whatever my value judgments make of these goals, they are *economically* feasible. If the voters and the Congress backed up the President, he could cut tens of billions of dollars of nondefense expenditure programs. That would leave room to cut taxes by almost as much. The result could be some reduction in the degree of inflationary pressure, as resources are released from the public sector to the private and as the deficit is limited by spending cuts that match overall tax cuts.

No one I met conceded this scenario to be *politically* feasible this year. Cheese paring won't achieve it. Some big programs would have to be hit hard.

Many argued: cut tax rates now while the President enjoys novelty and conservatism is popular.

"Surely tax cuts greatly in excess of achieved spending cuts will swell the deficit, adding to inflationary pressure and forcing the Fed to be that much tighter in its interest rates and money-growth targets," I tritely observed.

"Not if there is a supply-side miracle," someone responded. "If that occurs, lower tax rates will bring in even higher tax receipts and the deficit will diminish."

Hard-headed Republicans would not run their own private businesses on the basis of such hoped-for miracles. What I encountered was little genuine belief in Laffer-curve miracles. It is expedient to reserve judgment on that issue, so that one can continue to dangle out hope to help sell the program of tax cuts now.

Underlying Realities

The most Machiavellian of my informants helped me make sense of the inconsistent components of the fiscal program.

"The future is longer than the present. Better to risk a little more inflation now if that's the necessary price of bringing down taxes. Then in the 1982 election coming up, we can pin fairly on the Congress *their* responsibility for worsening inflation because of *their* flagrant refusal to eliminate the deficit by *cutting expenditures.* With stronger Republican control of both houses of Congress, and with the remaining Democrats chastened by the electorate, we can then achieve our full program in all its economic feasibility."

To a conservative, this is a no-lose deal. If productivity and capital formation pick up, fine. Even if they do not, you have scaled down the scope of government. If some poor people get hurt, who said life is fair?

INTELLECTUALS

February 23, 1976

BILLY Graham's book on angels sold well, one presumes primarily to non-angels. Intellectuals have a propensity to write books that are read only by intellectuals and therefore do not sell so well. This despite the propensity of intellectuals to read books. That is all intellectuals are good for: to read, write and talk about books and ideas.

The complaint has been made that although each intellectual has at most one nose, intellectuals as a group have an influence on the climate of opinion disproportionate to their numbers. The indictment is a just one.

In this respect intellectuals are like plutocrats, each of whom also has but one nose. Still, because money talks and can command a hearing, those with economic interests must tend to exert a disproportionate influence in a democracy. All that the majority have to wield in self-defense is their preponderance of noses and of votes under universal suffrage.

The balance in favor of plutocracy would be the greater were it not for the fact of involuntary servitude of the young in school and college. When people are at their most impressionable ages, they are at the mercy of intellectuals—from whose clutches a few never escape.

High-school students read Galbraith; some are even *made* to read him. Then at college dangerous doctrines like those in the Samuelson textbook are assigned for reading; in addition, your chance of getting a good job at Sullivan & Cromwell may even depend on how faithfully you regurgitate their contents on quizzes. Since, as some sages observe, you can't touch pitch without getting mired, is it any wonder that departures from the sound doctrines that made this republic great are so frequent and so flagrant?

Pesky Conscience

Intellectuals, let us face it, are a nuisance to have around. They set themselves up to be the conscience of the community. Instead of following a rule of reason—which the court pragmatically interprets to mean that sometimes one must go along to get along—intellectuals let reason dominate and buffalo them. And they wish to apply its lash to us as well.

Vilfredo Pareto, a pointy headed intellectual if there ever was one, hated intellectuals and regarded them as undermining the bourgeois order. Harvard's Joseph A. Schumpeter, no practitioner of the fine art of meeting payrolls, heartily concurred. Kristol, Bell and Buckley are Johnny-come-latelies in the camp of intellectuals who deplore the influence of their own class.

One column cannot begin to enumerate the many discontents of intellectuals today as they look around the world. My purpose here is to discuss the restrictions on Indian democracy imposed this last year by Mrs. Gandhi's rule.

By measure of decibel count of oral complaint, one might infer that there is more indifference in the United States to what has been happening in India than there is now in connection with the repressive regime of the military in Chile. And that American intellectuals care less about loss of Indian freedoms than they do about restrictions put on freedom to emigrate from the Soviet Union of scientists, dissidents, religionists and ethnic nationalists.

It is time to redress the balance.

The Mussolini Pattern?

A court case provided the immediate occasion for Mrs. Gandhi's introduction of censorship and jailing of opposition leaders. A broader background involved some weakening of her electoral majorities and, objectivity requires one to say, some increase in strength of some opposition forces not themselves enamored of democracy. However, an informed jury would not agree with her contention that a conspiracy was afoot, posing an immediate danger, and requiring temporary strong measures in the interests of preserving democracy in the long run.

What followed is sadly familiar: rigid censorship of the press; systematic and capricious jailing of thousands without trial, sentencing, or even public acknowledgment of the fact. An inefficient police state invites an underground, and there now appears to be a cooperating underground in India.

Mrs. Gandhi complains of a double standard, in which China is forgiven worse offenses than India. She misses the point that well-wishers of India expected more of India, and hoped for more for her.

Public Choice and American Political Parties

CLASS POLITICS
February 2, 1976

MR Dooley, our turn-of-the-century Art Buchwald, would have loved Gerald Ford's State of the Union address. With the grace Ron Nessen has called our attention to, the President quoted generously from Tom Paine, the radical populist dismissed by Teddy Roosevelt as "that filthy little atheist."

Who is the common man the proposed program should appeal to? You should optimally have a half-million-dollar ownership in a "small" business or farm to take full advantage of the proffered estate-tax goody, which is available even if the farm is in the end going to be sold to a city slicker. (Under present law you don't get forgiveness of interest on your tax liability; but, as you'll find by checking with your local friendly banker, an interest rate that is to be set at 7 per cent is generous in an epoch when prices rise nearly that much a year.)

It would have tickled Mr. Dooley's peculiar sense of humor to observe Secretary of Treasury William Simon proposing to close all tax loopholes, lower all tax rates, and greatly simplify the taxing process at the same time that his Chief is dangling new election-year loopholes before the upper- and middle-income classes.

Wouldn't the common man like to be able to tax-shelter an extra $1,500 in stock investment? He would if he had it; and it might add something to capital formation. It would also add to the complexity and inequity of the tax code. And its proposal comes at the same time that Ford wants to impose minimal Medicare fees lest there be frivolous overuse of our limited hospital and physician resources.

Partitioning of America

Rhetoric aside, we Americans are going through a great political debate. If you are a believer in rationality and scientific method, you try red dye No. 2 until evidence tells you it is harmful; and, when new evidence tells you that cyclamates are not as harmful as alternatives, you change your mind about their prohibition.

So it ought to be with political decisions. If a welfare program is inefficient and turns out not to be able to accomplish what it hoped to do, you change your mind, dropping it for some better alternative.

The crisis of New York City, plus the fact that people resent tax burdens in a decade during which real incomes have not managed to make their usual advance, has attracted some new recruits to the camp of conservatives who have always thought that *the public sector should be reduced in the*

American society. Ronald Reagan, Richard Nixon, Ford and George Wallace have been spokesmen for this viewpoint.

Reagan is the most extreme. His notion of being able "to vote by your feet" means, and its logic intends it to mean, that any group of affluent people be allowed to form their own community within the U.S. and limit the support they give to others less affluent. But, of course, one person's privacy is another person's exclusion.

Refighting Old Battles

Reagan's logic must involve vast ghettos of those who are not affluent and who have been left by the others. Like a partitioned Lebanon or Ulster, one can envision enclaves in the Middle Atlantic states, the Midwest, parts of California, in which blacks, Puerto Ricans, Spanish-Americans, Indians, immigrants and ordinary poor people work out their problems on their own grass-roots basis.

New York City's root problem came about precisely because those with taxable capacity used their feet to walk out of the city, and those with needs walked in or were pressed into the corral. The pathology of Gotham is now to be generalized over the nation at large. The Hoover and Roosevelt battle over the federalization of humane welfare burdens is to be fought all over again. The clock of history is to be turned back to A.D. 1932.

Australian and New Zealand voters have drawn back from laboristic governments. The Danish welfare state has been in crisis. Even the Swedish labor party, after some 40 years of rule, is faced by opposition parties of almost matched parliamentary strength.

Were the Democratic Party to nominate a Fred Harris, or some other serious populist who would scare the bourgeois voters the way George McGovern rightly or wrongly did in 1972, the Republicans could probably win the White House with ease in November. One deems such a nomination unlikely.

Since the affluent are few, reactionary programs run real political risks.

PARTY ECONOMICS

April 26, 1976

NEITHER the candidates nor the voters are playing up economic issues in this election year. Still, it does make a difference economically whether Reagan, Ford, Jackson, Carter, Humphrey or Udall is elected.

An informed reader will realize that I have listed the six men with the best chance of being elected in rough order of their "conservatism." Such a listing can be only approximate.

For one thing, it has been difficult to infer from Carter's rhetoric exactly how "liberal" or "progressive" he would turn out to be as President. Then, too, there is the complicating fact that although Jackson may be on the right in national-defense matters, his stands on domestic matters have often been populist.

If you had closed your eyes and listened to the literal 1932 words of Franklin D. Roosevelt on budget balancing, you would hardly have been prepared for the New Deal programs of his first 100 days in office. But the electorate knew better when choosing FDR over Herbert Hoover. The two men's lifetime records and the interests supporting each made it clear which was the true conservative.

Humphrey and Udall, whether they call themselves "progressives," "liberals" or "middle-of-the-roaders," can be expected to espouse more expansionary fiscal and monetary policies in years of significant unemployment—i.e., in the remaining years of the 1970s. Despite their differences on defense and détente, Ford and Reagan can both be expected to favor tax and welfare-expenditure decisions that resist the modern trend toward egalitarianism. These ideological differences between Republicans and Democrats would be the more apparent were it not for the limits imposed on Republican Presidents by Democratic majorities in Congress.

Class Interests

At the core, American political parties are oriented along class lines, to represent either those who have or the larger number of those who don't. Hamilton, Adams, Madison and Jefferson understood this even before Marx. Money is much. But it is not everything. There are also religion, race, region and social class (as distinct from income class).

Still, looked at from the standpoint of the paradigm that economic interest defines parties, the line-up of candidates does make sense. Each Democrat is a greater threat to the affluent than any Republican. But remember there are always a sizable number of voters in the middle, not sure where their economic interests lie. It is these shiftable voters who must be wooed.

That is why the party of property ever seeks an attractive leader—a Disraeli, Churchill or Eisenhower—to draw some of the masses away from their preoccupation with using the powers of government in their own favor at the expense of the more affluent.

Many are called to this role, few are chosen. Because Goldwater was the darling of the right, he scared away the shiftable voter in 1964. Ronald Reagan now suffers from this same disability. He should have shut up about his hope of emasculating federal-determined welfare programs until *after* he got elected. His distrust of Russia is shared by plain people. But they do not wish to lose sleep over what an impetuous President might do in this regard. Perhaps his function in nature's grand design is to make Gerald Ford look moderate and sagacious.

The Old FDR Magic?

My paradigm also has implications for the Democratic nomination. The shiftable middle classes must not be repelled by Democrats' seeming to become a threat to their status. Udall's nemesis is thus the McGovern who made a Nixon landslide possible just four years ago.

What shiftable votes can Jackson attract? Perhaps some Jewish vote that strayed off from Nixon in 1972. His trade-union vote seems little tempted to defect toward Ford.

Here, as Humphrey must realize, is Jimmy Carter's strength. Like FDR and JFK, Carter has broad appeal. He has shown that he has the ability to draw votes from (1) blacks, (2) Wallace supporters, (3) rank-and-file Democrats and most significantly of all from (4) the Democrats who voted for Nixon in 1972.

Carter is all things to all men, you will object. Precisely. That is my point. And, I suspect, his point. Can he bring it off?

ECONOMIC POLITICS

November 18, 1974

To help understand the implications of the 1974 elections, I had a chat with an interesting friend who is a Republican. Let's call him Adams, after John Adams, who didn't have to read Karl Marx to understand that there is a recurrent class struggle between the rich and poor, and that political parties come into existence to represent those rival interests.

First, I asked him to sum up the Nixon Administration. "Better than Hubert Humphrey's," he replied, "and certainly beats anything of George McGovern by a thousand country miles. Let me give you just one for instance. As a successful businessman, I used to pay 77 per cent in taxes on my last dollar of income. No wonder I was paying 50 to 60 cents for tax shelters to avoid paying 77 cents in taxes. During the first Nixon term, almost while nobody but me was noticing, the tax rate was cut so that no one ever pays more than 50 cents on a dollar of earned income. That's the kind of thing I like: *quiet* delivery of benefits."

Tactics

Being incorribly academic, I raised an objection: "Yes, but what about the indexing of Social Security benefits during the Nixon term? This helped the lower-middle classes more than it helped you."

"Touché!" he replied. "But never forget that there are more middle-class people than rich, and we've got to give something to get something."

"So, all in all, Richard Nixon's Presidency was not so bad?" I asked.

"Wrong," he replied. "After Watergate, Nixon was a loser. From my viewpoint it was necessary to have him eliminated. I wouldn't have come so far in life so fast if I hadn't learned when to cut losses. In that connection let me point out that even if Rockefeller's confirmation squeaks by, he's dead for what counts—the 1976 Presidential election."

Being able to stand only so much cynicism, I hastily changed the subject to the safer topic of Gerald Ford, expecting to hear that the shift to an open Presidency was good business.

Adams was not to be diverted from the high road of principal. "Let's discuss Ford against the background of my favorite game plan for the GOP. That 1972 landslide was too much of a good thing. The GNP got overstimulated. Therefore, 1973 should have been made to be our recession year.

"Instead, by 1974, Ash, Simon, Stein and Greenspan were advising the President to fight inflation by cooling off the economy. Result: he led his party into the election with unemployment heading above 6 per cent, and growing fast before voting day. Autos and housing are now disaster areas. The recession disease spreads to steel, paper, aluminum, the capital-goods industries and other sectors that earlier held up well."

Ever anxious to serve as angels' advocate, I sprang to the defense of the Administration experts. "After all, you can't make omelets without breaking eggshells. Suppose the current sacrifices do cut the inflation rate in half by next summer. Suppose we do then have a V-bottom recovery. Suppose the economy is expanding vigorously for a full year before the 1976 Presidential elections. Won't that be a good scenario for the Republicans?"

"Suppose, suppose . . . ," Adams broke in impatiently. "The trouble with you academics is you have no proper appreciation of risk. Maybe things will work out that way. Maybe not. After all, Nixon's team told him in spring 1970 that the inflation would be seen to be on its way to solution by the fall, and the GOP would come into the 1970 elections smelling like a rose. They were wrong then. This time they may be right. But also, they may again be wrong. I had our corporation in-house economist do a survey of what the economic experts with the best forecasting records over the years are predicting concerning the benefit return in lower inflation rates that we can expect for our incurred costs in permitting the recession to develop. He reports: each extra million of unemployed workers will reduce the inflation rate by only trivial amounts."

Strategy

Challenged to set forth a constructive program for the Administration to adopt, Adams opted for safety:

· Begin to fight the recession.
· Stimulate housing.

- Step up optional federal spending.
- Soft-pedal the tax surcharge.
- Bad-mouth inflation.

Not a very exciting prescription, I told him. And not one sure to work.

He had the last word. "We still have our secret weapon—the Democratic Party."

ROAD TO 1984

August 13, 1973

WE live in an unlucky age. When the times call for a Walter Lippmann, we find ourselves with a glut of Bill Buckleys and Kenneth Galbraiths. Outflanking them at the ungolden extremes are the Hayeks of the right and the Marcuses of the left.

Why have the Watergate hearings brought so little joy? One should have thought that the discomfort of the President's admirers might at least have been offset by the *Schadenfreude* of his critics. The reason why the never-ending disclosures out of Washington have been so disquieting is that we begin to see, on the TV tube darkly, the face of Fascism. True, to use the vernacular of the King James Bible that has come so much into fashion, Fascism is still a cloud on the horizon no bigger than a man's hand. But if a George Orwell were alive to sniff out the signs of Fascism on the left or the right, he would be sounding the 1984 alarm.

Twin Errors

When the Nazis were still riding high, there was a tendency to lay the blame for evils that came to light on men around Hitler. "Der Führer is all right; but watch out for Göring and Goebbels"—so went the alibis.

There is the same understandable tendency now for some to attribute what were standard operating procedures in the Administration to convenient scapegoats like Ehrlichman, Mitchell, Haldeman or Dean. Or to Liddy, Hunt, Stans and whichever is the favorite scoundrel of the week.

The truth is otherwise. When Dr. Kissinger comes to write his memoirs, his preface will have to contain that empty tag so beloved of authors: "For any mistakes in foreign policy, I am solely responsible; for any triumphs, credit must go to President Nixon." Such caveats are not expected to be taken seriously.

Thus far I have been speaking of those who try to be favorable to Richard Nixon. There are plenty of other people who go to the opposite extreme: they attribute the wiretapping, break-ins, cover-up payoffs and other misdemeanors and felonies to the wickedness of the President and his alleged psychological instabilities. To them it is ever a case of "Tricky Dick, the paranoid"—who just happened to get caught at Watergate, but who is the same infighter who defeated Jerry Voorhis in 1946, Helen Gahagan Douglas in 1950, who climbed to prominence as a McCarthy Communist witch-hunter and who escaped political oblivion by the contrived "Checkers" TV apologia.

I find this a shallow diagnosis. The truth may be more disquieting. For if our troubles come only from one rotten apple in the barrel, then having eliminated it we could look ahead to politics as usual.

To Turn Back the Clock

When we were secretly bombing Cambodia, I doubt that Henry Kissinger and Melvin Laird, who must have been in on the secret, regarded the President as the madman that many of Adolf Hitler's aides thought him to be. I beg leave to doubt that Richard Nixon is psychologically more abnormal than the late J. Edgar Hoover. I see little evidence that he is more rash or chauvinistic than, say, Sen. Barry Goldwater. And far from his suffering primarily from opportunism, I think the key to understanding the Administration is to realize that Mr. Nixon is a man of principle, an ideologue and not a mere vote-seeker.

Unfortunately, the principles that Richard Nixon believes in represent a minority view that cannot be imposed on the country without departure from standard democratic procedures. The old-time religion of a budget balanced at a low level, and of the government leaving key economic decisions to the marketplace, is no more the ideology of most Americans than is Billy Graham's version of religion the standard U.S. code.

Thirty years ago, Friedrich Hayek wrote *The Road to Serfdom*. It was not a bad book, even though its principal thesis was wrong: Hitler's Fascism and Lenin's Communism were not, as Hayekians believe, the inevitable consequences of Bismarckian-type social security, Lloyd George–type tax reforms or FDR New Deals.

What the Nixon team wished was to turn back the clock of history to the pre–New Deal days. If Congress and articulate segments of the American people got in the way, then the awesome powers of the Presidency must get rid of the roadblocks.

People say we should be grateful to Watergate because it shows the American system at work to cure its own evils. What rot. But at least it has stopped the President from exercising that mandate he never got.

The Mixed Economy

ADVICE TO CANDIDATE KENNEDY
October 15, 1979

GIVING economic advice to Kennedys is the story of my life. It's a habit hard to break.

I began with Sen. John F. Kennedy. I continued with candidate and Democratic nominee Jack Kennedy, and ran a task force on the state of the economy for the President-elect. As with Moses, it was not given to me to enter into the promised land of the White House. Other duty called. But I was able to serve as out-of-town designated hitter, backing up the magnificent on-the-site all-star Council of Economic Advisers: Walter Heller, James Tobin and the late Kermit Gordon. It was only natural when chief Bobby sounded the pipes to call out the clan that I should leave the furrow of pure economic research and grab my abacus in that good but abortive cause.

First Elective Bid

As far as Teddy Kennedy is concerned, my credentials are in good order. It is important in politics to be early. Back in 1962 when the youthful Edward Kennedy made his first bid for elective office, I was one of the half-dozen academics in Massachusetts who favored him for the Senate.

Friends asked: "Don't you know that it's only the Kennedy name that is giving this 30-year-old the chance to serve in the Senate?" Of course I knew that. But, as I pointed out, the great William Pitt did not become Prime Minister of England at 24 because of his baby-blue eyes. The question

I had to decide for myself was this: "Will Edward M. Kennedy make a good senator? Will his advantages of luck be put to good or bad use?"

Kennedy's superlative record over seventeen years in the Senate exceeded my sanguine hopes. I wish that all the bets I made twenty years ago had paid off as handsomely in dividends and capital gains.

Let me now turn to advice for 1980 in the form of an open letter to Senator Kennedy:

You should pre-empt the center in economic policy. The 1964 Goldwater and the 1972 McGovern campaigns have pointed out the way to lose. Shun their examples.

This is not a counsel of opportunism. It is a cool program of optimizing the humane cause in terms of political feasibility.

Comprehensive medical insurance meets a genuine need and strikes a resonant chord in the electorate. Your name, the Kennedy name, is properly associated with that good cause. But it is also true that the middle classes are apprehensive lest they be further squeezed in this age of inflation by a quantum rise in taxes to pay for public services. The present, incomplete system is already sure to mount in medical costs. Strategic planning to control costs of a comprehensive system is not only good politics, it is good economics and good ethics.

So far, Mr. Carter is not to blame for the economic slowdown under way. Accelerating two-digit price inflation is no laughing matter. But it is not too soon for contingency planning to be sure that a recession does not get out of hand. Even Wall Street will drink to that. People on Main Street could sleep easier if they knew the Federal Reserve won't repeat its usual caper of keeping money tight for too long.

So my advice in the area of macroeconomic policy is: avoid the overdramatic. Defending some pegged parity rate for the dollar is not the ultimate goal. What needs guarding is the *real* solvency and smooth running of America's plant and human capacities. The life signs here are good. Indeed, our profitability and competitiveness in the 1970s is something that the Germans and Japanese can well envy.

From the direction of the left, avoid the temptation to get a short-term lift from mandatory price and wage controls. They did work politically for Nixon in August 1971 and guaranteed his already-likely electoral landslide in 1972. But it was President Ford and all of us in the country who inherited the economic whirlwind that Nixon had sown under the political advice of his then Secretary of the Treasury, John B. Connally.

Energy is an intrinsically hard question. Conserving its future use is an absolute must. I know of no way to bring this about without making oil and gasoline more expensive to the bulk of the consumers.

The most stupid Republican knows that. The problem for statesmanship is to mobilize the electorate's will to recognize this fact of life by devising a social contract to share the windfall burdens and gains. This is language few Republicans understand. Your challenge as a poll leader is to shape a program of aids to the poorest and windfall taxes for the luckiest that will bring an end to the political impasse on energy.

The center way is the hard way. But for 1980 it's the only way.

PLANNER IN PERU

September 1, 1980

WE have become accustomed to hearing nothing but bad news from South America: more atrocity stories from Chile, a new military coup in Bolivia negating its recent election outcome, terrorist activities in Argentina and Uruguay. I therefore wanted to see with my own eyes the remarkable return this summer of democracy to Peru.

Peru was ruled by a military dictatorship for the last twelve years. One morning in 1968, tanks rolled up to the Presidential residence, President Fernando Belaúnde Terry was rousted out of his bed and put on a plane for Argentina, and most of his key officials escaped imprisonment only by slipping quietly over the border.

What was different in this all too familiar story was the fact that Gen. Juan Velásco Alvarado, the usurper, represented a left-wing rather than a right-wing ideology. The so-called 80 families of the Peruvian oligarchy were stripped by expropriation and confiscation of much of their holdings. Foreign investors—such as the Chase Manhattan Bank— were bought out through offers they couldn't refuse. Large land holdings were divided among workers' cooperatives. The state expanded its role in the ownership and control of the means of production.

Economic Chaos

Regrettably, noble intentions are not enough. After an initial binge, Peru's economy foundered. General Velásco was rusticated and replaced by a less demagogic general. But despite the fortuitous discovery of oil, real wages and income deteriorated steadily after 1975.

Peruvian inflation, which had always been under relatively good control by Latin American standards, began to accelerate as the government printed money to finance its huge deficits. Peru's lavish borrowings from abroad finally caught up with it, and Peru appeared on everyone's short list of nations likely to default on their foreign obligations.

At this point the armed forces apparently tired of trying to run the economy. In the second surprising feature of the recent Peruvian experience, the military permitted a free election last May and acquiesced gracefully to the overwhelming victory at the polls of ex-President Belaúnde and his middle-of-the-road Acción Popular Party.

Belaúnde is an architect and city planner who spent his exile years at Harvard, Johns Hopkins, Columbia and George Washington universities. A dreamer of dreams, he has a strong appeal for the masses, winning 45.3 per cent of the popular vote against a field of eleven opponents, a feat almost without precedent in Latin America and one which quite surprised the departing military. The Marxist parties, splintered among pro-Peking, Trotskyite and other cliques, totaled a mere 15 per cent of the vote, a fraction that does not adequately reflect their actual strength within the trade-union movement.

Democracy

It is clear the people are tired of military rule. They feel free to criticize and express their aspirations, and are enjoying the remembered air of democracy.

"Will the present honeymoon last?" This is the question I kept asking myself and the many members of the Peruvian establishment I met on a recent lecture tour that took me to Lima and the Andes.

There are pluses and minuses in the picture. Here are some pluses.

Peru has favorable long-term natural resources: hydroelectric power; copper, silver, lead and zinc; the probability of further rich oil finds; a potential for tourism in the jet age, as yet barely tapped.

The departing military team, aided by good prices for exports of copper, silver and oil, cleaned up the payments deficit in 1970 and turned the international reserves position around.

Playing Sancho Panza to Belaúnde's Don Quixote is the new Prime Minister, Manuel Ullos. As chief of a new team of Cabinet officers, many of them newly returned from exile, Ullos must try to reduce inflation from its present annual rate of 60 per cent to 40 per cent. This will be hard to do while, at the same time, reducing the subsidies that give Peru's consumers gasoline at one-third true world costs.

What worries me most are the unrealistic levels of expectations endemic in the developing world. It's just not feasible to pursue austerity à la Margaret Thatcher or Chile's "Chicago boys." The middle way is a hard way but in my view the only way.

Expecting the impossible will not get it for the Peruvian populace. Let's hope that democracy in Peru will luck it out.

BRITAIN: DON'T EXPECT A MIRACLE

May 28, 1979

Now that the dust has settled after the resounding defeat of the Labor Party in Britain, analysts are studying the personalities and ideologies of Prime Minister Thatcher and her selected team. Will she and Sir Keith Joseph, the new Minister of Industry and exponent of limited government, adhere in office to the stern programs they proposed while in opposition?

When so many are concentrating on the doctors, I think it profitable to take a close look at the patient, the British economy. Miraculous cures are more to be expected when we face a clinical case of paralysis for no anatomical reasons than when all the signs are of malignant metastases.

Britain is clearly a rather poor European country. London looks a bit tacky where Paris, Stockholm and even Milan look up-and-coming. But this is no new thing. Twenty years ago, most European countries had left the U.K. behind. Britain's slow real growth rate since 1960 has only widened the gap between her and the other welfare states of Europe.

Holland, France and Sweden take a larger tax bite out of total income than does Britain, but they still make greater productivity progress than she does.

Anticlimactic Diagnosis

When the Brookings Institution did a study in depth of the United Kingdom economy, its experts found mediocrity aplenty but no striking breakdowns. Tired blood, rather than pernicious anemia, was, in effect, their anticlimactic diagnosis. The forthcoming sequel to the Brookings study, I understand, rather confirms the earlier conclusions.

If true, this finding is important. It suggests that *one should not bet on a Thatcher miracle* comparable to the 1949 Erhard miracle—in which Ludwig Erhard boldly cut out German price and wage controls and was rewarded with an explosion of entrepreneurship and material progress.

Nor are there grounds for a Franklin Roosevelt 1933 miracle of spirit. If the patient is not moribund—merely lackadaisical and sluggish—no magical resuscitation would seem in the cards.

Where in historical experience might one find a useful analogue? The election of General Eisenhower in 1952 ended two decades of New Deal rule. Ike's Administration did bring business some relief from heavy taxation. But it did not return us to Herbert Spencer's world of man-eat-man or to Herbert Hoover's world of rugged individualism. The cutbacks of the public sector by the Eisenhower team were not without their toll. No fewer than three full-fledged recessions are recorded in the annals of the Eisenhower terms. Taming inflation turned out to involve slowing U.S. real growth down to an average rate of but 2.5 per cent.

This is not to argue that the Thatcher victory was for no reason and will make no difference. The last few years have shown poor performance even for England. I think the trend of government spending and taxing can, and will, be changed by a determined Tory majority in Parliament. Gardeners who prune know that sometimes less is actually more. Worthwhile welfare programs ought to be able to stand up to unsparing scrutiny and audit. Not all the initiatives of recent years can be justified on a cost-benefit basis.

Even from my liberal and egalitarian standpoint, it is absurd for the U.K. to have maximum marginal tax rates of 98 per cent along with glaring loopholes so that these need not be paid. Callaghan's one accomplishment while Prime Minister was to cut in half an inflation rate of more than 25 per cent a year. To halve it once again by a dose of monetarism will in all likelihood not be a painless procedure.

How to Get Your Way

The "inevitability of gradualness" was a tactic appealed to by the Fabian left. It is a tactic that can also be worked by the property-owning right.

Periods of social-democratic rule were brought to an end in Sweden, Australia, New Zealand and elsewhere by electoral victories of more conservative parties. As I pore over the subsequent years' indexes of production and prices, I am not able to report remarkable improvements. But that has not meant loss of office or even of Gallup poll support for the new governments.

Continuity within change is as important economically as it is politically. It will be tragic if the British trade unions throw down the gauntlet to the new government. Lebanon and Ireland have taught us how fatal to the GNP is civil strife.

It will be a blunder if the zeal to restore the free market provokes an outburst of class warfare and strikes. Benjamin Disraeli was a conservative leader who measured nicely just what the political market would bear. Pray that Margaret Thatcher will have inherited some of his canniness, along with a little of the proverbial Disraeli luck.

U.S. STILL THE RICHEST?

August 18, 1975

A scholar gains fame if he establishes a new thesis to explain American history. When this century was young, Frederick Jackson Turner identified the Frontier as pivotal in the U.S. past.

The late David Potter, of Yale and Stanford, proclaimed this to be the Land of Plenty. U.S. culture has been formed in the self-image that we are the most affluent people on earth. Henry Ford, as much as Davy Crockett and a deal more than Ralph Waldo Emerson, is our archetypal hero. We pity the poorer foreigner who lacks our resilient youth, our free institutions, our Yankee, melting-pot ingenuity and, yes, our frontier's plenitude of resources per person—and who therefore lacks the treasures in this life flowing therefrom.

The trouble, though, with being rich is that someone else may become richer. I do not refer to the odd sheikdom which, by virtue of a lucky oil strike and the forming of the export cartel, finds itself with a per capita income many times that of the U.S. After all, we have enclaves in Houston, Manhattan and Grosse Pointe with similar aberrations of income.

Nouveaux-Riches Parvenus

I refer to the ugly rumors that Sweden, Switzerland and perhaps even West Germany are beginning to top the U.S. in real GNP per capita. If it is capitalistic free enterprise that made us wealthy, how come the regulated economies of the effete Old World threaten to outstrip us where it counts—on the bottom line? And what lesson does one infer from the indication that Japan, Inc., will after X years overtake and pass the U.S., as it has already done to Britain?

Before we explain the facts, let's be sure what they are. When Sherlock Holmes wished to know more about a rare alkaloid poison, he knew just which professor of forensic medicine to consult (the one at Edinburgh, of course). When I want to learn about regional income comparisons, I go to Prof. Irving Kravis at the University of Pennsylvania. To cap his classic studies made a score of years ago for the Organization of European Economic Cooperation, Dr. Kravis and three of his Penn colleagues, together with the United Nations Statistical Office and supported by the World Bank, surveyed and analyzed prices of 1970 for ten countries. Their newly published book, *A System of International Comparisons of Gross Product and Purchasing Power,* is a gusher of information.

Although it does not deal directly with Sweden and Switzerland, with the help of some calculations by Kravis colleagues Drs. Robert Summers and Sultan Ahmad, presented in a paper for the Econometric Society, I infer the U.S. is still No. 1. Sweden seems to enjoy only about seven-eighths of U.S. real per capita income, Switzerland four-fifths, France and West Germany three-fourths, Japan two-thirds, Britain three-fifths, Chile one-fourth, India perhaps one-fourteenth and Kenya one-seventeenth.

What's past is epilogue. What trends are suggested for the future?

Regressing to the Average

Whether or not we follow Satchel Paige's advice of not looking back, *most everybody is gaining on us.* Our defeated foes, Germany, Italy and Japan, have had per capita real growth at twice our rate since 1950. French growth has been two-thirds more than ours. Even Britain, for whom we feel so sorry, grew 10 per cent more than we in 1950–70 and, *mirabile dictu,* ended with capital investment at 22 per cent of national product as against our meager 19 per cent.

In case it is thought that having more planning with a capital *P* is the moral of the tale, one is given cautious pause by Prof. Abram Bergson's Harvard study: this shows that if you compare all Eastern European socialist economies of COMECON with all mixed economies of OECD of about the same real-income levels, the controlled economies do not average out with better growth over years such as 1950–67 or 1955–67.

The simple, but unsad, truth is this: it is easy, even natural, for the front runner to fall back to the pack. Ashes to ashes and dust to dust is just another way of stating the second law of thermodynamics and the remorseless increase in entropy and mixed-upness. New York State grows less than Texas, Boston less than Dallas, Athens less than Sparta.

Uncle Sam—and Dr. Kissinger—have to learn that the U.S. with one-quarter of world GNP in 1975 cannot do what it could in 1945 with one-half.

CAPITALISM IN TWILIGHT?

June 7, 1976

JOSEPH Schumpeter used to characterize the modern mixed economy as "capitalism in an oxygen tent." Had Schumpeter lived for a quarter of a century after the first publication in 1942 of his *Capitalism, Socialism, and Democracy,* I think he might have been truly astonished by the invalid's vitality.

For the world as a whole, the third quarter of the twentieth century outshone any epoch in the annals of economic history. As far as growth of total world output is concerned, we did not see its like before. Perhaps we shall not see its like again. But let us not fail to notice what its record did show.

The most dramatic performances were by the miracle economies: Japan, West Germany, Israel and Italy. But not very far behind were France, Scandinavia, the Low Countries and Canada. Schumpeter, I am sure, would have found virtually incredible the sprint of progress accomplished by his own native Austria, for whom he thought the knell had tolled with the death of the Emperor Franz Josef and the collapse of Schumpeter's own post–World War I Finance Ministry.

Minor Miracles

I am aware that it is fashionable to speak of the widening gap between the less-developed and the developed nations. And if one looks at the divergencies between humanitarian hopes and the sad reality for India, Pakistan, Bangladesh, Haiti and numerous former colonies in Africa, Latin America and Asia, one appreciates the poignancy of the shortfall.

Yet even within the less-developed economies, there are success stories to be told for Singapore, Hong Kong, Taiwan, Thailand, Mexico, and in a measure for Iran, Venezuela, Puerto Rico, Brazil and Nigeria. If one writes off each such case as merely an instance of lucky natural-resource endowments and fortuitous governments conducive to economic advance, one must be reminded that the prosperity of the United States was not merely a reflection of our steely-blue Yankee eyes.

It was King Alfonso X of Spain who said that, had he been in on the creation, he could have made a better job of it. Although I should have preferred that more of the recent decades' progress had occurred where it was needed most, I have to admit that the poorest countries grew even more slowly in earlier times than they have since World War II. Britain's economic growth is disappointing in comparison with that of France and Germany but not with that of Britain itself in Victorian and Edwardian times.

Too Much of a Good Thing?

However, has the modern evolution of capitalism, the mixed economy, run out its string of luck? Is the realistic outlook for the final quarter of the century a more somber one?

It is not the worldwide recession that prompts these queries. Nor is it the quadrupled price of OPEC oil, which the Club of Rome reads as the first signal of a Malthusian age of scarcity to come. The Keynesian methods of the mixed economy worked tolerably well to contain the virulence of the recession. The lights will not soon go out in Frankfurt, Chicago and Stockholm.

My queries come from reading doleful comments on our times in the European financial press. The May 1976 issue of *Vision*, published simultaneously in several languages, gives a sampling of lachrymose statistics like the following:

· Concerning ownership of the capital of leading firms in sixteen European countries, "the state crops up in 40 per cent of them." We may add the fact that in Germany, Sweden and even the United States, workers are coming to be represented on the boards of directors.

· The Dutch, German and Spanish governments respectively now take in 46, 39 and 22 per cent of their GNPs, spending about half for welfare purposes (pensions, health, etc.). Ten years ago the numbers were 36, 33 and 16.

I do not interpret these and kindred facts as omens of *Götterdämmerung*. Is Spain more stable than the Netherlands and Germany? Is the Spanish pattern more to be envied or is it to be feared?

Markets can respond to penicillin or bubble gum, to police cars or Cadillacs. Corporate executives can live with minority unionists much as with minority capitalists.

Please omit flowers and black cloth as premature.

ECONOMICS AND POLITICS

January 15, 1979

NONECONOMISTS often exaggerate the importance of economics. In saying this, I am not denying that India's next harvest will be crucial in determining how hungry—and unhappy—its teeming millions will be. Nor am I laughing off the differences in American suffering involved if the 1970s decade ends in a rip-roaring economic recession.

I am glad to render unto economics that which is itself economic: production trends, levels of profitability and the relative share of wages in the national income, price-level inflation, and per capita living standards. Many, however, go further. They find an economic basis underlying sociological behavior, power relations of government and even religious belief.

"When capitalism dies, women will become free for the first time. Anti-Semitism will wither away, along with neurosis. When there is bread for all, no one will need to steal or want to." Here I have merely vulgarized the effusions to be found in the writings of Friedrich Engels, Leon Trotsky, Paul Baran and other Marxian romantics.

My present concern is not with the validity or lack of validity in grand theories of economic determinism. Instead, I wish to try to understand the possible relationship between the unrest now going on in Iran and its recent economic history.

Pocketbook Voting

Let me begin with what seems to be a clear case in which deteriorating economic conditions led to the overthrow of an administration and to a new epoch of social legislation. The Great Depression of 1929–32 undoubtedly caused Herbert Hoover to lose the 1932 Presidential election to Franklin Roosevelt. With unemployment everywhere, bankruptcy and bank failures rampant and the middle classes not spared the ravages of economic collapse, the electorate turned radical by American standards and rallied around the New Deal welfare state that still prevails.

It is also a reasonable hypothesis that Germany, with an unemployment rate of 25 per cent in the 1930s, might not have turned to Adolf Hitler's Fascism if the Weimar Republic had forcefully pursued countercyclical stabilization policies. Had John Maynard Keynes's *General Theory* appeared in 1930 and not in 1936, World War II might well have been avoided.

The plot thickens, however, when we bring in new facts. The French Revolution occurred not in the poorest country of Europe, but rather in the richest. The late historian Crane Brinton used to emphasize that those really famished are too lethargic to rebel; coming down from a high living standard leads often to irrepressible discontent.

Joseph Schumpeter, one of the giants in economics during the first half of this century, pointed out that the signal economic triumphs of Victoria's capitalism did not buy off dissent. The rationalism that brought steam and electricity also brought insistence on universal suffrage, a reform that led remorselessly to welfare redistribution of incomes and to Fabian socialism. Dickens's Oliver Twist put the matter succinctly when he asked for "more."

Oil Not Enough

Prof. Richard Easterlin of the University of Pennsylvania has studied the question of whether material economic progress makes people feel happier. Surveys report that people are happier with a job than without one, happier if they have had recent raises in pay and improved living standards. People apparently do feel happier in the short run from economic progress. But Easterlin finds no evidence that we are in the long run happier than our fathers and grandfathers, even though we enjoy demonstrably higher real income than they did.

Now we can dispel any Iranian paradox. Purely because of the accident of oil discovery, Iran is one of those backward countries that has been able to register tremendous progress in the last decade. The Shah has been its Stalin. Granted that Iran has the skewed income distribution typical of developing countries, its real wage has risen markedly, at a rate unmatched in American history.

Thus the simple thesis that progress mutes discontent simply will not wash. Schumpeter's cynicism proves considerably less misleading. The Shah's very successes helped breed his decline.

Alas, one perceives no Roosevelt, Masaryk, Nehru or even Kemal Ataturk to replace the Shah and create in Iran a Swiss or Swedish paradise.

ECONOMIC SCARES

September 11, 1978

"ANOTHER worldwide crisis of capitalism is upon us." With these dramatic words Robert L. Heilbroner, one of our few interesting writers on economics, opens a survey of boom and crash in a long *New Yorker* magazine article.

As the new economic year begins this fall, what message could be more important than Heilbroner's—if his conclusion were credible? Why am I puzzling over next quarter's Federal Reserve discount-rate policy if the Age of Welfare Capitalism, which succeeded the Age of Monopoly Capitalism, is itself about to shuffle offstage in favor of the Age of Planned Capitalism? Why am I fiddling with inventory trends if the fires of the American imperium are being extinguished around the globe? My academic colleagues prescribe salves for the acne of post-Keynesian business cycles while the patient may be succumbing to the insidious cirrhosis of the 50-year Kondratieff Cycle.

I once lost patience with my firstborn as she viewed a soap opera, in which before our eyes a chap of my age was experiencing a heart attack following his indictment for embezzlement and discovery in adultery. "Give me one reason, Jane, why you like looking at such stuff," I asked in irritation. I have always remembered her answer: "Because it's so scary."

Somber Likelihoods

Sometimes nightmares do come true. Even paranoids may have enemies. Following upon the miraculous 1950s and 1960s, the 1970s have been years of disappointing growth abroad, exchange-rate dislocations and economic travail.

A middle-aged writer with a skillful pen may be pardoned for despairing over the likelihood that modern mixed economies will soon find a cure for their syndrome of chronic stagflation. But what has all this to do with a "crisis of capitalism"? Even Professor Heilbroner, when you read his words carefully, does not believe—as Marx and Engels did in the early 1850s—that the knell is tolling for the imminent demise of the established order. What he believes is that modern humans, like the characters in soap operas, do face plenty of problems.

One and a half books back, Dr. Heilbroner opined that

scarcities of natural resources would require more centralized planning. Observing the fortunes since then of planners like Sweden's Olof Palme, India's Indira Gandhi, Britain's Harold Wilson, Germany's Willy Brandt, the World Bank's Robert McNamara—to say nothing of the fortunes here of Howard Jarvis, Jimmy Carter, James Schlesinger, Sen. Russell Long and Gov. Jerry Brown—one realizes it is too soon to concede that planning's time has yet dawned.

A turn toward planning seems politically doubtful. One of many reasons for this is the difficulty of showing that planning in its traditional form has much to offer toward alleviating our present discontents.

1979 Growth Recession

It is cheap sport to lampoon the forecasts of others from a safe perch of noncommittal agnosticism. Here is my assessment of the probabilities for the next twelve months of whatever you want to call the present epoch.

I fear that the American economy will register only 2.75 per cent real growth from this Labor Day to that of 1979. This will leave the unemployment rate uncomfortably above 6 per cent.

Such a scenario for a growth recession, rather than for a downright recession in which real output declines for a couple of quarters at least, is by no means guaranteed. There is a quarter-chance that a money crunch, engineered by the Federal Reserve or occurring when its tight money policy runs out of control, will trigger a decline in housing and inventory expenditure grave enough to bring on a genuine "recession" (not to mention a "crisis").

There is an equally significant chance that the system has enough steam left in the boiler to enter upon its fifth year of the present recovery.

Stagflation will not be permanently routed by the likely

mini-recession. There will still be a long and painful road ahead before we succeed in curing our sizable basic deficit of international payments.

Middle-class backlash and taxpayer revolts will not achieve restoration of Herbert Spencer's laissez faire. There is a science fiction of the rights as well as of the left and center. Read it and enjoy. But don't bet your nest egg on wishful fantasies.

TOO MUCH DEMOCRACY?

April 9, 1979

MANY American voters are fed up with taxes. They see prices rising at double-digit annual rates. As their real wealth melts, they fear for their future living needs.

The governmental share of the national income seems to them to grow remorselessly. Four months of the year are now spent working for the Washington octopus, the state-capital politicians and the town-hall bureaucrats. If the trend of the twentieth century's middle two quarters continues, by the year 2000 the people best educated and most industrious in the arts of commerce and production will be turning over to the rest of the community half the fruits of their effort.

John Adams and Alexander Hamilton warned against democracy. So did Edmund Burke and Thomas Babington Macaulay. Universal suffrage, they prophesied, would inevitably mean that the poorest 51 per cent of the population would pillage the property of the frugal middle classes.

Conservative Lament

Present-day Jeremiahs are even more gloomy. They expect no part of the public to reap net benefit from the logrolling inherently involved in the legislative process. Even the poor do not receive what the rich lose.

The deadweight loss of inefficient and unresponsive representative government simply decimates the total social pie that we call real gross national product. The pace of economic progress is brought to a veritable halt as the government fritters away the resources needed for producing new capital equipment and plant, and as inept regulation poisons the wellsprings of technological advance and entrepreneurial innovation.

Workers are hurt along with owners of property, since any rise in real wages must come primarily from the accumulation of capital and the improvement of skills and managerial techniques. At best, it is only the politicians and bureaucrats who fatten and thrive under populist democracy.

I believe that the above paragraphs fairly summarize what many Americans have come to believe. My own analysis of the causes underlying our chronic stagflation has to run along different and less-simple lines. If only it were true that old-fashioned demand-pull inflation was our primary problem!

Nor will historical experience with the political economy of social choice bear out the diagnosis that democracy by its nature must produce overlarge public spending. The economic principles of collective decision making and of competitive game theory demonstrate that there is as much an inherent tendency for governments to spend *too little* as too much. What is everybody's business may be nobody's business. The pursuit of private profit will not keep carcinogens out of our rivers and atmosphere. Self-interest will not lead you and me to hire an army and navy to preserve the system that lets us be go-getters and private-utility maximizers.

As the philosopher John Rawls has reemphasized in his *A Theory of Justice,* we do not vote for Social Security and welfare assistance out of love for Washington civil servants. Being human and realizing we are subject to the unknown perils of unemployment and destitution, we cannily opt for the mutual reinsurances of the modern welfare state, knowing that, but for the grace of God, the bell that tolls could be tolling for us. Your typhoid is my typhoid and we are all, so to speak, citizens of the same Hiroshima.

Bearing Witness

When I was asked last week to testify before the Rodino congressional subcommittee dealing with constitutional amendments for balancing the budget, all the above conflicts came up. On such occasions I do not deem it my function to press my value judgments on those with different ethical views. My duty as an economist is to present as accurately and objectively as I can what will be the likely costs and benefits from each proposed policy decision.

Even from the standpoint of those anxious to contain and reverse the trend toward an expanding public sector, historical experience suggests that it is unwise to use the Constitution to fix upon the nation for all time some particular formula of macroeconomic policy.

Only recall 1930–32. Herbert Hoover tried disastrously to raise tax rates in the teeth of a worsening depression in order to balance the budget that inevitably had gone into deficit because of reduced tax collections. Had Roosevelt been forced by the Constitution to do the same, blood would have run in the streets.

Economics is an inexact science. Rules that first seem good wreak havoc later. Winston Churchill was right. Democracy is a poor system; but no one has ever been able to design a better one. If a preponderant majority permanently want less public spending, they'll get their way!

Government by law and not by men means flexible evolution through due process. It doesn't mean freezing into the Constitution each passing economic fad.

Chapter 2

TOUGH CHOICES IN SUSTAINING GROWTH

MACROECONOMICS deals with the economy as a whole, and the three generally accepted macro-economic goals are economic growth, full employment and price stability. These goals, which at times are mutually exclusive, must be pursued by a method that is consistent with the moral and ideological framework of the policy maker and, hence, the public at large. However, from a strictly economic point of view, maintaining and increasing output per capita is primary. Healthy growth, as well as a reluctance to tolerate less than full output, is the dominant theme of Samuelson's writing. The charge to maintain general economic well-being and growth, by whatever means available, is taken seriously by Samuelson. The ups and downs, as well as the long-term growth path of a particular nation, are not due exclusively to government policy, according to Samuelson. However, he does admit to a political cycle. A particular economy is subjected to crop failures, oil cartels and business cycles abroad, as well as to internal hysteria. Although the propensities toward major depressions and hyperinflations still exist, Samuelson believes sophisticated economic analysis makes them unnecessary, and political expediency will not permit them.

Therefore, the appropriate role of the policy maker is not to counter a recession with inflation or vice versa but rather to minimize deviations in both directions from the long-run growth path. The fiscal policy tools available are executive and congressional control of the government budget by changing government spending and taxation. The monetary tools are selective credit controls and the Federal Reserve's control over monetary aggregates, which in turn affect interest rates. In general, Samuelson advocates neither austere nor consistent use of one or the other of these tools to adjust for recession or inflation. He emphasizes the need for government policy that is countercyclical to the economic cycle. In the case of stagflation, in which widespread unemployment and price rises exist simultaneously, he is above all pragmatic but leans toward an expansionary policy as one that is both humane and least likely to choke off growth. Cautious restraint is sometimes indicated, but only when the forecasters agree that a boom is overstrong.

Econometrics expresses economic theories in mathematical terms in order to verify them by statistical methods. In addition, econometricians seek to measure the impact of one economic variable on another in order to predict future events or advise on the choice of economic policy. On an even bet, Samuelson goes with the consensus of government, academic and business forecasters. However, he sees himself as a judgmental forecaster, which *means that he will modify econometric results to account for real-world conditions not built into the economic relationships specified mathematically in each econometric model.*

Policy making transcends economics as a science and hinges on value judgments. Samuelson is candid about his concern for unskilled and minority workers at those times that contractionary government policy allows the labor market to slacken. But he is equally and repeatedly candid about the cost in terms of inflation that must be tolerated if relative full employment is used as a target for fiscal and monetary policy.

Samuelson certainly makes no major break with Keynesianism in his Newsweek *articles. Nor is there even a hint that Keynesianism was excessively used or misused. Neither does he seem to be concerned that the post–World War II economy has built up an immunity to fiscal policy, which perhaps nullifies the short-run effects that the government budget could have on the economy. In "Vital Public Spending" (November 29, 1967), Samuelson strongly advocates a tax increase as a contractionary fiscal measure to control inflation. In the seventies, he proposed tax cuts to avoid serious recession.*

Oil cartels and crop failures generate real supply effects. Inflation, on the other hand, is a rise in the average price level. Therefore, if some prices declined at the same time fuel and farm prices increased, there would be no inflation. Policy makers have not permitted or forced declines in prices, but rather have accommodated price increases. In general, Samuelson recommends such policies, primarily because he has trouble justifying recessions designed to correct inflation.

Prior to the Reagan election, several economists

*introduced the concept of rational expectations,
which means simply that people form their expectations on the basis of available information on the
probable future actions of policy makers. If the
public knew and believed that the government was
not going to accommodate inflation, the economy
would adjust downward in terms of the inflation
rate without suffering a protracted recession. Samuelson does not accept the contention that inflation
is mainly a psychological problem, and he suggests
in these articles that the real cost of controlling it
would be extensive and politically unacceptable. At
present, he admits to being wrong in forecasting
that Americans would be living with inflation for a
long time to come. Samuelson probably under-
estimated the will of the public to control inflation
and the extent to which many, but not all, families
have insulated themselves by taking in two, not one,
paychecks. However, Samuelson was certainly correct in warning that the cost of reducing inflation
would be severe and protracted in terms of high
interest rates, unemployment, and forgone production. He did not anticipate any supply-side miracle
and, hence, has not been disappointed.*

Economic Development and Growth

A BURNS DEPRESSION?
March 3, 1975

NOMENCLATURE changes. Originally the word "recession" was used to describe one of the four phases of the
business cycle: the phase of decline from the peak of the

boom. By this definition, the year 1930—following the boom of the late 1920s—was a recession year in the Great Depression of the 1930s.

Then, in the age after Keynes, we ceased to have old-fashioned depressions. But we still did have periods of greater unemployment and of negative real growth in the economy. We needed a euphemism for these unpleasant punctuations of the economy's advance. The word "recession" served nicely for this purpose, and it has come to be defined as "a period of *mild* depression."

Now that we seem to be in the worst recession of the whole post–World War II period, the time has come to dust out the old word "depression." I submit that a sensible usage would be *to define any recession that involves more than 10 per cent of the labor force as a depression.*

By this test we may or may not now be in a depression. That depends upon whether later this year the unemployment rate tops out around 9 or 9.5 per cent, or whether, as is quite possible, the unemployment rate goes above 10 per cent at its peak.

To say that we may be in a depression is not the same thing as to give an affirmative answer to the question that economists are increasingly asked these days: "Will we have a *great* depression like that of the 1930s?" The 1930s depression was the depression to end all depressions. The U.S. in 1975 could go into a depression like that of 1873 or 1893 without going into a Hoover depression like 1932.

A Legend Forged

In discussing the mounting attacks on Dr. Arthur F. Burns, the strong-minded chairman of the Federal Reserve Board, Leonard Silk wrote in the *New York Times* that, at 70, Burns now has nothing to lose but his reputation. With respect, that is an odd and empty comment. In my experience, all that one has to lose in Washington, regardless of age, is one's reputation. All Presidents, except on those rare occasions when they are fighting desperately to stay out of jail, work with the thought in their mind of how they will be judged in the history books.

So it is with Burns. As the leading disciple of the late Wesley Clair Mitchell (America's foremost student of the business cycle), Arthur Burns built up over half a century a deserved reputation for eclectic critical knowledge of economic fluctuations. Whatever applause academe can bestow on a scholar, Burns has received.

As economic adviser to President Eisenhower in his first (and best!) term, Dr. Burns showed himself to be a skilled policy analyst, conservative but nondoctrinaire. I have often said, as a Nixon watcher, that Arthur Burns is the only adviser that Richard Nixon had who invariably gave him good advice. Greater praise it is not in my power to bestow.

Anyone who knows the American political scene and knows Henry Kissinger must agree that the position of dominance that he reached by the middle of last year was unexpected and even unprecedented. Little wonder that his mystique has begun to wane since then. Next to Kissinger, and admittedly in a smaller historical role, Burns has risen to a remarkable pinnacle of power and respect. Barney Baruch was always, to insiders, a lightweight authority; but the position of respect that Baruch's name commanded is as nothing compared to that now attaching to Burns's. That a flaming populist like Rep. Wright Patman got along better with Burns than with former Fed chairman William McChesney Martin, Jr. is a measure of Burns's skill in personal relations and of Patman's naïveté.

Paradise Lost?

Who is given credit for the sun must be prepared to be blamed for the rain. History judges a man by how he acted in his most critical hour.

Since last summer it has appeared to most economists that Dr. Burns has lost his touch in weighing the risks of inflation and recession: they indict him and his *frères* for putting too tight a tourniquet of real money on the economy. They charge him with not "pushing hard enough on the string" of credit expansion.

Unfair to blame Burns for the economy's bad luck? Perhaps. But who says that history is ever fair? And who thinks the Federal Reserve does not help to make the luck that afflicts our 200 million people? If we do go into a depression, the Fed will justly bear much of the blame.

B FOR THE ECONOMY

February 26, 1979

EVERY few years when I buckle down to revise my introductory textbook in economics, I undergo a crash course in the basic facts of American economic life. It's a record worth reviewing, since the real picture tends to get lost in the crush of headlines—either good or bad. This time, I have been rather pleasantly surprised by the amount of genuine progress recorded since the tenth edition of the book was prepared in the mid-1970s.

The story, of course, is not all good. So let me mention at the beginning the bad news about inflation. Although the worldwide recession of 1973–75 did finally bring down the double-digit price rises of 1974, one discerns as we move toward the 1980s no significant progress toward a satisfactory solution of America's stagflation problem. Living with inflation of 5 to 10 per cent per year has become the hard reality of modern life.

Shouldn't the decline in the exchange rate of the dollar also be put in the column of debits? I believe that would be an oversimplification. Given the improvement in world harvests and what that implies for U.S. agricultural exports, and given the disappointing development of nuclear and alternative unconventional energy sources, it is a good and not a bad thing that exchange depreciation brings down American costs enough to make our goods competitive in world trade.

I am also happy to report that the Club of Rome problem has not worsened in recent years: we aren't being overwhelmed by sheer numbers of people relative to natural resources. Discovery and development of new geological resources seem to have about kept up with a somewhat reduced trend rate of exploitation. Worldwide drops in the birth rate offer hope that global population might level off in the next century. Actuaries record that life is generally now a bit less short, nasty and brutish.

Growth in Jobs

Since 1975 America has been in a vigorous recovery, the envy of Europe and Japan. Much of this antedates Jimmy Carter's Inauguration, going back to the Ford Administration. New records for longevity of peacetime expansion are in sight.

The prosperity shows itself in expanded employment. Female participation in the paid labor force is swelling. New entrants onto the job market, attributable to the last baby boom, by and large find the jobs they're looking for.

By contrast with rising unemployment rates in Germany, Britain and France, ours dropped from 9 per cent to the neighborhood of 6 per cent, a stubborn floor. More jobholders per family means higher real disposable incomes, as department-store cash registers have been attesting.

One disease associated with affluence is a disappointing trend in productivity growth. There is a mystery here inasmuch as the rate of productivity growth in manufacturing seems not nearly so bad as in services.

Aggregate corporation profits, even after we correct them

properly for inflationary revaluations, have been quite buoyant in recent years. Indeed, foreign enterprises now envy the American performance.

But common-stock prices continue to wobble in the doldrums. Our middle classes complain that their savings have not been able to keep up with inflation. Their only substantial capital appreciation has come in connection with home ownership, not a gain that very many can cash in on.

Diffusion of Benefits

Mere growth in economic aggregates wouldn't do much good if it came, as it did in the 1920s' "new era" of Calvin Coolidge, against the background of increasing economic inequality. How have the unskilled fared, black Americans and other minority groups, those who live on farms?

It is reassuring to see that black Americans have been maintaining the improvements in their relative income attained in the Kennedy-Johnson years. While they still earn only about 60 per cent of what whites do, this is perceptible progress from the 50 per cent levels of the Truman and Eisenhower years. Fortunately, the gains do not represent mere tokenism because they occur more at the bottom of the income scale than they do at the top. Despite the parade of tractors in Washington, average farm incomes came close in 1978 to urban incomes.

But as always, there is a caveat to much of this economic progress: the gains can still be jeopardized by a serious future recession or a prolonged period of slow growth.

MARGARET THATCHER'S TRIALS

June 16, 1980

THERE is said to be a swing to the right in American politics. Admirers of Ronald Reagan hope that this is the case, for Reagan's policy positions consistently lean in the conservative direction.

The United States is not alone in experiencing something of a backlash against the welfare state. The Swedish Labor Party, after four decades in office, was unseated by a coalition of non-socialists. Voters in both Australia and New Zealand have turned against labor parties in office. Norway tried a fling with a more bourgeois government a few years back.

To Americans, Margaret Thatcher's current Tory rule is the most interesting of these many political experiments. The British are our longtime allies—our cousins, at least by language.

Some of the symptoms of "the British disease" afflict us, too:

- Slow economic growth and high inflation—stagflation.
- High consumption, low savings and investment.
- A sense of being heavily taxed.
- Disappointing productivity trends.

To learn more about how the Thatcher crusade is working out, I recently paid a visit to Britain. I realize one must not exaggerate the value of evidence gathered from direct personal observation. There are only so many persons in the street one can sample. And after you have talked to one investment banker, you've pretty much talked to them all.

Still, if anyone believes in the moonshine of "supply-side economics"—that reducing tax rates across the board and freeing international trade from exchange controls will unleash a miracle of market growth—a trip to London will cure such delusions.

British price inflation still rages despite pedantic allegiance to a naïve monetarism. The financial community finds it credible that Thatcher's team will keep a tight rein on the money supply. But that doesn't make the financial experts expect that inflation can be lowered without years of austerity in macroeconomic policy. Any rewards from the campaign against inflation are still to come.

The good luck of Britain's finds of oil and gas in the North Sea has shielded her against the shocks of OPEC price increases. But oil has not been enough to offset the weakness of British manufacturing production. By strengthening the exchange rate quoted for the floating pound in relation to world currencies, Britain's oil revenues actually serve to undermine the international competitiveness of her export industries.

I have skipped over the already familiar fact that London is just about the most expensive city in the world for the business traveler. And it is no longer newsworthy to comment on low British wages. It is sad to learn how little an experienced teacher or a trained accountant or clerk is paid. Whatever they earn, they are taxed pretty heavily and cannot buy many of the comforts of life at prevailing prices. When the minimum lending rates go up at the banks, householders are automatically charged a higher interest rate on their old mortgages; people learn without seeming to flinch that they must pay something like 15 per cent of their outstanding liability.

One can't blame any current political party for the fact that Britain is a poor country. No fair person expects Thatcher's laissez-faire program to repair in a year or in half a decade what a century of custom and legislation has brought about.

Not Finding

It is fair to examine the trend of events since the Tories came into office. Social Darwinists are forever bombarding us with anecdotes on the marvels of the marketplace: how Ludwig Erhard's currency reforms brought war-devastated West Germany into miraculous recovery or how San Francisco rebuilt herself after the 1906 earthquake—back in the good old days of limited government and unlimited acquisitive enterprise.

So, although I realize that anecdotes don't constitute science, I tried to keep my eyes open to any signs of Thatcher success. Perhaps if I had traveled more widely I'd have found some gems to report. Or it may be that I lack the faith to believe in things unseen. In any case, neither in the impressions of one's immediate senses nor in the statistical data do I find noteworthy signs that the market magic has yet begun to work.

There may be a moral for U.S. voters. Higher living standards do depend on more efficient supply. But don't believe the rhetoric of those who claim that the policies of Cal Coolidge will soon deliver the goods.

GOOD NEWS ON DEVELOPMENT
July 23, 1979

OUT of my subconscious came the memory of my mother's old saying:

> *I complained that I had no shoes,*
> *Until I met a man who had no feet.*

What brought this to mind was my reading recently, during the worst of the gasoline shortage, the World Bank's survey of economic progress since 1960. Entitled "World Development Report, 1978," and with a foreword by bank president Robert S. McNamara, it is a treasure-trove of hard-to-come-by data on 125 countries.

The report brings tidings of considerable joy—some slight consolation now that my weekend trips to Cape Cod are in jeopardy. At long last, the percentage income gap between the developing and industrialized countries is ceasing to widen. Let me sample the findings.

Life Less Nasty and Short

Begin with vital statistics. With no exception, people in every country can look forward to a longer average life. Even in Ethiopia and Mali, life expectancy at birth has risen by four years to 38 years. To be sure, this is barely half the 75 years of Norway. But it beats the actuarial odds back in glorious ancient Athens or splendid Elizabethan London. And, most germane, it represents palpable progress since 1960.

Next time you hear a Groton senior or Bennington freshman lisp against material things, remind yourself that higher per capita income does indeed buy longer life and better health. Small may be beautiful. But poor most definitely is not. (The accompanying table shows the relationship between poverty and longevity.)

Does a system of public-health provision atone for a lack of economic advance? Perhaps the fact that the centrally planned economies come so close to the top actuarially despite their considerable shortfall of material affluence may point in that direction.

The birth-rate data are not so cheerful. Birth rates are declining in the developing countries, but they are still high enough to keep populations growing at about 2.5 per cent per year. These regions are expected to have a two-thirds increase over their already swollen numbers by the year 2000.

There are lessons to be mined from the data. The low-income countries fail to plow back into investment as large a fraction of the gross national product (GNP) as the middle-income and industrialized countries—only one-sixth as against the latter's one-fourth. Chalk up one for the apologists for capital formation.

BUYING TIME

	Real per capita income (1975 dollars)	Life expectancy
Industrialized Countries (U.S., Sweden, U.K., etc.)	$6,200	72 years
Centrally Planned Economies (U.S.S.R., China, Poland, etc.)	$2,280	70 years
Developing Countries Middle Income (Brazil, Mexico, Egypt, etc.)	$750	58 years
Low Income (India, Kenya, Mali, etc.)	$150	44 years

The record does not, however, bear out the thesis that the poor stay poor because their governments usurp in frivolous public consumption a larger fraction of the GNP. Again, the low- and middle-income countries have lower government expenditures as a fraction of GNP than the industrialized countries!

Tackling Poverty

Robert McNamara is not universally popular. Like Herbert Hoover, he parts his hair in the middle. Like Hoover, he developed a reputation for efficiency in business (Ford Motor Co.) and public service (the Pentagon). Like the Herbert Hoover who helped to feed the starving Europeans at the end of World War I, McNamara has recognized poverty as an enemy to be fought.

The World Bank has successfully promoted, under both McNamara and his predecessors, the development of total product in poor nations, encouraging the use of market incentives and profitability tests to do so. I take off my hat to Robert McNamara for what has been his unique vision—his recognition that successful market forces alone can't be relied on to mitigate flagrant inequality and abject poverty.

His own words are worth quoting:

"The past quarter century has been a period of unprecedented change and progress in the developing world. And yet despite this impressive record, some 100 million individuals continue to be trapped in what I have termed absolute poverty, a condition of life so characterized by malnutrition, illiteracy, disease, squalid surroundings, high infant mortality, and low life expectancy as to be beneath any acceptable definition of human decency.

"The twin objectives of development then, are to accelerate economic growth and to reduce poverty."

ANOTHER GREAT DEPRESSION?
October 28, 1974

KARL Marx used to like to quote a tag from Hegel: history has a tendency to repeat itself, the first time as tragedy, the second time as farce. The American people apparently now feel that history will indeed repeat itself, but both times as tragedy.

The Gallup poll reports that 51 per cent of the American people think we are moving into a depression. This fear is not a monopoly of the uninformed lay public. Last June, the prestigious London *Economist* published an article, later widely quoted, to the effect that the massive balance-of-payments deficits created by the high price of oil would plunge the world into depression. Some large institutional investors who seek my opinion on the state of the economy now keep their liquid balances in Treasury bills. When I asked why they didn't seek 11 rather than 7 per cent yields available on the certificates of deposit of our largest and safest banks, they admitted that they were scared of the risk!

Are fears of a depression like that of the 1930s well grounded? I do not think they are. But this is not a subject upon which one can entertain certain or even confident opinions. So let me go over the evidence you will need to form a rational judgment in the matter.

What It Was Like
Not 20 per cent of Gallup's sample know what the Great Depression of the 1930s was really like here and abroad:

• One in four persons could not get a job, here in America and in the Germany that turned itself over to Adolf Hitler.

• So many thousands of our 15,000 different banks failed that Franklin Roosevelt's first act as President was to close down all the banks—as a first step before reopening the most solvent under a new set of government rules.

• In what we now call, rightly in my opinion, a recession, our money GNP still grows at a 10 per cent annual rate. Between 1929 and 1933, money GNP virtually halved.

• Today we debate with Arthur Burns and the Federal Reserve whether the money supply should grow these next twelve months at around 7 per cent (as I would think), or whether it should grow 4.5 per cent (as many monetarists think). In the early 1930s the money supply was falling by every definition.

I could go on and on, recalling how very bad the Great Depression was here and abroad. And how very much worse it was than anything we are yet experiencing today. But that will not necessarily reassure a thoughtful person concerned lest our present situation will develop into something much worse than we have yet seen. You can cogently argue, after all, that 1930, the first year after the 1929 debacle, did not look so bad; yet we now know that it was the precursor of a grim decade of less than full employment growth in the U.S. economy.

But was it inevitable that the recession of 1930 had to degenerate into the depression of 1931–33—or for that matter into the decade whose depressed conditions did not really come to an end until the world was plunged into the bloody ordeal of the second great war?

I used to think the answer to this question was yes. I no longer think so.

History is a onetime thing. You cannot prove how events would have been different if Hitler had not attacked Russia, or if Napoleon had not stopped to dally with Josephine. But the art of the good historian who essays to be more than a rattling good storyteller of antiquarian tales is to form out of all the available evidence the best betting probabilities on each contingent event.

Good-By Hooverism

The basic reason why the Great Depression was not inevitable, and why anything really like that depression is improbable now, is that in those days governments all over the world hewed to the lines of orthodox finance. As things got bad, they tightened their own belts and forced the populace to do likewise.

It is more than an empty cliché to repeat that populist democracies all over the world have bitten deep in the apple of the tree of knowledge: we live in the age *after* Keynes, and there is no going back to Herbert Hooverism.

I see troubles ahead. But not those of the 1930–33 type.

POLICY FOR STAGFLATION

October 15, 1973

THERE are only two times in the business cycle when proper policy is easy to formulate.

At the bottom of a recession, the Federal Reserve Board is supposed to expand the money supply and keep interest rates low. At that time any President, budget director and Secretary of Treasury should understand that a deliberate budget deficit is in order. Since political pressures work at such a time to reinforce simple common sense and the findings of scientific economics, there is not much danger that sound advice will be then ignored.

The other easy time for policy prescription is when an

economy is sprinting ahead on an obvious collision course with a full-capacity and full-employment ceiling. Then a budget balanced at full employment may not provide enough fiscal restraint. Then the Federal Reserve authorities must try to ignore the cheap-money populisms of a Congressman Patman.

At all other times the lot of the economic policy maker is not an easy one. If he has been doing his job right, the mixed economy will always be walking the tightrope between inflation and unemployment. Most of the time the jury of experts will be disagreeing on the proper mix of policy.

Different Value Judgments

Does this disagreement mean that economics is not yet an exact science? Well, of course, economics is not yet an exact science. But the measure of its factual and analytical inadequacies is not properly gauged from the decibel count of disagreement among the expert jurors.

Prof. William Fellner is the new man on the Nixon Council of Economic Advisers. He and I are old friends. I have long been one of his claque of admirers. Yet Dr. Fellner and I often find ourselves in disagreement on the desirable degree of tightness of fiscal and monetary policy.

Usually, as now, I would counsel that the system aim for a lower target for the rate of unemployment than he would. It is not that we differ much in our forecasts on where the economic system is heading. Probably, neither of us would give odds against the experts who think we are now moving into a mini-recession, where that term is defined as a year in which the growth rate in real GNP is positive but well below the 4 per cent rate that corresponds to long-run population and productivity change.

Two equally good scientists can differ in their value judgments. Professor Fellner with his vivid memories of Continental inflations has a natural concern for those retired people who are the principal victims of inflation; and a concern lest the last half per cent of employment be purchased at the cost of reaccelerating inflation.

I, with my vivid memories of the Great Depression, have a natural concern for those unskilled and minority workers who are called on to shoulder the burden of fighting creeping inflation by means of the nation's running a relatively slack labor market. So, be warned of my possible biases.

1974 Program

1. *Don't try to fight food inflation by fiscal and monetary policies.* That is putting a tourniquet around the patient's neck to check his bleeding chin. In the next couple of years the same factors of supply and demand that sent up prices of food and fiber will send them down.

2. *The current boom is too old to introduce new taxes,* as the Fed's Arthur Burns recently recommended. Also, the time is past for draconian cuts in budget spending in order to cool off inflation.

3. *Do permit the economy to slow down its growth rate from last year's unmaintainable 7 per cent sprint.* To keep the average rate of unemployment below 5 per cent in the period from now to 1976, we would do well to let it rise temporarily above recent levels (repeat, *temporarily*).

4. *The signal for beginning to restimulate the economy ought to be any manifest tendency for the growth rate to stagnate toward zero.* A few quarters of growth at only a 2 per cent annual rate will cause the unemployment rate to climb toward 5.5 per cent. For women, youths and unskilled urban workers, the climb will be steeper. Resist the counsel that what this country needs to break the back of inflation is a salutary recession.

5. *Price controls cannot cause meat or fuel scarcities to disappear.* But jettisoning the control program is a prescription for a disastrous reactivation of the quiescent wage spiral.

These are hysterical times. But what is called for in the economic sphere are cool decisions that don't try to cure all our problems overnight.

THE ECONOMIC OUTLOOK

March 25, 1974

ANY intelligent person following current economic events might be forgiven if he despairs of making any sense of the situation. There seem to be more contradictions than ever in the developing trends. Let me therefore try to provide a guide to where we seem to stand as the winter of 1974 draws to a close.

Yes, the economic experts were right in saying last spring that the U.S. was then moving into a "growth recession." Since last Easter we shifted down from boom expansion to far below the 4 per cent annual rate of real growth that is the par needed to provide jobs for a growing labor force in a technologically progressive economy. The unemployment rate is on the rise, and by next fall the odds favor its being nearer to 6 per cent than 5.5 per cent.

Yes, the experts were right who predicted that 1974 would be a year of "stagflation"—stagnation along with serious inflation. Price increases have been accelerating and spreading. This quarter's rate of inflation is hovering just below the 10 per cent level. And the end is not yet in sight. I have been talking recently with businessmen all over the land. And virtually all tell me they are panting for an upward adjustment in their prices—to compensate them for what they consider a profit-margin squeeze as their raw-material costs have soared. I presume that a survey of trade-union officials would show a similar desire on the part of workers for a "catch-up" in their wages.

Yes, there is an actual "recession" in real output this first quarter of 1974—perhaps at as much as a 4 per cent annual rate of decline. For the second quarter, the bets are about even among the experts on a further decline in output or a leveling off. Little money is being offered on the long-shot bet of a "V bottom" and a sharp upsurge in business.

Cold Comforts

No, there is no cogent evidence to support the view that the U.S. is about to plunge into depression. A worldwide depression is primarily a fabrication of free-lance journalists, gold bugs and financial sensationalists who have had a miserable track record as forecasters in the past.

No, the typical forecasters from banks, industry, universities and governments do not expect the inflation rate to be as bad at the end of 1974 as it is now. (I don't know quite how to square this with Fed chairman Burns's recent congressional testimony warning of two-digit inflation of the Latin American type. Perhaps there is something infectious in the job that makes its holder succumb to the temptation that so often seduced former chairman Martin—namely, to issue warnings that go beyond the evidence in order to shake voters and congressmen out of policies deemed to be unsound. But perhaps Burns has cogent evidence and ways of analyzing it that will gradually become available to the public at large.)

Uncertainties

The foregoing appraisal exhausts the easy side of my current audit. Much harder to answer are the following questions:

· Will unemployment peak out at 6 per cent? Will it be stable or falling by the year's end?

· Will the upturn in business come soon enough, so that

1974 will not go down in the history books as a "genuine" recession? And will any improvement in the stagflation come soon enough and be significant enough to take pressures off Republican candidates in next November's election?

The jury is still out on these issues. And until they are clarified by the passage of time, legitimate debate about desirable policies can go on. Therefore, I would urge the following cautious programs:

1. Regardless of what happens to the oil boycott and to the continuation of a recession in real incomes and output, personal tax exemptions should be immediately raised. Even in World War II, the exemptions were $500 per head; in view of the inflation since then, $900 or $1,000 would be a fairer exemption than the present $750.

If such a tax cut were to be done, well it were done quickly. Now, while unemployment is growing.

2. Now is also the time for monetary policy to ease. It would be folly to try to roll back energy prices or raw-material prices by contriving recession or encouraging a maintained level of unemployment above 5.5 per cent. After healthy growth is restored, gradual anti-inflationary pressure will again be in order.

This, I submit, is a sober and cautious program. I believe that it is also a humane one.

QUESTIONS AND ANSWERS

June 17, 1974

MY mail reveals that people are today unusually worried. I shall give here my best replies to their most common queries. More important than yes-or-no answers is the delicate task of indicating, within the limits of my space, the uncertainties that are inherent in even the best economic analysis of the thorny problems we are now facing.

Q: Isn't the economic system as we have known it going to pot?

A: Dostoevski, Carlyle, Henry Adams and Spengler foresaw unspeakable horrors written in the palms of modern civilizations. When you read about Watergate, contemplate the doomsday print-outs of the Club of Rome, tick off the heads of state who have recently lost office and sample the collected works of Fed chairman Burns, you might well begin to wonder whether the prophets of disaster are not coming into their own.

Yet as I turn the pages of an annual roundup by the State Department of growth around the world, I discover that 1973 was a year of unusually successful economic growth: real world GNP, after corrections for inflation are made, turned out to rise by 6.9 per cent, a rate that economic historians will consider to be a high one.

In the remaining years of this century, we shall have Sahara droughts, bad Asian monsoons, increasing relative costs of exhaustible raw materials. But the best betting odds from available trend data are that the globe's economy will provide the wherewithal for rising life expectancies—if only those with economic power choose to make nature's plenty available to those most in need.

Recession or Recovery?

Q: Mr. Nixon keeps insisting that we are not in a recession. Yet unemployment grows and headlines portray many industries in distress. What is the truth?

A: Most experts think we hit bottom in the spring. But they still expect 1974 to be a year of stagnation relative to the growth rate we need to keep unemployment and excess capacity from growing.

The important debate is not on the semantic definition of whether a "recession" has taken place. It is on how weak or strong the recovery is likely to be, and whether government policy should try to increase the vigor of the recovery.

Q: If I can stop worrying about a depression or even a serious recession, what diagnosis can you give me about the inflation we're in? When Dr. Burns warns against double-digit inflation that will ruin us if we don't take this last chance to eradicate it, chills run down my spine. Should I stockpile wheat and get out of the melting dollar? The Administration keeps saying inflation will be better by the end of the year, but I've been hearing that tune so long that each repetition makes me scared.

A: Let's ignore government PR. What are the best forecasters saying—economists such as Eckstein (Harvard and Data Resources, Inc.), Evans (Chase Econometrics), Greenspan (Townsend-Greenspan), Klein (Wharton School computer model)? As against the 11.5 per cent annual rate of general price increase of early 1974, the experts expect a fourth-quarter inflation rate in the range of 7.3 and 8.3 per cent.

Economics is an inexact science. So I must prudently allow a one-third probability that at year's end inflation will still be in the 10 per cent range. Bad? Yes. But no rational reason for talk about us as a "banana republic" or on the verge of a 1923 German hyperinflation.

Policy Debate

Q: How are you able to make the future seem so uncontroversial?

A: The real dispute is not about our different forecasts. Behind the scenes, the debate is between (1) those who think that the fight against inflation makes it *desirable* for a year or two that unemployment *not* average out below 5.5 per cent and (2) those who think this is a higher price than the American voter will, or should, pay.

Q: Which school is right?

A: No simple answer can be given. In part the issue hinges on value judgments that transcend economics as a science. But in part, resolution of the policy debates must hinge on precision of forecasting that no jury of experts can yet pretend to. Thus, some forecasters think the recovery will be overstrong even if the Fed keeps money dear. Others think tight money will do little to dampen down inflation a year from now, but can put such a damper on housing as to make any recovery anemic.

In short, lack of agreement is a proper response to uncertainties.

THE NEW RECOVERY

July 28, 1975

IT is now official: the U.S. economy hit bottom in May. The new data on second-quarter 1975 GNP have confirmed what the economic experts have been confidently predicting.

Not only are the experts happy, but the Ford Administration is also relieved. The only people managing to avoid euphoria are the unemployed. The rate of joblessness will continue to deteriorate a bit until late summer or fall, when the economy has again attained the 4 per cent annual rate of real output growth needed if we are to *offset the normal increases in population and the normal displacement of labor by productivity advance.*

What is the outlook for the next twelve months? That is a more interesting question at this stage of the game than "What is the outlook for the decade?" or "How long will the recovery last?"

I shall give my opinion on probable output growth and probable inflation from mid-1975 to mid-1976. But opinions are cheap. You can collect a sheaf of them in a morning; and their opposites in the afternoon. It will perhaps be more useful—and it will certainly be more novel—to describe how one forms a reasoned judgment in these matters.

Digging Evidence

The Chinese were right: one peek is worth a thousand finesses. If it is not given to us to peek into the future, we must pore over the facts of the past.

Since there has been a business cycle in capitalist history about every three and a half years, we have some 40 recoveries we could look at. But as the Good Book says, there is a time to remember and a time to forget. What has the world of Martin Van Buren, or even of Calvin Coolidge, to do with the present-day world? Let's stick to the postwar years.

There have been five recognized recessions since 1946: a Truman recession, three Eisenhower recessions and a Nixon recession. The first four quarters of recovery from each of these have shown real output growth respectively: 14 per cent ('49–50), 8 per cent ('54–55), 9 per cent ('58–59), 7 per cent ('61–62), 5 per cent ('70–71).

So taking a simple average, par for the course would seem to be about 9 per cent—or, if 1950 is eliminated because of the Korean War distortion, 7.5 per cent.

This is but a first step. The second step is to examine whatever seems special about the situation at its beginning. Thus, failure to take this second step contributed to gross overestimates of strength for the Nixon recovery in 1971.

Three special features now seem present:

• Autos, which have a rhythm of their own, seem unlikely to experience a normally vigorous recovery. Energy concern plays a key role here.

• Housing seems to lack zip, even under the sunshine of easier credit.

• Fighting inflation remains a prime policy concern. Until Richard Nixon tore up his old game plan in August 1971, government determination to fight inflation contributed to the weakness of the post-1970 recovery. Although the present rate of inflation is only about half that of last autumn, no watcher of President Ford, Arthur Burns or Alan Greenspan can fail to observe their continuing concern that the recovery *not* be too exuberant. And they are in a position to get much of what they desire. Sometimes too much.

Not all is gloomy. The stock-market advance is a favorable factor. So is the sharpness of the inventory decumulation behind us. The sheer length of the recession should leave consumers hungry and, other things equal, eager to spend.

The third step is to survey what the forecasters with the best batting averages predict: the Wharton-Pennsylvania Model, Chase Econometrics, Data Resources (DRI), your own favorite soothsayer.

Summing It Up

The consensus forecasters seem to average out with a guess of 6 to 7 per cent real growth over the next twelve months; price inflation of 4 to 8 per cent; unemployment a year from now to be little below 8 per cent (as against about 8.9 per cent this May and June).

As for me, this time I must generally go with the consensus forecasts. But I think they underestimate the likely spread of probabilities.

Here is my appraisal:

· Real GNP growth—4 to 9 per cent.
   Price inflation—4 to 8 per cent.
· Profits rising smartly, interest rates slowly.

BONANZAS FROM DEMOCRATS

July 26, 1976

THE Republicans are the party of property; the Democrats are the party of the lower-income populace. This pat statement fits most of the facts.

But, surely, this creates something of a paradox? For all the polls now show that Jimmy Carter is most likely to lead a unified Democratic Party to victory in the fall. And yet business is buoyant. Executives are purring in the executive suites. Even the Dow-Jones averages play peekaboo with their all-time record highs.

How can we explain this complacency on the part of the business and banking community in the face of what one would expect to be to them a displeasing prospect?

In my opinion there is no paradox, and precious little that needs explaining, or explaining away. The brute truth is that Democratic Administrations have been good for profits and business these last 50 years. What is bad for the country at large is bad for General Motors. And it has been during Republican Administrations that most of our recessions have tended to come.

The Unvarnished Record

Let's pose a little history test.

Since Hoover's time, which President has been most unlucky in terms of bad performance of the U.S. economy during his Administration?

The answer is not Richard Nixon. The jury might argue between Gerald Ford and Dwight Eisenhower. Although the Ford recession was the worst of the postwar period, my own verdict would have to go against Eisenhower. During his two terms we managed to have *three* recessions. Worse than that, from the standpoint of stock-market values, business profits and full-employment opportunities, the sad fact is that the Eisenhower years were years of chronic growth stagnation. And only the first of his recessions can be explained by the Korean War.

For each four years of Republican occupancy of the White House, the annals show at least one full-fledged recession. By contrast, Franklin Roosevelt, taking over at the depths of the Great Depression, presided over only one recession in his four terms of office. Aside from post–World War II reconversion, one can properly debit against Harry Truman only the recession of 1948–49. Kennedy and Johnson had no recessions in their years. (However, Johnson did have a "mini-growth" recession in 1967; and some of the blame for the Nixon recession of 1969–70 must probably fall on Johnson's Vietnam finance policies.)

There is nothing mysterious about these regularities. Nor are they mere coincidences. They follow remorselessly from the ideologies of the two parties.

An Eisenhower, Nixon or Ford appoints for his Secretary of the Treasury and budget director Wall Street or industrialist types like George Humphrey and William Simon. The roll call of economists appointed by Republican Presidents includes names of scholars known to be of the conservative wing: Arthur Burns, Raymond Saulnier, Gabriel Hauge, Herbert Stein and Alan Greenspan.

Of course these choices matter. That is what elections are about.

To the Victors . . .

Gradually each President gets the kind of Federal Reserve Board that is in his own image, just as he eventually gets the Supreme Court he wants. And we the electorate get these same Federal Reserve Boards and Supreme Courts that, in effect, we have opted for when casting our ballots between the contending party candidates.

Some Democratic candidates are more frightening to men of affluence than others. William Jennings Bryan was deemed to have unsound views on money. Franklin Roosevelt's New Deal was hated, even though he did more for the recovery of business profitability and capital values than any President in the history of the republic. George McGovern was identified, rightly or wrongly, with extremist groups and their programs.

Jimmy Carter is perceived by management groups as not one to rock the boat. They reason that anyone so sanctimonious must be sound in his basic attitudes toward the need of business to earn a profit.

Other things equal, businessmen prefer a Republican President. But they know when to cut their losses and live with the acceptable second best. Particularly when that second best might turn out to be first best with respect to longevity of the economic recovery and juiciness of profits.

RECOVERY SIGNS

September 22, 1980

JIMMY Carter's bad luck with the election-year recession is beginning to end. I doubt that the signs of upturn will be strong enough to eliminate this Reagan advantage, but Charles Schultze and the White House economic advisers must be breathing easier now that the stage of free fall has come to an end.

Although the economy's growth has been stagnant since

March 1979, the actual recession is dated from January 1980. Best guesses were that it would last until Election Day and be followed by a weak recovery in the early years of the 1980s. Realists did not expect so limited a recession could end inflation permanently. What they did hope for was some deceleration of what had become an inflation rate of more than 15 per cent per year.

Experience has confirmed the dictum "If you must forecast, forecast often." When I left the country this summer for visits to Peru and Norway, events looked on schedule. If anything, the dismal collapse of auto sales and housing starts in late spring, coupled with negative growth of the money supply, gave comfort to the pessimists who expected what candidate Reagan calls a "depression." By the time I returned to God's country, though, the worst was clearly over.

Automatic Stabilizers

The parachute had opened in our modern mixed economy. The prospect of a government budget that would stay balanced in the face of a recession happily disappeared as fiscal policy automatically began to resist the fall. The Federal Reserve Board permitted interest rates to fall, ending what had been a money crunch and enabling the reeling housing industry to make an upturn.

The stock market advanced serenely through it all. This time share prices failed to forecast the recession before it arrived. And, so to speak, up to this moment, the common-stock indexes have not accorded diplomatic recognition to the recession in being.

Some economists are troubled by this puzzling behavior of Wall Street, but there are precedents for it in history. In September 1953 the stock market began its fifteen-year boom right in the teeth of the first of the three Eisenhower recessions. Money managers can apparently forgive Republican recessions, and by 1953 the suspicion finally jelled that postwar share prices were cheap. Similarly, many investors have now begun to be impressed by the gospel of MIT's Franco Modigliani that years of inflation have raised the true value of ownership in American plant and equipment and that ultimately this must show itself in a much higher level of common-stock prices.

Mr. Dooley said that the Supreme Court *follows* the election returns. Wall Street *anticipates* the election returns. Ronald Reagan is the pinup boy of the brokerage crowd. They go to bed at night with visions of tax credits and dream all night of capital-gains tax rates down to 20 per cent. One of the current perils of holding a leveraged position in equities is that Ronald Reagan will shoot himself in the foot with some unguarded remark about abolishing the farm subsidies or going to war with Mexico. But who ever promised the risk taker a bed of roses?

The recovery is not assured, of course. Here is the latest forecast of the Wharton Econometric Forecasting Association, the academic group from the University of Pennsylvania that has been taken over by a commercial corporation:

· Fourth-quarter real output will be above this quarter's. I reckon that means the upturn comes by Columbus Day, early October.

· Consumer prices will be rising at a 12 per cent rate on Election Day, falling for the next year and a half to below a 9 per cent rate.

· Fourth-quarter unemployment is expected to peak at 8.3 per cent of the labor force, only slowly falling back toward the present 7.6 per cent rate.

Wall Street would be glad to settle for this horoscope. Other consensus forecasters—McGraw-Hill's DRI and Chase Econometrics—are less sanguine on a fourth-quarter turnup. There are still others who speak direly of a "double dip," in which a weak fall upturn later goes into reverse.

My own fear is stagflation. I see no evidence that we are

on the road back to price stability. Recession concerns will all too soon turn into recovery concerns.

But who ever promised the policy economist that life would be a bed of roses?

YEAR-END QUESTIONS

January 1, 1979

LAST week, I was asked certain basic questions in Washington. They were essentially the same ones I was asked abroad last month. From my mail, I know that these are queries bothering people everywhere.

Here are my best answers to them. Besides indicating how I interpret the relevant evidence, I shall do my best to describe the range of differing opinions. Ours are complicated times and economics is not so exact a science that readers will be able to rely on one person's opinions alone, however plausible his analysis may seem.

Q. How is the year 1979 looking?

A. Since President Carter's Nov. 1 adoption of tight money and austere budget programs to fight inflation and steady up the dollar, best informed opinion now expects a mild recession beginning about midyear and ending by early 1980.

Q. Why will it be mild?

A. This time the rest of the world need not, and probably will not, join America in the contraction. Japan, Germany, France and the other principal nations have not yet had the vigorous recovery enjoyed here; so their expansions may still have a way to go.

Price Prospects

Q. Will such a downturn do the trick and lick the inflation threat?

A. I don't think so. And economists more conservative than I—Drs. William Fellner and Herbert Stein of the American Enterprise Institute are two excellent examples, each worth listening to—also doubt that so mild a recession can accomplish very much. If people can look beyond the dip to a pre-election sprint promoted by Washington, they'll not find a stable price regime credible.

Q. Why bother then with programs to send unemployment up a full per cent at least?

A. The polls show most people do fear inflation, particularly when it accelerates. Our recovery will be 50 months old by summer, making it one of the oldest on record.

The private economy still looks pretty strong. Consumers, despite more debt, still buy cars, still crowd the stores. Housing holds up. Inventories seem balanced. It is argued that, if the Fed does not bring the real growth rate down below our long-run trend rate of 3 to 4 per cent per year, the inflation that accelerated in the last half of 1978 will further accelerate in 1979–80.

Q. Though a recession will not cure inflation, some slowdown will help keep it from getting worse and will improve the inflation rate a bit. Is that the argument?

A. Precisely. I would add that Swiss roulette is a dangerous game. The avalanche you touch off may take the garden *and* the unwanted weeds.

Dire Threats

Q. I hear talk of depression. Should we worry about the so-called Kondratieff Cycle?

A. Walt Rostow says we should. So does MIT's Jay Forrester. They could be right. But as I and the bulk of economists read the evidence, save your worrying time for more likely evils. Two centuries of capitalism's history is not long enough to establish the statistical reliability of long economic waves. The Rostow and Forrester versions do not agree with each other, and neither agrees with Nikolai Kondratieff's original 1926 theory.

Q. I hear rumors of impending galloping inflation. If not cataclysmic slump, what about the danger of catastrophic collapse of the monetary system?

A. The asthma of stagflation rather than the galloping pneumonia of hyperinflation is what seems indicated by the history of the '60s and '70s.

Q. Have the interest rates peaked?

A. I doubt it. The January and February inflation numbers will look bad. OPEC's oil-price increase will be pushing prices up, too. Social Security payroll taxes and the minimum wage go up Jan. 1. That will raise prices and make many people think all the government programs are a failure. So I suspect bond prices will stay weak until spring. Lots of people are betting I'm wrong in this. We'll see.

Q. What about common stocks?

A. Weak bonds breed weak stocks. But before a recession hits bottom, stocks usually turn up. In 1979 this could happen even sooner.

Now for the $30 billion question: Will the dollar exchange rate hold?

A. For now, probably yes. The trade deficit's all-too-slow improvement keeps the longer prospect iffy.

COPING WITH STAGFLATION

August 19, 1974

PRESIDENT Ford's taking office is not likely to have any great effects on the U.S. economy one way or another. This anticlimactic conclusion does not, however, rule out the following prospect:

With a little luck, the U.S. economy is likely to do better in President Ford's first year of office than it did in Nixon's last year.

On analysis, I find no merit in the common view that our economic troubles were appreciably due to the fact that Richard Nixon was so busy fighting for his political life that he was unable to devote the time needed to devise government policies to cure inflation. If he had all the time in the world, we'd still face our present problem of *stagflation*.

There are no feasible policies that President Ford can now be expected to formulate with the help of a cooperative Congress that will succeed in doing much about such inflation. If you don't believe this sober fact of life, gather a jury of the country's twelve best economists. Provided you have sampled a broad spectrum of political opinion, their lack of agreement will corroborate the one basic fact about stagflation:

No mixed economy—not the U.S. or U.K., Sweden or Switzerland, Germany or Japan, France or Italy—knows how to have sustained full employment with price stability.

Galbraithians will tell the new President that price-wage controls administered by a President who believes in them can do the trick. Gerald Ford will not agree with them, and neither will their academic colleagues.

Hayekians will tell Ford that the free market plus control on the supply of money is the only way to deal with stagflation. But a majority of their colleagues will read in the evidence of the modern world greater costs and less benefits from such policies than are dreamed of in these philosophies.

Continuity

What then will the new President do? He will listen to the cacophony of advice offered. Being essentially conservative, and being a believer in continuity, he will presumably follow the advice of people like Dr. Burns and the inherited staff of Administration economists.

So long as the unemployment rate stays below the politically critical levels of, say, 5.75 per cent, Ford will give his blessing to tight money and austere fiscal policy.

The dozen forecasters with the best batting averages in recent times expect that, under these policies, *real growth will be anemic from mid-1974 to mid-1975*. To be sure, that would be better than recent negative growth. But it would be significantly less than the 3 to 4 per cent growth rate needed to employ a growing labor force.

Gerald Ford, being a political pragmatist, can be expected later to talk increasingly about the stagnation part of our stagflation problem—as the electorate begins to react to the growing level of unemployment. Once the 1976 election comes into view, the dynamics of populist democracy will tend to reactivate the only business cycle left in the modern mixed economy—the political cycle, in which policy is expansionary just before major general elections.

The Middle Way

How would I advise a new President?

1. Set yourself realistic sights. Best feasible policy is to try to reduce this year's low two-digit inflation to high one-digit inflation by next year.

Most relief will come about not from government's austere macroeconomic policies but from abatement of the rash of exogenous factors that sent prices up in 1974: no new strength to the Mideast oil monopoly; with luck, no worldwide rash of crop failures; no simultaneous flare-up of overheated economies all over the world.

2. Realize that the inflation you inherit is tougher than what Nixon faced in 1968–69. Now cost-push inflation, not demand-pull, is on us in force. The President of all the people, who wishes to end the divisiveness of our political life, should speak softly and put aside his big stick lest he rouse sleeping dogs of the class struggle.

3. Apply a simple test to any counselor who presses an all-out religious crusade against inflation. Ask what his program is likely to achieve in terms of percentage-point reductions in inflation, and make him set out its costs in unemployment and living standards.

In short, replace ideology by cost-benefit analysis.

A NOBEL FOR FORECASTING

November 3, 1980

THE recession ended in late summer, making it the shortest one on record. If it had been any shorter, the game warden would have made us throw it back.

Autumn had scarcely begun when we knew the upturn had commenced. We have the giant computer to thank for this promptness in knowledge.

In 1798, when Malthus was warning that England faced overpopulation and mass starvation, no one had a clue to what was really happening to the total size of the population.

Dr. Richard Price, an eminent authority, was convinced that the British population had shrunk by a third since the Glorious Revolution of 1688. We now know that Price was wrong, but no one then had any way of resolving the issue.

As recently as 1937 the United States was surprised to find itself in a steep recession. Gen. Robert Wood, then the head of Sears, Roebuck and Co., testified that when he went into the Canadian bush on a hunting trip everything looked all right. When he emerged, the economic heavens had fallen in. Accurate data, promptly available on a broad sector of the economy, are indeed a post–World War II development.

Age of Klein

Of software and the man I sing. On Dec. 10 in Stockholm, Prof. Lawrence R. Klein of the University of Pennsylvania will justly receive the Nobel Prize in Economics for his scientific innovation of macroeconomic forecasting.

We are all in Klein's debt: not just the hundreds of econometricians who ply their craft at banks, consulting firms, universities, corporations and government agencies but also judgmental forecasters like me who eschew formal mathematical models.

A malicious colleague once asked, "Paul, how soon will the computer make you obsolete?" Since he was malicious, I let him have the truth: "Not in a million years." Even if I am wrong by a factor of 10, the point is made. Inside every computer is a fallible human being, the person who wrote its program, who specified its important variables and designed their general structure.

I retell the story so that it can be provided with its needed correction. It is idle to pose the debate in the form of judgment versus quantitative science. For in plain truth every judgment of the modern age rides piggyback on the output of hundreds of operating computers. When, abacus in hand, I confront the blank back of an envelope, my views are already contaminated by knowledge of what is being said by Klein's Wharton model, Otto Eckstein's model at Data Resources, Inc., the UCLA and Ann Arbor models and a dozen other econometric systems.

As Larry Klein's graduate-school teacher at MIT, I must recognize that water can rise above its source. It does so every academic generation. Klein was MIT's first Ph.D. in economics. It's been down the hill of diminishing returns ever since.

America is a great country. Klein got to MIT on the basis of his straight-A record. (*All* A's? Well, he did get one B in practical typing at Central High, Omaha. And one B in economic history at the University of California at Berkeley.)

Work to Do

Science is a process of creative self-destruction. Nobel prizes mark not completions but milestones on a continuing journey.

Economists forecast better than they did. They forecast better than chance, better than do naïve rules like "Same tomorrow as today," better than non-economists can do, whether they be astrologer, banker or candidate for public office.

Nevertheless, economics remains an inexact science. Most of the consensus forecasters, those few dozen analysts with a batting average worth following, expected that 1979 would be the year of recession, not 1980. They were not completely wrong. The history books do show 1979 to be a year of *growth recession*—a growth rate well below the trend. But it may turn out to be that the difference between a growth recession and a full-fledged one is just enough to make President Carter lose the election. Whether the new recovery will be the weak one most forecasters expect is still a matter of betting odds.

Although forecasting has improved, we may be reaching

a plateau. An *indeterminacy principle* seems to dog us, beyond which we cannot penetrate.

Somewhere in Consolidated High or Los Angeles State there is a future laureate who will make Lawrence Klein obsolete. More power to her!

Fiscal Policy

VITAL PUBLIC SPENDING
November 29, 1967

THE case for a tax increase is based upon the premise that aggregate dollar demand is likely to be so excessive this coming year as to produce undue inflation. Purely as a matter of economic mechanics, inflation can be fought by two kinds of fiscal restraints: higher tax rates, or lower rates of government expenditure—or, of course, a combination. This truth most economists are agreed upon. (Pragmatically, I define a truth to be that which at least two out of three *Newsweek* experts on economics are agreed upon!)

Now, just which of these two fiscal weapons should be used? Should we rely exclusively on higher tax rates? Exclusively on expenditure cuts? If both weapons are to be used, what should the quantitative mix be?

Need for Value Judgments
Actually, these are not questions that can be given an answer in terms of economic principles alone. Any jury of three economic experts might legitimately come up with three quite different policy recommendations. And such disagreements would be no reflection on the *technical* competence of any of the scholars.

On what then *does* depend the proper policy recommendation? Ultimately, the choice on such matters must depend on the value judgments of the majority of the citizenry.

If the people give high priority to using economic resources to clean up our polluted rivers and atmosphere, the fact that we are waging a war in Vietnam and are facing a problem of inflation should not stand in the way of their getting the program they want. If the people preponderantly desire that minimum standards of welfare be maintained and that the battle against poverty be vigorously pursued, neither war nor inflation provides legitimate economic obstacles to attainment of these goals.

Of course, the fact that more of the nation's resources are being devoted to Vietnam, and the fact that there is such a scramble of spending on goods as to lead to tight labor markets—these are legitimate reasons for taking a fresh, hard look at national priorities. But the following technical fact cannot be overemphasized:

The United States is not today remotely near any limit of tax capacity. If the people desire more of government programs that they deem vital, there is vast scope in the 1968 economy for expansion of *the public sector.*

Note that I have spoken loosely of "the citizenry" and "the people." You can never expect unanimity of the value judgments we are talking about. Some people couldn't care less about the poverty program or redistributive taxation. Others burn for such reforms. And some burn more than others.

So, in a mixed economy like ours, it boils down to the expressed views of the electorate. Majorities come and go. And we have to hope that E. B. White is right in saying:

"Democracy is the recurrent suspicion that more than half of the people are right more than half of the time."

It is necessary to remind ourselves of these abstract philosophical considerations because there seems to be a genuine

confusion in much current political discussion. Too often it is taken for granted that cuts in government expenditure must precede or go hand in hand with any rise in taxes. There is no such necessity and it is economic nonsense to postulate that there is. Compared with other Western societies and compared with our affluence and public needs, I find it easier to make the case that America today spends too little rather than too much on government.

The Good Society

When resources are tight, one might suppose that there is some presumption that all frills be eliminated. Thus, we justify a tax surcharge on the ground that the last dollars taken away from us will cut down on our least important private use of resources. At such times government programs of marginal worth—the supersonic airplane, our confused farm program, and much of our aerospace expenditure would be on my list—are also candidates for the knife.

However, and here I am presenting my credo for the good society, I believe it would be tragic if the new campaigns we have been waging against poverty and inequality—both at home and abroad—were to be abandoned or even curtailed because of the myth of economic necessity.

Newsweek readers know that I favor a tax increase. Let me make clear that I do not favor it at any price. If its costs were a legislative deal to cripple important welfare programs, I would have to point out that a degree of open inflation is not the greatest evil.

ALVIN H. HANSEN, 1887–1975

June 16, 1975

AS far as political economy is concerned, the golden age of the Harvard Yard might more appropriately be called the Age of Hansen. Alvin Hansen, who died last week full of years and honors, was often called the American Keynes. But the title does not do him justice.

It is true that Hansen was the leading interpreter in America of the path-breaking and novel methods of economic analysis of John Maynard Keynes. And this is all the more remarkable since Hansen was already middle-aged when the 1936 Keynesian classic, *The General Theory of Employment, Interest and Money,* was written. As the great Max Planck, himself the originator of the quantum theory in physics, has said, science makes progress funeral by funeral: the old are never converted by the new doctrines, they simply are replaced by a new generation. Hansen was an exception. He read Keynes, and disagreed. He read again, and agreed.

More important, he worked out the implications for economic policy—primarily fiscal policy, but monetary policy too—of the new Keynesian paradigms. The U.S., being an affluent and vast continental economy, turned out to be actually a more appropriate object for Keynes's new theories than his native England.

Depression Therapy

Franklin Roosevelt was, in the beginning, not at all a Keynesian. He stumped against Hoover on a promise to balance the budget. His early brain trusters were, at their most radical, Veblenian planners as innocent of the intricacies of modern macroeconomics and econometrics as the elderly bankers they inveighed against.

By Roosevelt's second term, the facts of life had sunk in: the NRA and fireside chats would not themselves restore prosperity; planning rhetoric could not provide the monetary demand industry needed to provide jobs for the quarter of our population who were involuntarily unemployed. Budget deficits, far from being an unfortunate concomitant of the Depression, were something deliberately to be contrived if the country was to get moving again. It was Hansen, and his Harvard-trained economists, who gradually converted the President and the Congress to an understanding of these facts of economic life.

To the public at large, Alvin Hansen's fame stemmed from his theory that an affluent country like ours was likely to face a long-term problem of stagnation. The frontier with its free land was gone. (Hansen, brought up on the farm in South Dakota that his Danish parents had homesteaded, understood the significance of this.)

Along with growth of land, Hansen's dynamic version of the Keynesian system required, for its vigorous balance of saving and investment, buoyant growth in population. Yet to informed demographers, the pre–World War II evidence pointed toward a continued decline in birth rates and rates of population growth. Finally, Hansen and his Harvard colleague Joseph Schumpeter stressed the role of innovation and invention in providing the motives for private investment spending. Scanning the record on corporate saving to provide internal sources of finance, on capital-saving as against labor-saving technological change, Hansen formulated his doctrine of possible long-run stagnation under undiluted capitalism.

Fiscal Rx for Maturity

This message made Hansen unpopular in conservative circles. Few love the prophets of doom. But even more unpopular is a prophet who proposes that the government do something about the problems he warns against. Hansen was the militant apostle of positive fiscal policy, both to stabilize the ups and downs of the business cycle and to maintain long-run balance of full-employment saving and investment.

World War II banished all these concerns for a time. Alvin Hansen was one of the honorable few who correctly foresaw that the end of the war would not bring mass unemployment, but instead a restocking boom. And Hansen was one of the first to discern—no less than 30 years ago!—that no mixed economy can simultaneously have full employment, steady price levels and free-market wage and price determination.

Hansen lived to see his vision fulfilled. The Employment Act of 1946, which put the government on record as responsible for job opportunity, is his permanent legacy.

SHOULD WE CUT TAXES?

May 6, 1974

THE first quarter of 1974 was dreadful. Real GNP we now learn fell by almost a 6 per cent annual rate. This is 2 percentage points worse than the better-informed analysts had expected; 4 points worse than in Mr. Nixon's own implied forecast.

But that is not all the bad news. We experienced stagflation with a vengeance in the first quarter. The annual rate of general price inflation was almost 11 per cent—again, 2 percentage points worse than the better forecasters had guessed.

Little wonder then that Senators Walter Mondale and Edward Kennedy have called for a tax cut in order to alleviate the stagnation, and to insure that we not move into a really serious recession that would be hard to reverse once the vicious spiral of unemployment and reduced incomes were to undermine business investment and consumer spending.

Kennedy and Mondale are known to be liberals who are acutely sensitive to the burden of unemployment and the poverty it brings. You realize how serious the first-quarter numbers were when you learn that such middle-of-the-road congressmen as Speaker Carl Albert and Majority Leader Mike Mansfield have also begun to espouse an antirecession program of fiscal expansion.

The Money Crunch

There are two ways to fight threatening recession: by *fiscal* tax cuts and expenditure increases; or by Federal Reserve expansion of the money and credit supplies sufficient to bring down mortgage rates on housing, interest rates on funds needed for investment and durable consumer goods, and the cost of equity capital to corporate employers.

Yet, at a time when the ground swell for budget deficits is getting under way, the Fed permits interest rates to skyrocket upward: the prime rate that banks charge is making records around 10.5 per cent; the federal funds rate soars above 11 per cent; long-term corporate and government bonds go begging unless their coupons are sweetened to levels that will be a drag on borrowers for years to come.

This rise in interest rates has many causes. Each speech of Fed chairman Burns adds 50 basis points to quoted yields. This in turn weakens another Real Estate Investment Trust's credit status and casts doubt on the commercial paper market generally. And this drives business borrowers to the commercial banks. Then the upsurge in bank loans evokes another speech from Dr. Burns. So it goes. The hysteria about long-run double-digit inflation, shared by zero out of 24 forecasters with good track records in recent years, fortunately, is unlikely to bring on such inflation. But it may well knock the bottom out of the housing market.

Indeed, why should any prudent person be keeping his money in the savings and loan associations that finance housing when at this time the short-term interest rates he can earn elsewhere are several percentage points higher than the 6 to 7 per cent they pay on their longer accounts? In my very next column it will be my duty to inform *Newsweek* readers how they can successfully "disintermediate"—i.e., pull their money out of the banking system and get a higher short-term yield with safety.

The Greater Enemy?

From the recession dangers I have described, one might think that all people would now favor tax cuts and easier money. Why don't they? Obviously, it is the recent II per cent inflation that scares Establishment decision makers most. The majority of businessmen think the recession will have hit bottom by midyear. The probabilities are still on this side; but one's confidence in imminent recovery has to be less than it was earlier. Until unemployment reaches nearer to 6 than to 5 per cent, conservatives will buy the argument that anything done to fight recession will only make inflation worse.

Where do I stand? I agree that inflation is no joke. But I also understand that the rises in oil and energy prices, and in food and raw material prices, are *not* the result of overloose fiscal and monetary policy. Concretely, whatever we do, the odds favor a retreat of inflation by year's end to well below the present two-digit range. A stitch in time to prevent the risks of a more serious recession will not, by any reasoned analysis I have seen, propel us into a pattern of uncontrolled inflation.

A modest tax cut can even contribute something toward preserving wage restraint in this year of labor unrest. A pragmatic easing of credit is now the better part of wisdom.

INFLATION TRAUMA (II)

May 21, 1973

THE economy has been strong—overly strong. Price infla-tion has been accelerating all this year (despite April's pause in wholesale food-price rises).

Why, then, aren't the economic experts urging on the Federal Reserve, and the government, tight credit policies and restrictive budgets and taxes?

Of course, a few experts are urging precisely that. But they are in the minority. And most of them would frankly wel-come a mini-recession toward the end of the year.

Why do they want a mini-recession? It is not really be-cause they are sadists, cruel to their wives and families and wishing suffering on the American people. Instead, they tell us, they favor a mini-recession or growth recession now be-cause it is too late to tame the excesses of the boom in any other way. And, they argue, if we don't have a short-lived recession in the next ten months, this only means that some-thing more than a mini-recession will be waiting for us later in 1974—a full-fledged retrogression of production, with the usual accompanying upswing in the unemployment rate back to the 6 per cent level or more.

Sustainable Growth

The majority of the experts do not share this desire for a preventive recession in the good cause of containing the rate of inflation. All they desire is that the economy taper down from its recent unmaintainable 8 per cent annual growth rate in output to a healthy 4 to 5 per cent pace that can be held in the longer run. That way job opportunities will stay favorable.

To be sure, no one is expecting a utopia in which the price level will be stable. Anyone with a good track record in analyzing the post-1950 developments in North America and Europe realizes that the only cure now known for creeping inflation is decidedly worse than the disease itself.

Whenever I write this simple fact, I am subjected to a torrent of abuse, quite devoid of rational rebuttal. Such irate rough-handling of the messenger who brings the truth of bad news diverts attention from the important problem of our times: how to devise policies that minimize the unavoidable degree of creeping inflation without sacrificing long-run living standards and work opportunity.

I've said that most experts want a gradual approach to a maintainable high-employment growth path. Do they think we are likely to get it?

To answer this question I've been looking over about fifteen different forecasts. Forecasts by academic computers. Forecasts by banks and brokerage firms. Forecasts by government agencies.

With rare exceptions they are in fairly close agreement. And all fear by the last quarter of this year the onset of at least a mini-recession. That is, almost without exception the forecasters are predicting that real GNP will be growing at less than a 4 per cent annual rate in the period from the coming Thanksgiving to the following Easter.

From whence comes the weakness?

· The experts believe that housing will be down.

· Car sales have been borrowing against the future and will be down in the next model year.

· Many experts think that inventory accumulation will be done in the quarters just ahead, at the cost of an ensuing downward swing in inventory investment by the turn of the year.

· Some of the experts think that this timetable will be helped by a monetary crunch that is already getting under way.

This puts me into a quandary. For more than six months I have been counseling policy makers to lean against the wind of an overstrong economy. The fact that my advice was ignored only adds to my feeling of superiority and self-righteousness.

Policy Dilemma

But that's idle vanity and water over the dam. In the face of near-universal expert agreement that we're about to move into slow growth, do I dare continue to advise restrictive programs?

On the one hand, I don't have so much confidence in my own judgment as to be happy to stand up against the whole chorus of experts. On the other, I don't have so much confidence in forecasts as to stifle my suspicion that the current excess of heat in the economy may still be with us all year long.

After soul-searching I come out with the counsel that we still lean against the wind of an overstrong boom. We can do so with better conscience if we drop the nonsense of gradualism and prepare to act fast once signs of recession are more than a gleam in the eye of the computer.

INFLATION FALLACIES

July 29, 1974

THESE days the world has proved itself too complex for simple economics. The cure for this is not the abandonment of economics. The only cure for oversimple economics is refined economic analysis. But the rub is to find the correct combinations of causal mechanisms.

One must clear the air of two pervasive misunderstandings if any progress is to be made in understanding and prescribing for inflation.

1. "Failure to control inflation has lowered real wages this last year." This is a fallacy. The real wage for a standard workweek has indeed declined since a year ago, but this is primarily because energy, food and other basic raw materials have become more scarce.

To understand this, suppose that by a miracle we were back in a 1900 flexible economy and could keep the overall price level constant, avoiding inflation by having other prices fall as much as food and energy prices rise. What wages could the system then afford to pay urban workers? *Reduced* money-wage rates. Thus, control of inflation could not prevent the rise in real incomes of sheiks and Iowa farmers and the fall in urban real wages. How fortunate it is that last year we didn't already have comprehensive indexing and escalation, which would have futilely tried to preserve an unmaintainable real wage.

Half of the recent two-digit inflation has been this *real supply* effect. Even if Treasury Secretary Simon had the political clout to impose a brutal budget cut, that could not undo the rains during the recent planting seasons in the U.S. and the U.S.S.R. And if Simon offset the budget cut with equivalent tax subsidies to business investment spending, the package would do nothing for that fraction of the *current* price inflation which can be touched by fiscal and monetary policy.

Felt Pains

There is a second, more subtle, fallacy. To understand it, suppose that somehow the OPEC oil monopoly were to weaken and real energy prices come down a bit. Suppose good crops all over the world were to replenish our low food reserves and depress prices of food and fiber. There would still probably remain a true, balanced inflation to the tune of say 6 or 7 per cent a year.

2. "My money wage rises at 8 per cent per year. But my cost of living rises by 6 per cent. So inflation cheats me of my rightful living standard."

Consumer surveys report this as a pervasive current frustration. This provides a perplexing complaint for economists and psychologists to analyze. The frustration is real. As Governor Wallace and other beneficiaries of political discontent know full well, it cannot be shrugged off.

But, on reflection, you will realize that Fed chairman Burns could not possibly restore to people that 6 per cent of real wages they were "cheated" out of—even if he were successful beyond his wildest dreams in stabilizing the price level at full employment. People seem naturally to look on the *whole* 8 per cent increase in money earnings as attributable to *their* just deserts. They cannot be expected to realize that it is only because of the balanced inflation which is occurring that the labor market metes out to them more than the 2 per cent wage increases provided by long-term productivity gains.

The Moral

Exposing these fallacies does not mean that inflation is harmless. Or that we should be soft in the fight against it. Such a view would be bad economics and disastrous politics.

What is implied is that *we make a careful cost-benefit analysis of any proposals put forward to fight inflation.* Were this done, I suspect prosecutions for false representations might be sustained by the Federal Trade Commission against some of the Washington leaders who have been making the headlines.

The most flagrant example is that of Secretary Simon's recent program to cut humanitarian items in the Federal budget to the tune of tens of billions, and at the same time provide tax subsidies for corporate investment. At a time when real wages have already been squeezed by material scarcities and by catch-up increases in prices to restore profit margins, it would be a risk to political consensus to deliberately skew the already unequal distribution of incomes. Such a program is well designed to rouse the sleeping dogs of the class struggle. Prime Minister Heath and his Tory Party came to grief in Britain essaying just such a policy. Can't we learn from that example?

WARM AUTUMN FOR THE WEST

July 18, 1977

THE Organization for Economic Cooperation and Development (OECD) represents the 24 leading market economies: the U.S. and Canada, Japan, Australia and New Zealand, and the European non-Soviet-bloc countries. Under the chairmanship of Paul McCracken, eight eminent economists have just completed for the OECD an important report, "Towards Full Employment and Price Stability."

It makes for gloomy reading at first glance. The potential output producible by these leading nations in 1980 has been written down by about one-twelfth from that confidently projected for 1980 at the beginning of this decade.

Even these reduced levels of full-employment income will not be realizable during the rest of the 1970s if the advice of these economic experts is followed. The McCracken report, fearing lest too rapid a recovery reaccelerate inflation, counsels the OECD bloc to pursue a real-growth target of 5.5 per cent per annum for several years, calling this "the narrow path back towards full employment and price stability."

This recommended path is one, the authors admit, that will leave unemployment and excess capacity high until well into the 1980s.

The Brightest and Best

Mark you, this octet is not a covey of elderly bankers, delivering the kind of stale sermon we have come to expect from bankers and businessmen. McCracken was the least conservative, the most eclectic, of all the Republican chairmen of the Council of Economic Advisers.

On the average, the age of this stellar sample of economists from France, Britain, Germany, Italy, Japan, Turkey and Sweden is as much less than mine as my age is less than Arthur Burns's. Friedrich von Hayek would consider this jury of economists hopelessly "liberal," just as John Kenneth Galbraith and Gunnar Myrdal would consider them hopelessly staid.

The panel's balance is all the more reason, I believe, to ponder over its diagnoses, evidence and logic to determine whether its degree of pessimism is warranted. And, since a certain degree of pessimism can also be regarded as a certain degree of optimism, we need to weigh its analysis to judge whether the West can still grow at all in these days of OPEC cartelization and natural-resource limitation.

Is it really the case, as the McCracken report authors seem to believe, that following their narrow path will leave us at its end in a state of "price stability"?

I must confess to doubt on this matter, particularly since they seem to base so much of their argument on the airy notion that our present inflation problem is much the product of a pesky state of "inflationary expectations." If only these could be conjured away, to be replaced by some better expectations, then, presto, much of the inflation problem would disappear. Can they really mean that?

Sunny Spots

Fortunately, civilization will not grind to a halt if the price level fails to level off in the early 1980s.

The United States has been living up to both the spirit and the letter of the report's guidelines. If only we could be as certain that West Germany and the nations of Northern Europe are achieving their recovery goals as that the United States has been fulfilling the new President's economic targets!

It is fruitless to discuss solemnly at this time whether the first part of 1979 will be stronger or weaker than the last of 1978. But it is well to know that there would be no defiance of the laws of technology and the lessons of history if the Carter Administration were able to stretch out the post-1975 recovery to the end of this decade and beyond.

Slower population growth does mean slower future economic growth. But there is nothing to grieve about in that. Affluence itself tends to reduce the effort devoted to production of material things, which is a deucedly sensible reaction. Only ostriches can ignore the permanently higher costs of energy and the likelihood that raw materials may become effectively more scarce. Sensible observers will take account of this by some reductions in their forecasts of productivity trends.

Happily, a careful second glance at the McCracken report will confirm that autumn can be a pleasant season indeed for a mature industrial society.

A NEW ECONOMIC TACK

February 5, 1979

DURING the 1976 Presidential campaign, puzzled observers sometimes said, "Will the real Jimmy Carter please stand up?" Now the President has done so and revealed himself to be essentially a conservative Democrat.

Franklin Roosevelt, Harry Truman, John F. Kennedy and Lyndon Johnson could not have written Carter's State of the Union Message. Jerry Brown could have done so, emphasizing the need for government to retrench and dodging the hard questions of how to compromise between the evils of inflation and those of stagnation.

Can Carter steal the Republicans' clothes? Or will he have abandoned the constituency of the poorer half of the nation without winning over the middle- and upper-income classes? Will his low-keyed economic proposals have any significant chance of scoring success against inflation in the twenty months left before the 1980 Presidential election? And can they do so without exacting a heavy human—and political —cost?

Let us examine precedents. Helmut Schmidt heads the Social Democratic Party of West Germany, the party that historically corresponds to America's Democratic Party and one which is certainly not more conservative than ours. Yet Chancellor Schmidt has been pursuing an austere economic program that tolerates unprecedented unemployment in the determination to fight inflation. Schmidt's political popularity and viability seem not to have been jeopardized by such a program.

President Valéry Giscard d'Estaing of France has encouraged Prime Minister Raymond Barre to pursue measures of deregulation and austerity that reach draconian proportions. Yet so frightened is the bulk of the French population by the prospect of leftist incursions on their privileges and property that they tolerate a sluggish economy.

Perfection Not Required

Granted that there are successful precedents for the leader of a liberal party to turn conservative, can Carter's ploy work?

If to be re-elected he must be as successful in conquering inflation as the Germans have been, then Carter's new game plan hasn't the ghost of a chance. The new austerity will at best reduce our 9 per cent rate of inflation to 8 or 7 per cent, not to zero or the German 2 to 3 per cent rate.

I do not believe the President's fate, and that of his party at the polls in 1980, hinge upon his effectively curing inflation. If only it could be perceived by the public that inflation will not get worse and that some slow progress toward its amelioration is taking place, the Administration's stock could rise in the public-opinion polls. (Again, the example of France is in point: the fact that Prime Minister Barre's program has failed to bring the French inflation rate down below that of the United States has not damned it.)

Not Overdoing It

I have personal reservations about the wisdom of the President's new shift to the right. But on this occasion, I shall not let my own value judgments intrude upon the discussion of how macroeconomic policy ought best be formulated to fight inflation.

You hear debate about whether the Carter budget is truly an austere one. Often, those who deny that it is are saying only that they would prefer a substantial long-term reduction in the fraction of the national income that passes through the hands of government. Likewise, those who regard the budget as unmercifully tight are usually merely reiterating their belief that human need ought to be taken care of out of the economic capacity of the whole country.

It is more fruitful to ask: Will a deficit of $29 billion, taken together with next year's Federal Reserve policy, realize the Administration's announced goal of low positive real growth? Or is a larger deficit inevitable if an outright recession is to be avoided?

Despite the surprising strength of 1978's final quarter, the whole evidence makes me bet that the Carter forecast errs on the optimistic side. As business weakens in 1979, tax-revenue shortfalls and unemployment-compensation add-ons seem likely to send the deficit above $30 billion.

Such a rise in the deficit I believe to be economically sound. Indeed, Carter and the Fed ought to guard now against such tightness as will make a recession likely. An all-out war against inflation, which gives no heed to real consequences, will only invite political backlash later. Moderation wins out in the long pull.

RECESSION: MADE IN WASHINGTON

December 24, 1979

THE private U.S. economy shows remarkable strength, fighting hard against falling into a recession tailspin.

Gasoline hysteria has cut into automobile sales. Tight credit and expensive interest rates on mortgages have undermined housing construction.

Yet, as I write, the jury is still out on whether we are now in a genuine recession.

Many economists find this uncertainty frustrating. Their vanity would be better served if their magic money formulas could pronounce with precision just how the economic winds are blowing. They feel less secure in their science when the factors they must assay come out of Washington—from the committees of Congress and the Federal Reserve rather than from the business rhythms of 10,000 Main Streets.

I have to dissent. Evolution did not conspire to make a paradise for forecasting economists. We are paid to endure —and evaluate—ambiguity.

More important, I much prefer for the country a recession contrived by Fed chairman Paul Volcker and President Carter rather than one created by blind Mother Nature. What man does, man can undo. Acts of God and the King's enemies are harder to diagnose and reverse.

The Year That Was

To justify what you will correctly indict as optimism, let me review 1979. Christmas is a culmination of the economic year, so that we can now strike a trial balance.

The history books will record 1979 as a time of mini-recession. Real gross national product failed to grow at the U.S. trend rate of 3 per cent per annum.

Employment held up surprisingly well. So 1979 productivity must have been terrible.

Does this mean that profits took it on the chin? Correcting for inflation, we find profits held up surprisingly well. Businesses found they could generally pass their higher costs on to the consumer in the form of higher prices.

I see only one way to reconcile this drop in productivity. Real earnings—per person, per hour or per day—will be found by economic historians to have declined significantly. And all this happened without unusual strikes or class bitterness. To appreciate how singular this scenario has been, note that workers in Western Europe have not yet experienced any such commensurate fall in their real wages.

Polls of the American people show that we all blame the drop in our real earnings on "inflation." As one shopper put it to the TV camera: "I'm fed up with this inflation. It's taking the meat out of my stew and leaving me with potatoes and turnips."

With respect, she has misidentified the sources of the drop in Americans' real earnings. Those sources are (1) higher real energy prices, (2) higher real farm prices incident to harvest supplies here and abroad, (3) low industrial productivity.

Suppose the Fed and the Treasury had successfully avoided *all* general inflation. Then the shopper would still have less meat in her stew—for the same triad of reasons.

With a stable price level, that triad would have had its impact via a reduction in our money wage rates. Blood would run in the streets before a modern mixed economy would accept so visible a wage cut. So, in a sense, the inflation that we all understandably damn has helped make possible an inevitable adjustment in living standards.

The Year to Come

There is little optimism in my 1980 horoscope on inflation. If the consumer price index grows but 11 per cent in the twelve months ahead, instead of at its present annual rate of about 13 per cent, my best hopes will be realized.

If the private economy is fairly strong, with few apparent distortions, why do I expect a recession in 1980? I have faith in things still unseen: tight enough money can deliver the goods of recession, and I expect there will be enough inflation to motivate the Federal Reserve to keep money tight enough to do the job.

In my reading, President Carter promised the world a U.S. recession on Nov. 1, 1978. On Oct. 6, the occasion of Paul

Volcker's "midnight massacre," the President's I.O.U. was presented for payment.

I do not recognize an effective political will to engineer a *severe* recession. That's why my bets are on a mild U.S. contraction in the next nine months. Unless Iranian instability undermines the world oil supply, Western Europe and Japan should at worst experience growth recession.

Will such a scenario as this stampede Wall Street? Who can say? To my mind, a recession is not incompatible with an upward explosion in equity prices—with all the new problems that would entail.

LIVING WITH INFLATION

February 25, 1980

IN my youth I saw a performance at the Brattle Theatre in Cambridge, Mass., of the Clifford Odets proletarian drama *Waiting for Lefty.* We in the audience were part of the play. The suspense builds up unbearably at our union meeting as to whether we will or will not strike. And then, as I remember it, comes the grand climax. A messenger enters the back of the theater with the news that Lefty has been shot: the strike is on and the walls of capitalism are to be put in jeopardy.

To managers of bond portfolios, a similar build-up of anxiety has been taking place as they wait for the promised recession to bail them out of their losses in long-term bonds. To the consensus forecasters, who have been predicting a recession since April Fool's Day 1979, the debacle cannot come too soon. Although members of the President's Council of Economic Advisers used to keep stiff upper lips and wield a duplicitous pen when denying that a recession was in the offing, chairman Charles Schultze in the recent Economic Report of the President is resolutely optimistic that we shall have the recession needed to dampen down the fires of double-digit price inflation.

Stalemate

Meantime, the American economy labors and labors but thus far has been capable of producing no more than a mouse of growth recession. Detroit has cooperated by not having a supply of small cars to sell. Chairman Paul Volcker at the Federal Reserve has kept the faith and a rein on the money supply. Housing starts are down and the speculative real-estate bubble has encountered stable or falling home prices —at least for the moment.

But consumers have been cutting down on their saving rates so that their living standards won't fall as much as their real after-tax incomes are falling. There are but few signs of excessive inventories. The stock market acts as if it wants to have an excuse to go up. Plant and equipment investment remains fairly firm. The smell of new defense orders helps to ward off recession blues.

There is no reason why the suspense should not go on for a long time. And things could be worse than a flat economy, you may be tempted to argue—as, for example, in a serious recession or an overheated boom.

What is so frustrating about the present phase of mini-recession is the patent fact that the United States economy is not yet showing any signs that the rate of inflation is abating. The whole purpose of the game plan being pursued by the monetary and fiscal authorities is not to choke off growth for its own sake. The slow growth envisaged for the unemployment rate is not motivated by sadism or by malevolence toward the unskilled, young and non-white workers. The name of the game is to fight inflation.

With oil prices rising abroad and rising at home to catch

up with world levels, with metal and fiber prices being bid up on organized futures exchanges, it would seem that once we get the hoped-for mild recession, it may do disappointingly little for the base rate of inflation.

I've quoted conservative economist friends who have said at Washington meetings: "If you're contriving a teensy-weensy recession for us, please don't bother. It won't do the job. What's needed is a believable declaration that Washington will countenance *whatever* degree of unemployment is needed to bring us back on the path to price stability, and a demonstrated willingness to *stick* to that resolution no matter how politically unpopular the short-run joblessness, production cutbacks and dips in profit might be."

Harsh Truth

I suspect that the American political system will not give them the experiment they desire, even if the electorate turns conservative in November. But going by the economic evidence, I cannot share their optimism that the short-term price would be only a modest one that society will have to pay to wring stagflation out of its system.

I am forced to the conclusion that, whoever is elected President, Americans will be living with inflation for a long time to come.

This is a hard fact—hard on us who must live with it, hard in the sense of being well grounded in reality. If you are not an ostrich, you will want to know it.

Most Presidential candidates duck this issue. One infers that the Republican contenders would be prepared to incur higher short-term costs in unemployment than President Carter would. Only Edward Kennedy is ready to ration gasoline and freeze prices and wages—but will that sell? Jimmy Carter sits in the not-uncomfortable middle.

THE CASE FOR CONTROLS
March 3, 1980

THE Carter economic game plan is obviously off course. Inflation is worsening, not abating. The planned recession continues to elude Washington.

That is what Henry Kaufman, senior partner and respected economist for Salomon Brothers, told bankers last week. When he came out in favor of a whole new game plan, one including drastic resort to outright economic controls, panic hit Wall Street.

Few economists favored wage-price controls until recently. But the ranks of the camp that does are growing. Two more months in which the cost of living rises at annual rates like 18 per cent will greatly increase the probability that President Carter will be forced to ask for controls before 1980 is over.

Barry Bosworth, now of the Brookings Institution but earlier head of Carter's wage-price apparatus, recently put those odds at 99 to 1 against controls—and Dr. Bosworth is sympathetic to giving them a trial. I would put the odds closer to 1 to 2 that Mr. Carter will be forced into a reversal of his opposition to direct controls. That makes the issue worth discussing—at length and objectively.

Tough Choices

What alternatives to wage-price controls are there? They boil down to these policy options:

· The Federal Reserve and Administration authorities can abandon their gradualism, and *act now to tighten credit and fiscal policies severely.* It is one thing to say that present macroeconomic policies cannot bring on a recession. It is another thing, and a ridiculous thing, to say that the authorities are powerless to produce a recession if they want one badly enough. (That could mean prime rates that rise briefly to 20 per cent; a decline in the money aggregates for several months, and a drastic rein on nondefense spending this year.)

· The authorities can *continue on their steady-as-you-go policies of gradual restriction.* With luck, 18 per cent inflation might work back down to 13 and then down to the hoped-for 9 per cent rate. Five to ten years of austerity, in which the unemployment rate rises toward an 8 or 9 per cent average and real output inches upward at barely 1 or 2 per cent per year, would be hard on our political system. But it might accomplish a gradual taming of U.S. inflation.

· We could *muddle along with stagflation.* Unwilling to tolerate more than a mild recession, we would accept the risk that the core rate of inflation might exceed one-digit rates in the mid-1980s, and might be still higher at the decade's end. Just because stable prices become only a historical memory doesn't mean grass must grow in the streets and civilization come to an end.

Against these alternatives, more and more economists are coming to accept controls.

Do direct controls provide a viable alternative? To answer this, I must first distinguish between different controls: *selective credit* versus *wage-price* controls. Henry Kaufman, like many conservative and middle-of-the-road New York experts, has long warned that getting rid of interest-rate ceilings and relying solely on high-interest cost of *freely available* credit will mean weaker control of activity by the Fed and must entail *wider swings* in interest rates. (If Presidential powers had been used in 1972–73 and 1978 to have the Federal Reserve and other agencies set priorities in the use of credit and impose direct limitations on borrowing, any desired slowdown in overall activity could have been contrived with interest rates not having to peak so high.)

I agree. But do we wish autos and housing to go lower in 1980 than seems likely? The surprising strength in consumer spending is in nondurables. So the merits of credit controls are not now critical.

Main Debate

The key issue now dividing Carter and Kennedy is a wage-price freeze and gasoline rationing. If the electorate had the stomach for gas rationing, that would be a way of enforcing genuine energy scarcity without having that scarcity become a cost-push force on the official price index. So, this becomes a question of political feasibility and I leave it there.

There is much experience with direct wage-price controls in a score of countries and over four decades. It reduces to this:

Controls work well for a year. After that, mandatory controls become increasingly ineffective, inefficient and inequitable. Query: Isn't the inflation problem we face the *recurring dilemma* of stagflation in the mixed economy rather than something unusual? After a year, what then do we do?

STAGFLATION (I)

September 3, 1973

MONTH after month the cost of living rises. High food prices merely dramatize the fact that all the items in our budget go up and up and up. Even with raises for seniority and excellence, your higher paycheck barely stretches over living costs, and it certainly doesn't bring the average worker that steady improvement in real wages Americans have grown used to. As for the less lucky, they are really hurting.

So 7 per cent inflation is today's prime economic concern. If the President could do something about it, that would raise his stock more than any other single act. If Congress could use its post-Watergate powers to cure our inflation ills, the Democrats would bounce back nicely.

But, of course, there are no easy solutions. Price controls, short of outright rationing, will not make meat plentiful and cheap to buy. Draconian cuts in government spending are not politically feasible and would in any case have dampening effects only after some lag.

If there were easy solutions, they'd have been tried long ago. It is thoughtless nonsense to keep referring to Watergate as paralyzing obviously needed actions. If President Nixon had nothing to think about at Camp David all seven days of the week, he and his advisers still could not come up with a plan that would convert the present inflation into lasting prosperity with stable prices. Nor could Congress. Nor could a jury of experts from the Ivy League, Zurich banks or McSorley's Saloon.

The Perfidious Fed

Doesn't that leave things up to the Federal Reserve, which is supposed to manage our money supply? Well, the sad truth is that Dr. Burns and the other governors of the Fed also doesn't know how to control that money supply so as to (1) keep unemployment below 5 per cent and (2) cause the rate of increase in the price index to taper down toward 5 per cent by year's end and 4 per cent by the following year. Much less do they know how to restore us to what euphemistically used to be called "reasonably stable prices."

These past few months the Fed authorities have come under a crossfire. The monetarists think they have lost their marbles and wantonly engineered a 7+ per cent growth rate in the money supply when inflation calls, at most, for a 4 per cent growth rate. From the other side, people in the money market criticize the Fed for letting interest rates soar so high as to produce a near money crunch. Mortgage and other funds are becoming hard to get, and monstrously expensive. If the crunch is allowed to go on and develop, practical financial people predict that ominous and irreversible reductions in investment and consumption spending will be just around the corner.

I am not one loath to criticize the Federal Reserve. There is no other activity that so much adds to an economist's professional and self-esteem. But simple reason, if not charity, requires one to recognize the thin line of compromise responsible monetary authorities must walk.

Scylla and Charybdis

On the one hand, the central bank must not validate into perpetuity the high rates of recent inflation. So rates of M growth that matched the 10+ per cent growth rate of money GNP would be unacceptable.

On the other hand, the Fed has been taught—and not least by the monetarists—that monetary policy is subject to lengthy lags. So if it is excessively hawkish to fight current price inflation by rates of money growth below, say, 5 per cent, the effects of this policy will be registered about next Valentine's Day, when almost every forecaster with a good track record expects us to be well into a growth recession.

Those now clamoring for a highly restrictive macroeconomic policy have missed out on their timing. Where were they last fall when excessive strength for the year ahead was causing some of us fine-tuners to counsel macroeconomic constraint—reduced growth rates of money, even below 4 per cent, and reduced defense and other expenditures of low social priorities? Do any of the contractionary hawks really expect U.S. real growth in the next twelve months to even keep up with our working-force and productivity increase? None who will bet their money on it.

The real reason why critics are so vociferous is that most of them, privately, think that a recession is both inevitable *and desirable.*

Next time, I want to explore the merits and demerits of this view.

Q AND A

May 6, 1975

HERE are my best answers to the questions economists are most often being asked these days.

Q: Is inflation cured?

A: Evidence suggests that now, and by the year's end, the annual inflation rate will have abated from 1974's two-digit rate to around the 4 to 7 per cent annual rate. If luck holds out on world harvests, Mideast peacefulness and normal productivity trends, next year at this time the inflation rate can hold in this range.

There is no cogent evidence that we are on our way back to steady price levels. And no guarantee that inflation will never reaccelerate.

Q: How stands the recession?

A: The first-quarter GNP numbers are so bad that the experts are more confident than ever that the bottom is near at hand. At even odds, you should bet with the consensus forecasters: Drs. Eckstein of Harvard and DRI; Evans of Chase Econometrics; Klein of the Wharton model. A swing in six months from $18 billion inventory accumulation to that much decumulation gives hope that inventories are nearing a satisfactory level. This attained, total spending and production should tend upward.

Slower inflation also helps. Final insurance is provided by the tax cuts that are soon on their way.

It is no sure thing that recovery will come before midyear, or be at a satisfactory pace. Housing and autos may not rebound smartly in response to credit ease and fiscal stimulus. Also, historically unemployment rates lag, continuing to rise until real GNP grows at the 4 per cent trend rate. Even if we were now at the recession's trough, unemployment would probably peak out at more than 9 per cent.

Q: Economists no longer disagree?

A: A silly question. Now that we have our tax-cut bill, we naturally divide over whether it's *too much* of a good thing.

Q: Is the deficit too big? Will it induce an unhealthy, over-rapid expansion? Crowd out investment?

A: One question at a time. And please realize that value judgments as well as objective economic science must be involved in policy decisions. Rep. Shirley Chisholm, who has a minority constituency in New York City, will properly give different optimal responses than a Florida congressman representing a constituency of retired people on fixed pensions. Their respective tolerances for inflation and unemployment risks will differ. And even where they happened to agree on probabilities, they'd disagree on the proper compromise to be selected in the trade-off between more jobs soon and less future inflation.

Here are some key conclusions.

1. The deficit is not "unmanageable"; far from it. The bonds will sell.

2. Each dollar of deficit will not eat up one dollar out of a *fixed* pool available for private investment. So whatever a "crowding-out effect" means, it does not mean that each extra $10 billion of deficit displaces $10 billion of equipment, construction, and inventory capital formation that would otherwise take place.

3. A deficit is "too large" when it leads to too rapid a rate of production and employment recovery. When it leads to intensification of "demand-pull" price and wage inflation. When the financing of it leads to such a bidding up of interest rates that an inordinate number of capital-formation activities can no longer afford to acquire the credit they require. And the deficit is too large if it forces the Federal Reserve to create more money than is good for the economy in its recovery period.

Q: Well, is our deficit too large? You are telling me how I can go about answering this question. I want you, with your expert judgment, to answer it for me.

A: All things considered, I think the calendar year 1975 needs a deficit larger than we have ever had in peacetime. A deficit of 6 per cent of GNP would be about $84 billion—frightening to the layman but still 6 per cent.

The price level in 1980 will be a bit higher with such a deficit than otherwise. But singlemindedly seeking to minimize that price level would logically lead to your favoring continuation of the recession, and even a wish to let it slide into a depression.

A prudent target for annual real GNP growth in the recovery would be at least 6 per cent for some time. The rewards justify the risks. A reasoned look at the feasible patterns of experience will show that there is no satisfactory course of action that is without real risks.

MILTON FRIEDMAN
October 25, 1976

THE economics profession has long expected that Milton Friedman would win the Nobel Prize in Economics. His 1976 award is fitting recognition of his scientific contributions and his scholarly leadership.

There is no need for me to describe in these columns his important views as a conservative economist. His own words speak eloquently for themselves.

What I have to emphasize is that Friedman is the *architect* of much that is best in our conservative tradition and not merely the *expositor* of that viewpoint. Furthermore, the adjective "conservative" does not do proper justice to a thinker who would refuse the steel industry its import quotas, strip Texas of its oil subsidies and deprive the railroads and the trucking interests of their protective regulations.

Why is Milton Friedman "an economist's economist"? Let me point out the ways.

Curriculum Vitae

He started as an undergraduate student of Arthur Burns at Rutgers. No bad beginning. He went on to become a graduate-student star at Columbia and Chicago.

The "Chicago School," with its emphasis on human freedoms and the efficiency of market pricing, can be said to have been founded by Frank Knight, his revered teacher. Under Friedman it has been led to new heights of influence and profundity.

MIT, Harvard, Oxford and every topnotch economics department would today feel deprived and one-sided if the fruitful Chicago viewpoint were not represented on its faculty. This new fact is a tribute to one great leader.

Scholars are known by their original scientific discoveries. Friedman early made his mark in statistics and mathematical economics. Without being a Keynesian, he pioneered early budgetary measurements of income-consumption patterns and taught our wartime Treasury how to reduce the inflationary gap. Abraham Wald's great breakthrough in the statistical technique called "sequential analysis" stemmed in part from Friedman's realization that it is not necessary to finish testing every egg to infer that a batch is bad. Does this seem simple? So now does Newton's falling apple.

If it pays to reduce risk by insuring, how at the same time can it pay to increase risk by backing long shots? Friedman (with L. J. Savage) provided an answer. Also, Friedman (with Simon Kuznets, Nobel laureate 1971) first analyzed and measured "human capital," the investment we make in our medical and other education and the interest return on this investment.

Do not the rich save more from each dollar than the poor? If so, redistributing income from rich to poor will raise consumption spending and stimulate business. Friedman's investigation of "the *permanent income* hypothesis" revealed that, once we get used to being permanently at a higher income, we in fact save *much the same fraction* of income! That this finding stood up so well to adversary attack demonstrated his Nobel caliber.

Of course it is monetarism that marks Friedman's lifework of the last twenty years. His monumental *A Monetary History of the United States, 1867–1960,* written with Anna Schwartz, clinched his international reputation.

Missions Accomplished

The story the facts tell Friedman is that the price level is determined in the long run by the quantity of money. Contrary to the view of 1939 Keynesians and the stubborn 1959 view of many English economists, the short-run changes in the money supply provide the one factor reliably related to half the variance in nominal GNP changes. The rest being primarily noise, M growth is the only such significant factor. From this follows his basic prescription: *Keep aggregate M growth constant.*

What I have failed to convey is Milton Friedman's bounce and gaiety, his rapier intelligence, his unfailing courtesy in debate. The world admires him for his achievements. His intimates love him for himself.

The fact that he and I, despite our policy disagreements and scientific differences, have remained good friends over 40 years says something perhaps about us, but even more I dare to think about political economy as a science.

STILL A GOOD YEAR

January 9, 1978

WHAT changes in monetary policy should we expect now that G. William Miller has replaced Arthur Burns as chairman of the Fed? How should we second-guess the consensus forecasters in light of this news? Is there a widening uncertainty about all our estimates?

Just as Thomas B. McCabe of Scott Paper found chairman Marriner Eccles a hard act to follow when Harry Truman named him to replace Eccles, so Miller of Textron will have to compete with the mystique that Burns leaves behind.

The initial reaction to Burns's termination has been favorable. Common stocks recovered in a matter of hours. Foreign-exchange and gold markets moved less than had been feared.

My stock in Textron has done well in Miller's years at its helm. What is more germane, economists who have served with Miller on the board of directors of the Boston Federal Reserve Bank—such past Democratic advisers as Harvard's James Duesenberry and MIT's Robert Solow—think well of his intelligence, initiative and public spirit.

When we economists put our computer models through new runs based upon a new chairman at the Fed, it is surprising how minute are the resulting changes in estimates of inflation. Employing a variety of new reasonable assumptions, one comes out with less than half of 1 per cent of change in the 1980 level of consumer prices.

Uneasy Compromises

The other side of the coin is that vast improvements in the unemployment rate are also unlikely. A new Supreme Court has more genuine autonomy than a new Federal Reserve Board, for the reason that the Court does not have to report quarterly to Congress. The Fed under Miller can be expected to continue its uneasy compromising between holding down excessive monetary growth and excessive increases in interest rates.

All that being said, it should be a good year for the American economy. The evidence suggests these odds in 1978:

• 2 to 1 against a growth recession in which unemployment worsens.

• 5 to 1 against a recession in which the economy shows negative real growth.

• 100 to 1 against a 1930s-like depression.

• 10 to 1 against another bout of two-digit price inflation.

• 100 to 1 against real stability of the price level.

This is not good enough to realize Jimmy Carter's promises to create jobs for youths, the unskilled and minority workers. Those anxious about continuing inflation and possible weakness in the dollar exchange rate will continue to sleep uneasily. The stock market will still nervously contend with rising interest rates and fears for the future.

Still, for what is the fourth year of an American recovery, the scenario envisaged by 30 out of 40 of the leading consensus forecasters is not at all a bad one. German and Japanese forecasters only wish that they could be as sanguine about their own 1978 recovery as the evidence permits U.S. analysts to be about our prospects.

Complacency is the forecaster's greatest sin and most irresistible temptation. That's why I always find it valuable to pay close attention to the minority who doubt conventional wisdoms.

Chase Econometrics, which a year ago was also pessimistic, believes we are now in a growth recession. It expects unemployment to rise from the 6.9 per cent rate to 7.4 per cent by next fall. I agree that the recent weakness in auto sales bears careful watching, but the whole of the evidence does not suggest so extreme a deceleration in inventory buying as the Chase model predicts.

Recessionary View

Argus Research Corp., which gives its Wall Street customers forecasts loosely based on Chicago School monetarism, expects a growth recession in 1978 that is to be made all the worse by an accleration of inflation to an 8 per cent annual rate by the year-end, a rise in long-term interest rates to 9.7 per cent and weakness in the common-stock indexes.

On the other hand, monetarist forecasters at Citibank differ with the Argus pessimism. And the monetarists at the Harris Trust in Chicago are even among the most optimistic of the crowd.

Forecasters generally take for granted a sizable tax reduction for families and corporations by next October. I concur in the likelihood of this.

All told, I expect 1978 to continue the economic recovery. As to the longer term, Arthur Burns has left a sound legacy. I hail him and the passing of an era.

REALISTIC HOPES

October 23, 1978

AFTER recently briefing a financial group on current economic trends, I found myself charged with the heresy of optimism. Since economics has long been notorious as the dismal science, the indictment was a novel one and went something like the following:

"According to you, the weakness in the dollar is no worse than a bad cold. And now that 1978 developments are beginning to smell like the 1973 prelude to the worst international recession in the post–World War II era, you profess to discern signs of a revival in Germany and elsewhere. You don't deign to shed crocodile tears for the growing public debt and continuing deficit. Doesn't anything worry you?"

The questions raised are good ones. Mistrust a debonair surgeon and be wary of economists who, in William James's phrase, were born with a bottle of champagne to their credit.

Yes, I worry a lot. Indeed, I have to ration my 24 hours a day and concentrate on worries that genuinely matter, dispensing with false concerns and relegating minor anxieties to amateurs with excess capacity.

U.S. Weakness?

I am very disturbed by the increasing number of forecasts that come to my desk with expectations of a U.S. downturn in 1979—a downturn and not merely a growth recession involving a slowdown below our long-term average rate of growth.

As an example, George Perry of the Brookings Institution now expects negative growth rates next spring. I've been monitoring over the years his batting average as a forecaster for Walter Heller, and his is one of the better records in my files. So I pay attention when his signal flashes from orange to red.

Although some large banks also predict a U.S. recession next year, this is still a minority view among the consensus forecasters. Even the most astute judge must still reserve decision on this vital issue because, as I have often had to admit, it is almost as if there were a Heisenberg indeterminacy principle in economic science: beyond a certain degree of accuracy, even with the best computers and most up-to-date data, we cannot pierce the veil of chance.

What is the key unknown that will determine whether the Wharton and Data Resources, Inc., models are right and the recession-scenario models are wrong? In my judgment, it is not the outcome of the tax-cut debate. Federal Reserve policy on the money supply I believe to be important for estimating what the price level will be in 1985, but it is unlikely to be the element of surprise in the emerging business scene.

The great imponderable is *the future behavior of inventories.* DRI, perceiving that the levels of inventories look lean relative to the rate of business sales and production, forecasts no great deceleration in future inventory growth. The recession models of Perry and the Manufacturers Hanover bank disagree; and it is their expectation of a swing toward inventory reduction that seems to me to be the important element in their dissenting scenarios.

Dissonance Elsewhere

Abroad, there is room for greater optimism. Before World War II, all nations tended to have a common business-cycle pattern. When the U.S. boomed, so did Europe, Asia and

Latin America. Prior to 1973, it was beginning to look as if the new Age of Keynes had broken up the lockstep of a worldwide-consonant business cycle.

Alas, the recession of 1974–75 appeared to be a return to the older and more virulent pattern. Japan, India, North America and Europe jointly bid up prices in 1972–73. And they jointly went into a tailspin in 1974–75.

I perceive no compelling reasons why near-term weakness in America should be accompanied by similar weakness abroad. Quite the contrary. From early 1975 to the present moment, the American recovery has been a stronger one than those abroad.

After long resisting U.S. Government advice to join us in achieving vigorous economic expansion, the German and Japanese governments are admitting they were wrong. More important are the signs that their stimulative policies are beginning to catch hold. France, Italy, Britain, the Low Countries and Scandinavia can all more safely expand if the new German tempo can be maintained.

So, it is only to the charge of realism that I plead guilty.

AMERICA'S CREDIT CRISIS

March 17, 1980

WE are moving into a real money crunch. I just talked to a businessman who runs a fair-size leasing business. He is now paying 29 per cent per year for credit accommodation. And he is hurting.

One of our Eastern professors has taken a better job in the South. Rather than selling her house in a weak market in Boston, she is holding on to it. But her family needs a home in the new locality. So she made a deposit on a bargain buy there, intending to come up with part of the down payment by means of an 18 per cent second-mortgage loan on her Boston house. The dreadful news has just arrived that the Boston bank has stopped providing mortgage money on *any* terms.

A group of assistant professors at a Western graduate school of business like to put their money where their minds and economic models are. Convinced last month that the peak of interest rates had arrived now that auto sales and housing starts are down, their syndicate put up $5,000 each as margin money for a flyer in the market for Treasury bonds on the Chicago Board of Trade's futures market. They've been cleaned out: the syndicate is disbanded and their spouses are irate.

Strains

Savings and loan associations are losing money every month as prudent depositors transfer their assets to money-market funds that now pay up to 14 per cent. To slow down the outflow, the S&Ls are having to match market rates on Treasury bills. Some of them don't dare tie up the proceeds in mortgages and instead are themselves investing in the New York money market for the trifling differential profit to be earned on the funds. It is a nerve-racking way of life.

One can multiply such anecdotes. They are the stuff of which a tight-money epoch is constituted. Brutal as the impact of credit stringency must appear to its unprepared victims, fighting inflation by means of monetary restraint is supposed to work in the ways that I have described.

Slowly the medicine is working. Auto sales and housing starts are down. The boom in prices of houses has not turned into a collapse. But the index of prices for new and old houses, in ratio to the consumer price index, has at last turned down.

Back in the good old days, we should by this time have seen a rash of bank and broker-house failures. Mortgage foreclosures by the banks and insurance companies used to be the general rule in a financial crisis. Distress sales of inventories were part of the recuperative powers of the market system, purging itself of inflation by an overshoot into deflation.

Even the great mail-order establishment of Sears, Roebuck almost went to the wall in the recession that followed World War I. If Julius Rosenwald had not come forward to pledge his private fortune as collateral, it probably would have gone defunct, as so many other firms then did.

Is the crisis almost over? I distrust those who claim to call such turns with fine accuracy. To be able to predict when the peak of short-term interest rates will occur, you must be able to pinpoint when the expected recession will actually materialize. To be able to promise that interest rates will drop from their present range of 11 to 20 per cent back into a more normal range of 8 to 11 per cent, you must first discern signs that the price inflation is reverting to single-digit annual rates.

Rumors

Few forecasters any longer think that the first quarter of 1980 will record a drop in real gross national product. It is still only an even-money bet that there will be an appreciable rate of decline in real output in the second quarter.

The prospect for early abatement in the inflation rate is even dicier. The consumer price index will still have to register some uncomfortable rises in gasoline and home-financing charges. Rumors about an impending freeze on wages and prices and new selective credit controls are triggering some anticipatory price rises. Although union wage settlements were modest last year compared with the rise in the price index, rumors about the likely steel-wage bargaining are anything but reassuring.

We with no need to borrow and with flexible funds to invest will try to ride out the crisis, preserving what we can of our real assets. My advice last month on canny no-fuss investing came at a good time.

Much of my mail asked about *tax-exempt* money-market funds. Let me stress that only those with incomes well above $50,000 ought to be concerned with such esoteric items.

WHERE THE ECONOMY STANDS

April 28, 1980

WHEN I lecture in the U.S. and abroad, I am asked the same questions.

· Has the recession begun?

· When will interest rates reach their peak and recede?

· Will the inflation rate get worse? Or, if some relief is in sight, by how much can we expect inflation to abate?

· Will the banks go bust? Should cautious people liquidate their common stocks and purchase land, gold, diamonds, antiques, stamps, and stock a cabin in the woods with food and with a gun to fend off feckless predators? Is it smart to set up numbered accounts in Switzerland, Panama or Curaçao?

· How will the November election affect the answers to these questions? What will be the effect of President Carter's new credit and fiscal programs?

The above are quite enough to tax the most omniscient. But even tougher are these long-run questions:

· Will the 1980s ring down the curtain on economic growth, terminating the pattern of progress that has generally prevailed since the Industrial Revolution of the eighteenth century?

· Are we entering an era of conservative reaction, a wave that will move us back toward the pre–New Deal pattern?

Informed Guesses

With the usual warnings that economics is far from an exact science, here's how I read the evidence.

Twenty per cent interest rates will convert the growth recession of 1979 into the full-fledged recession of 1980. Production will be lower at the year-end. Unemployment will still be rising on Election Day. Corporate profitability will be down.

Is this a sure thing? Of course not. But at 2-to-1 odds it's a good bet.

I suspect we are now near the peak of interest rates. A worsening of inflation could reverse this judgment; but the collapse of staple prices in the wake of the Hunt brothers' failure to corner the silver market will probably advance the date when bond prices begin a sustained rise. The Federal Reserve will not resist a drop in interest rates brought on by a general weakening of the economy.

Falling interest costs and decelerating food costs, acting as offsets to still-rising energy costs, should begin by midsummer to work the inflation from its current 18 per cent annual rate down toward 10 to 12 per cent. This is still a vexing prospect but at least an improvement over the recent past. (Warning: the price level is the hardest variable for econometricians to forecast and they have chronically been too optimistic in their inflation estimates.)

Doomsayers are risky guides for those anxious to protect their nest eggs. I know only a few people who have been able to nail down gains in gold, leveraged real estate and the like. But I know many more who have jeopardized the security they sought by becoming Johnny-come-latelies left holding injudicious assets sold to them at gross markups by skillful alarmists.

The biggest and best investors do well in these days of stagflation to *minimize the rate of attrition in real wealth.* I can offer only cold-comfort advice.

Avoid crude mistakes. Diversify widely. Eschew perfection you can't attain. Then sleep well, knowing you've done your best.

Futurology

You must reserve judgment on how serious and long-lasting the recession will be until the election. I've studied several analyses of the new Carter programs. All tell the same story.

Carter's credit and budget tightening will subtract a bit from this year's real growth and add a little to this year's inflation rate. Any benefits from it will accrue only in 1981 and beyond.

If the next President decides to fight inflation by a dedicated program of monetary and fiscal austerity, the recession will be deep and long. As I read the evidence from Switzerland, West Germany and Japan, there is no comfortable way to move back toward reasonable price stability. I wish there were some new "supply-side economics" that could be relied on to tame stagflation. There is not.

I should report that there is a new school, the so-called rational expectationists. They are optimistic that inflation can be wiped out with little pain if only the government makes *credible* its determination to do so. But neither history nor reason tempt one to bet their way.

The United States economy still has the potential for positive growth. As a realist, I doubt we shall live up to that potential between now and 1985.

OUTLOOK FOR THE '80s

December 15, 1980

I am learning in a swing around Europe that foreigners were even more surprised by the magnitude of the Reagan victory than we were. It is remarkable how fast they are adjusting to the new realities.

A crack Austrian journalist asked me how Reagan's programs would be able to succeed in ending inflation at the same time that military expenditures are to be greatly expanded. He asked: "Do you, as an experienced economist, believe in supply-side miracles that will make all this possible, along with a balanced budget?" One should never believe in a miracle beforehand. It is hard enough to do so after the fact. I reviewed how flimsy the evidence is that capital formation will explode in the next few years or that the proposed Kemp-Roth 30 per cent cut in tax rates will generate higher rather than lower tax receipts.

Disillusioned

I then had to correct a basic misapprehension, one shared with business people I met in Denmark and England. Their view seems to be that Ronald Reagan enters office having built up high hopes in Americans of a new prosperity ahead in which our inflation problem is solved. That's not quite right, in my judgment. People are disillusioned with post-Keynesian programs not delivering the goods of full employment with stable prices. They know what they don't want, and they are sure that President Carter was not able to give them what they do want.

But this does not mean that the swing voters who gave the

Republicans their landslide victory have built up any real confidence that the new team will do much better economically. When you choose among evils, you don't kid yourself that better is very good.

A basic fact about present-day Americans is our scaled-down expectations. This seems a rational rather than pathological reaction to what have been the actualities of the 1970s. Now that we are into the 1980s, what is a reasonable economic outlook for the decade ahead? What, so to speak, is the average performance that Ronald Reagan's Presidency must deliver before it is found wanting by the voters?

Here, with the help of pre-election projections made in September by a prominent economic research department in the private sector, I shall take a peek into the future.

The good news is that real hourly earnings will be growing between now and 1987. This is a welcome reversal of the decline that began in 1973, as a result of prices rising faster than money earnings.

If the researchers are right, our economy will not be the zero-sum game that MIT's Lester Thurow has been warning against. With real gross national product rising at a 2 per cent average annual rate, there will be more social pie to be divided up among wages, profit and government. Corporate profits will be rising faster than the general price index.

Now for some bad news. The unemployment rate has been climbing since the 1960s. By 1987, the research team's computer projects, it will average 8.3 per cent of the labor force. That means one out of every twelve Americans looking for work will not be able to find an acceptable job.

Not only is the U.S. growth rate to be only half that sought in John F. Kennedy's Camelot, the unemployment rate in the years ahead is to be double the average of the 1960s. Such is the sad reality that Americans have been learning to live with in recent times. Do we at least attain the Holy Grail of price stability? That, many voters think, would be worth some sacrifices. But the projections of this research team are not sanguine.

Future Prices

According to its computer, the consumer price index grew an average of 3.2 per cent a year between 1960 and 1973. From 1973 through 1982 the forecast is for increases in the CPI averaging 9.3 per cent annually. Between 1982 and 1987, according to this forecast, the advance in the CPI will average 9.4 per cent a year.

Given the imprecision of the best forecasters of price levels, we see that two-digit price inflation is a distinct possibility for much of the decade.

Does the election landslide make these projections obsolete? That would depend on a still-unanswerable question: Is Ronald Reagan a relaxed Eisenhower or a crusading Thatcher? The front runners for the key Reagan Cabinet posts are well known to us. On their track records, I see no reason to write down a more cheerful horoscope.

Chapter 3

THE MERITS OF THE MARKET

C
*AN the market be trusted to provide the neces-
sities of life? Samuelson presents the case that private speculators tend to stabilize volatile food markets. Well-run stockpiles, in the hands of private
industry or the government, would not change the
average level of prices. Therefore, markets clear
efficiently in feast or famine, but generally at a
higher price than the poorest can afford.*

*Samuelson presents two clear-cut solutions to the
energy crisis: the free-market solution and comprehensive planning. He then laments that the actual
solution will be less than optimal. He demonstrates
in these articles that efficiency may be reached by
both paths. However, he recommends a program
that selects tools from both approaches.*

*According to Samuelson, the extent to which the
general American people should share in profits,
resulting from scarce resources, is a legitimate issue
of national concern. It is a non-issue for those who
hold to a strict interpretation of property rights.
Samuelson's view of society allows for a common
good in which reciprocity of effort is the rule. How-*

ever, Samuelson argues for permitting business dis-
cretion on the basis that consumers and earners in
general have a stake in efficient *business. Still, he*
does not believe that unrestrained self-interest will
necessarily result in the "public interest."

The Market Versus Planning

BUFFER FOOD STOCKS
June 6, 1977

WE all remember the run of bad harvests in the early
1970s. Again and again the Russian wheat crop failed. The
sub-Sahara ran particularly dry. The timing and nature of
India's monsoons was bad for its grain crops. Recurrent
droughts in Asia decimated the rice crops, and mainland
China's soybean yields plummeted.

Nor were we spared in the U.S. After we had put our faith
in a few hybrid varieties of corn, they proved susceptible to
fungus. When the Mississippi was not flooding at planting
time, Iowa was burning up from lack of midsummer rain.

The results we also remember: those Bangladesh babies
with bloated stomachs and toothpick limbs. Mass starvation
in the Sahel. Talk of bread at a dollar per loaf. Less steak for
American supper tables and more soybean meat stretchers
and chicken.

Economically, the worsening of the terms of trade between
urban wares and staple farm products meant a stagnation of
real wages. Along with the OPEC oil hike, this was the final
impulse pushing the Western world into the double-digit
price inflation that precipitated the worst recession of the
post–World War II epoch.

Market Chaos Versus Order?

So much is experience. Remembering history, George Santayana hoped, might parole us from having to repeat it. But what, exactly, are the lessons of history we are supposed to have learned?

Joseph of Egypt stored grain during the seven fat years against the seven lean years to come. Though cycles are no longer so regular as apparently they were then, today the developing nations in their South-North dialogues clamor for new and bigger commodity stockpiles: to stabilize prices of food, fiber and metals; to provide against future famines; to transfer real income from affluent industrial peoples to the teeming poor of Asia, Africa and Latin America.

Although Dr. Kissinger glimpsed some merit in such proposals, the economists in the Nixon and Ford administrations turned thumbs down on schemes that link development aid to commodity stabilization. (If put in charge of the 1846 Irish famine, they would no doubt have counseled decontrol of potato prices—to ration demand and to encourage supply!)

The new Carter advisers take a more tolerant view. Without conceding that our affluence is bought at the price of starvation in the LDC's, they want the U.S. to bear its share of costs in maintaining a larger stockpile of basic goods.

Oddly, it is American farmers who are apprehensive that such stand-by stocks will hang over and depress market prices. What they do not understand is the fact that scarcity can be alleviated only in the act of using up those accumulations of goods; and what they forget is that the purchase of goods in the open market to build up the inventories would raise prices or keep them from otherwise falling.

False Hopes

The average level of prices would not be raised or lowered by a well-run stockpile. The LDC's are as wrong to think such schemes would successfully raise raw-material prices as

American farmers are wrong to think they will lower average prices.

All that being said, however, the case for buffer schemes is not strong. The organized markets, data show, do work about as they should: after a rash of bad harvests, they cause world inventories to be depleted—just as in the early 1970s. After a rash of good harvests, futures-market pricing causes carry-over stocks to swell—just as now. Holbrook Working spent a lifetime at Stanford verifying these patterns.

But surely, government inventories will *further* stabilize prices and reduce the danger of world famine? The effect is likely to be small. Experience shows that it will pay industry to hold less in private stocks when government is known to be holding more in public stocks. Thus, the promise of a real Pharaoh's store for the lean years would be largely illusion.

The next time crops fail around the globe, what is needed for the humanitarian purpose of keeping people alive who would otherwise starve is *command over money* to buy them their desperately needed share of the limited global supply of grains. The best I can find to say for stockpiling schemes is that they might get us to budget now against the unknown date of our future need. To expect more is to court disillusionment.

ENERGY ECONOMICS

July 2, 1973

WHEN the gods look down to see how we humans handle our energy problems, they must chuckle with amusement. Or despair of social rationality.

We have neither engaged in perspicacious planning to meet the emerging and foreseeable problems, nor have we relied on the device of competitive pricing. Instead we have left things to oligopolistic industries, which themselves have had to guess about future government policies.

Follies

Here's the sorry tale.

· To use up our continental reserves faster, we long put quotas on oil imports. We gave tax advantages to domestic oil and gas producers.

· By deliberate regulation, we underpriced valuable natural gas—so that much of our best supplies of it have been dissipated in uses that might have been as well served by coal, oil and nuclear energy.

· When the Mideast oil monopoly was still weak, our State Department and oil companies knuckled under to it. Instead of joining with Europe and Japan in a united front against the Persian Gulf cartel while waiting on alternative supplies from Alaska, Canada, the North Sea and Indonesia, we turn the job over to multinational oil companies—which have every incentive to act as a tax collector for the monopolists.

· At the same time that the trend of demand for gasoline, diesel and jet fuel and residual oil has been surging steadily, there has been virtually no new refinery capacity built. And for years ahead, no matter what frenetic decisions are now made, there will continue to be a shortfall of capacity.

· For years we had no interest in the environment or human safety. Then suddenly out of belated concern over ecology, we've made it difficult (1) to carry through our planned program for nuclear-energy installations; (2) to expand coal mining, strip and otherwise; (3) to build long-overdue power-generating stations (thermal or nuclear).

· To meet requirements of the Clean Air Act, American cars will be fitted by 1976 with catalytic converters. (This is probably the *wrong* technology to achieve the act's purpose.) Since lead in gasoline will, after only a few tankfuls, contaminate the catalyst, every station in the land must by then be prepared to offer lead-free gasoline; and this in an industry that cannot find the refining capacity even to meet the normal growth of old-fashioned gasoline-energy demand. We vacillate between malignant neglect and rhetoric about standards which, if not literally unobtainable, are likely to be later reversed by an explosion of public opinion.

· After building colonial-style filling stations, often four to an intersection, and competing for high-margin sales by ingenious fibs in advertising and absurd frills of free service, the oil industry suddenly finds that it can shut down stations evenings and weekends. Spot shortages are met by doling out 10 gallons at a time. This merely multiplies trips to service stations and lengthens waiting lines.

Therapy

The old-fashioned solution would be to let the prices of gasoline, fuels, coal, gas and other energy go sky high. At 70 cents a gallon of gas, poorer people couldn't drive much. All of us might drive less. The trend toward smaller cars would be speeded up.

But also the oil industry, here and abroad, would make huge profits. Public utilities, freed from onerous regulation, would reap rich earnings as they raised our monthly electricity. That frost-free refrigerator, which just about doubles your monthly refrigeration bill, would no longer be worth buying. Instead of air conditioning, some people would stick to rotary fans.

Such a free-market solution would be bitterly resented by the public as inflationary and inequitable. Even if the government kept the oil industry from reaping the monopoly rents of the shortage by means of a stiff tax increase on gasoline —and an exceedingly strong case can be made out for precisely such an act—the increase in the cost of living would have macroeconomic repercussions on the inflation spiral.

At the other extreme, we could immediately introduce a comprehensive program of rationing. Each car gets only so much per month. Each household gets fuel supplies just adequate to keep it five degrees cooler in winter. Meantime, a crash R&D program could develop resource substitutes and more efficient techniques.

The gods in heaven know we will not adopt either clear-cut alternative. We will muddle through badly.

OIL ECONOMICS

September 29, 1975

LET me state two unhedged views on oil policy that are diametrically opposed to each other:

The only good price-control program is a repealed price-control program. The sooner we phase out *all* controls the better. And the same goes for Mr. Ford's tariff on oil imports.

According to this view, there is no long-run emergency. Provided we let prices rise and fall with supply and demand, there is nothing wrong with the U.S. importing half or more of its oil by the 1980s. Provided we let the different kinds of energy (natural gas, coal, oil, gasoline, fissionable uranium) be auctioned off at their market worths, the problem will take care of itself.

Moreover, it is argued, the temporary monopoly of OPEC —like any temporary monopoly—is going to disintegrate anyway; and having free pricing of energy domestically is likely to be the most efficient way of hastening that day of disintegration.

On the Other Hand

Quite different is this viewpoint:
Decontrolling oil and trying to promote U.S. independence

from imports are bound to increase the rate of inflation. They will do so the more if decontrol is allowed to take place suddenly. And the higher prices for fuels will tend to withdraw purchasing power from our consumers and thereby slow down the recovery.

Since wage rates tend to rise when consumer prices rise, it is to be feared that there will result a still further increase in costs and prices. And all this will be further aggravated by induced increases in airline costs and fares, and rises in prices of goods whose production depends on energy and which themselves set raw-material costs for production of other goods. Moreover, these days there is not only a pass-through of higher costs but also signs of a markup on such add-ons.

If government policy on decontrol and on insulating us from oil imports does substantially worsen the rate of inflation, it is to be feared that the Federal Reserve and Administration policy formulators will tighten the screws of monetary and fiscal policies on what already threatens to be a drawn-out and too weak economic recovery. Being stampeded into the wrong activistic energy policy will thus help to keep the unemployment rate high in the remaining years of this decade, and will thereby put an intolerable load on the unskilled earners and the minority workers most subject to unemployment. Etc.

This last point of view represents fairly closely the position of most Democratic congressmen who take an active stand on energy. The first comes closer to that of the Ford Administration. However, to represent the Administration concern for oil independence fairly, we would have to go to a third corner of a triangle.

Unlike the views of free-marketeers and proponents of continued controls or of only slow, unwinding controls, there is the Administration viewpoint associated with the name of Secretary Kissinger and his erstwhile Assistant Secretary, Thomas Enders:

This view holds that it is urgent that government policy promote independence of imports. Only by stringent measures, on our part and also on the part of other consuming importers of oil like Japan and Western Europe, can there be engineered reductions in OPEC exports and a hastening of the day when OPEC falls apart.

This school attaches importance to countervailing power against the cartel of sellers to be wielded by a cartel of consuming countries. Just as the Sinai settlement is a matter for skillful negotiation and promise, so the way to solve the oil "crisis," this school believes, must be by negotiation of floors and ceilings at open or secret international conferences.

Cooling It

Where lies the golden mean of policy? Here's my summation:

First, a slow phasing out of controls offers a good, perhaps the best, plan.

Second, even instantaneous decontrol needn't negate healthy recovery. The Wharton forecasting model ran a September calculation on "instant decontrol." It lowers the real growth forecast from mid-1975 to mid-1976 by 1 per cent; raises Election Day unemployment to only 8.1 from 7.9 per cent (or, optimists would say, to 7.2 from 7 per cent), and raises the price level on Election Day by only 1 per cent.

Moral: The energy debate is unnecessarily hot.

ENERGY BASICS

April 25, 1977

ECONOMISTS know how to lessen our growing dependence on imports of oil. Any assistant professor can provide President Carter with the following prescription:

"Free the price of oil. Stop taxing producers of 'old' oil to subsidize the low price at which we consumers and corporations can purchase energy and use it lavishly. Rationing total energy use by letting the competitive price rise will reduce the U.S. need to import. It will thereby slightly weaken the cartel power of the monopolists."

This cold-turkey solution fails to be adopted not because of ignorance of elementary economics by the President or his advisers. It is a solution simply *not politically acceptable to the American people and Congress.* Among other things it would involve a massive redistribution of income away from 215 million American consumers to some tens of thousands of oil producers and owners of domestic reserves.

Another possible solution would be to accomplish the same "rationing by the purse" through *heavy enough new taxes* on every purchase of fuel, gas or gasoline. Horsepower penalties on large new cars, accompanied by subsidies on small and efficient cars and on home insulation, will reinforce the reduction in total energy consumed. If the taxes are heavy enough, the enhanced profits to owners of oil could be largely siphoned away; at the same time, the inducement to explore and exploit marginal domestic wells would be weakened, but such an induced slowdown would at least have the implication that we are not so rapidly using up the limited geologic deposits located in North America.

The Rub

Why is this free-market-cum-taxation solution not politically feasible? Because, apparently, what the American voter wants in the last analysis is cheap energy—energy cheaper to him than what the U.S. economy has to pay for the stuff from abroad.

The voter really does not want our dependence on plentiful imported oil to cease—that is the nub of America's energy problem.

Here is where the genius of Presidential leadership is called for. I am reminded of the problem Franklin Roosevelt had: Americans did not want to go to war; but, also, we really did not want Hitler to dominate the world. How to get us to do what our own long-run wishes wanted done?

The analogy is an apt one. Although we now want the luxury of plentiful energy, we Americans really do not want to be at the mercy of some future withholding of supply; or at the mercy of some later repetition of the fivefold increase in the price of oil by the OPEC cartel.

Like Roosevelt, President Carter must temporize and compromise. He must *gradually* raise taxes on energy uses. He must *gradually* decontrol natural-gas and old-oil prices. He must propose subsidies to conservation and penalties for wasteful practices—subsidies and penalties that will not exceed what the political traffic will bear.

Naturally, such a tissue of compromises will be optimally pleasing to no one. To confirmed believers in *laissez faire* it will be anathema as still putting curbs on the beneficent operations of rising prices. To devotees of egalitarianism, its burdens upon the lower-income families will be all too obvious, as will its unfolding capital-gains windfalls to those who own resources that are gradually becoming ever more valuable.

The Final Test

I am writing these words before the details of Carter's new energy program have been disclosed. But, anticipating its general features, how shall we be able to judge whether that program is working out to be a success or a failure?

No program can solve our problems overnight. That's too much to expect. It is not too much to hope that a Carter program will succeed in reducing the total oil-equivalent consumption of energy in the next few years *below* the recent 38-million-barrel-per-day level, and will raise the fraction of that total provided by coal.

Finally, will it succeed in holding down imports to below the recent 7-million-barrels-a-day level? And succeed in tempering the ominous upward trend of imports?

Those are the bottom-line numbers to watch. But let's not forget to monitor which income classes are being made to pay the bill.

NOBEL LAUREATE LEONTIEF

November 5, 1973

I T used to be said that only twelve men in the world understood Einstein's theory of relativity, and all but one were Germans. Actually, that was an overstatement. But it did illustrate how rarely the general public can grasp the intricacies of a great scientist's work.

Wassily Leontief of Harvard has just been awarded the Nobel Prize in Economics for 1973. This is richly deserved for his pioneering work on the input-output structure of an economy's industries. Input-output is a fairly complicated statistical technique for analyzing both the anatomy and the physiology of the economy. Beyond its value as a tool of description, it is valuable as a device for prediction and for planning. On the theory that what one fool can learn so can another, let me try to explain the simple logic of input-output.

It takes labor and iron to produce coal. But to produce iron, along with labor, it takes coal. Don't we have a vicious logical circle here? Coal depends upon iron; but iron depends on coal.

No. There is circular interdependence. But the circle is a virtuous one. It can be resolved by solving the simultaneous equations of your high-school algebra class. (Recall Jack and Jill. Jill is half Jack's age. Jack is five years older than Jill. No vicious circle here. Since Jill will double her age in five years, she must now be five; knowing that, we calculate Jack to be ten. We've just solved two simultaneous equations by eliminating one of the unknowns—Jack's age—through a clever substitution, ending up with one easy equation for the one remaining unknown—Jill's age.)

They give $120,000 in Nobel prizes for this? Wait. Note the immensity of Leontief's statistical estimations.

The Grand Tableau

What Leontief did was to break down the aggregate gross national product into manageable industry subaggregates. At first he worked with but ten industries: agriculture, manufacturing, transportation, government, etc. From actual data, he measured how much each needs of the other per dollar of flow. To make the problem statistically manageable, he made the heroically simplifying assumption: when we shift from war to peace, from isolation to free trade, the ratio of inputs that any industry needs from other industries will either remain constant or will change according to trends that can be recognized and estimated.

Ten by ten coefficients is bad enough. But by the time he had data on 100 by 100 industries and 400 by 400, the number of his coefficients began to run in the hundreds of thousands; and the number of operations needed to solve them simultaneously to run in the millions. The giant calculator was invented just in time. And Leontief has been its leading customer.

Moreover, so far I have been describing only the Model T statistical version of Leontief's input-output. In recent years, he and his team—aided by grants from foundations, the Bureau of Labor Statistics, the National Science Foundation —have built a dynamic version that calculates the investment needs of an economy growing at various projected rates.

Fruits of Science

A prophet is with even greater honor outside his own country. The United Nations, the World Bank, government agencies in Scandinavia and Western Europe, the five-year plans of the developing countries—all have taken up input-output budgeting.

The supreme compliment came when the U.S.S.R. decided that input-output is o.k. (in Auden's verse, what is not forbidden is required) and, like wireless, is really a Russian invention after all. Since Leontief was part of the earlier wave of emigrant scientists who have enriched American scholarship, this nationalistic predating of the record is harmless enough.

I list some uses of input-output:

· After the Indochina war, what will be the effects on total employment and on skill requirements of a shift of $1 billion of GNP from war to peace purposes? (Leontief's result, an *expansion* of employment, must have specially delighted him, since he is one of the exceptions to the rule that as a scholar grows older he becomes more reactionary.)

· Leontief was the first to discover that U.S. exports are relatively more *labor intensive* than our imports—a paradox since reconfirmed.

· Congress used his tableau to detect the great weight of steel-price hikes on the 1950s cost-push inflation.

I could go on for pages. A great scholar's work is never done.

FRANK KNIGHT, 1885–1972

July 31, 1972

O NE of America's most influential intellectuals died recently. But few people would recognize his name.

Frank Knight was professor of economics at the University of Chicago for half a century. He never retired; when he died in his 80s his fountain pen was still full. Knight was the founder of the Chicago School in economics: if he was Abraham, Henry Simons was Isaac and Milton Friedman is Jacob.

Although, as far as I know, Knight was never invited to the White House, you can see his influence on Washington in the decisions that Secretary George Schultz will be making on foreign-exchange rates and in the mordant wit of Herbert Stein, chairman of the Council of Economic Advisers. But this is only the visible peak of the iceberg. Even radical economists, as I shall argue, bear the stamp of Frank Knight's thought.

Cracker-Barrel Socrates

How did *The New Yorker* miss doing a profile on so singular a personality? A profound philosopher and superb economic technician, he was also the village atheist and a sage of the Will Rogers vintage. These days professors tend to come from Exeter Academy or the Bronx High School of

Science. Knight was of that turn-of-the-century generation who—like Karl and Arthur Compton and Wesley Mitchell —came off the farm.

He used to say in his squeaky voice that he became an economist because his feet hurt him following the plow. Perhaps nearer the truth was the fact that when he was a graduate student in philosophy at Cornell, he was given an ultimatum: "Stop talking so much, or leave the philosophy department." This gave Knight no choice but to gravitate down into economics. (It also made him an authority on the laws of talk, as in his dictum: "Sociology is the science of talk, and there is only one law in sociology. Bad talk drives out good.")

Frank Knight was a skeptic who doubted the ability of man through government to better his condition. Capitalism —alas!—is the best we can settle for. Thus, if Dr. Friedman is one of those optimists who thinks that capitalism is the best of all possible worlds, Dr. Knight was one of those pessimists who is afraid that this is indeed the case.

I shall not argue here the issue of determinism versus free will. But if you believe that man can hurry forward the clock of evolution—that a Marx or Lenin can advance the date of the inevitable revolution—then you must concede man can regard that clock. From 1932 to 1945, faith in the market-pricing mechanism as the organizer of the economy sold at a discount.

The Counterrevolution

It was the priceless contribution of Frank Knight and the Chicago School to remind us of the market's merits. This is a message that falls on deaf ears in the common rooms of Britain's ancient universities. But it is one whose relevance a Russian, Yugoslav or Czech can understand.

And make no mistake about it. Rumors of the death of the market, like those of Twain's death, are greatly exaggerated.

In Britain and Scandinavia, socialist governments have in the last quarter of a century often been displaced from office. In America, too, the pendulum swings. The role of Frank Knight in this counterrevolution is pivotal.

A central feature of Knight's thought is his antipathy toward the mixed economy. As he put it, a planned economy is simply a well-managed penitentiary. It was this simplistic element that came to disillusion me with my boyhood idol. And I fear it made Knight a poor prophet of events that were to come after 1932, as when in a moment of despair, he declared that the only choice was between Communism and Fascism and he for one preferred Communism.

Knight's antipathy toward the prevalent post–New Deal world is not unlike that of a Herbert Marcuse. Many of the New Left are Knight without the market.

As a sage has said: "The ideas of economists and political philosophers, both when they are right and when they are wrong, are more powerful than is commonly understood. Indeed, the world is ruled by little else. Practical men, who believe themselves to be quite exempt from any intellectual influences, are usually the slave of some defunct economist . . . I am sure that the power of vested interests is vastly exaggerated, compared with the gradual encroachment of ideas."

Although, as J. M. Keynes also said, "in the long run we are all dead," Frank Knight lives on.

CORPORATE GIANTS
March 29, 1971

A. A. Berle, Jr. is dead. His passing provokes memories of the golden years before World War I when, reportedly, great scholars were great undergraduate teachers. When William James, Josiah Royce and George Santayana walked Harvard Yard, no man knew the language of FORTRAN and few lisped in differentials. But, I have it on high authority, every schoolboy savored the varieties of religious experience and to have heard Kittredge was to know Shakespeare.

More than Dutch elm disease has changed the face of college life. A feature of that bygone age was the presence of the prodigy: pygmies as well as giants strode the earth of Cambridge then. One would give much to witness the sight of precocious, knickerbockered undergraduates mingling with the Stovers and Merriwells in that gothic age of academe.

Berle was one such prodigy, at pretty much the same time that the mathematician-to-be Norbert Wiener and the musician Roger Sessions matriculated. Prior to the onset of puberty Wiener wrote an autobiography entitled *Ex-Prodigy;* but those who knew him, or have read the book, will realize that he never outgrew the scars of genius.

It is easier to pass from the ranks of precocity to the realms of generalized harmonic analysis and cybernetics than it is to mature into a man of affairs. Yet Berle, graduating from law school, practicing and teaching law, went on to become a New Dealer, an expert on Latin America and a successful force in the La Guardia reform movement and the formation of the Liberal Party in New York.

A New Genus

It is not for any of these, though, that A. A. Berle, Jr. will be remembered in the history of thought. It is for something that he discovered and analyzed as far back as 1933 that merits his fame.

I refer of course to the Berle-Means thesis that the large corporation in American life represents a new genus of life, a unit in which there is separation of ownership and control. As we go back to read the brief book by Gardner Means and Adolph Berle, *The Modern Corporation and Private Property,* its contents seem so familiar and true as to appear almost trite. To accept such an evaluation is to fall victim to the optical illusion of hindsight, like the boy who said, "Of course, Columbus discovered America—how could he have missed it?"

Fewer and fewer hairsplitters are left to claim that the corporation has no identity separate from its owners, workers and consumers. With the same lame logic, such reductionists regard Greta Garbo as simply a collection of DNA, and the solar system as merely nine something-or-others moving around the sun. The tax collector knows better. The corporation exists. (And, I may add, constitutes a good pooler of risks and therefore provides an excellent object for income taxation.)

The statistical evidence for separation of ownership and control—i.e., the evidence for the fact that in every democracy involving tens and hundreds of thousands of individuals, whether it be a trade union or a religious denomination, collusions of effective minorities exercise decision making—has become firmer with each passing decade. What follows from this unchallengeable fact?

Tracks of the Beast

Is it the case that the pre–Berle-Means unit of business, in which the owner of capital was all-powerful, adhered to the laws of profit maximization prated of in the economics textbooks? But that the modern corporate giant answers to a different drumbeat from the pursuit of cost reduction and profit (now and in the longer future)?

I used to go along with this fashionable myth. Study of the facts of life will show, however, that the old tycoon of industry was a capricious bird, with behavior to be understood as much from Freud (if not Krafft-Ebing) as from the handbook of operational analysis and managerial economics. If anyone in the universe minimizes costs and calculates present discounted values, it is committees in the large-scale corporation. To be sure, some inside managers, with minimal ownership, perpetrate hanky-panky and minor mayhem. But cheating on the boss did not begin yesterday, as the cuneiform tablets of Babylonia will confirm.

The boss they cheat we now know, thanks to Berle, is (1) the government, (2) the employees, (3) the consumers and, let's not forget, (4) those proxy-controlling owners. Our task is to insure that the giants remain responsive to the public interest.

BUSINESSMAN BLUES

August 8, 1977

FIFTY years ago, industrialists were the elite. When a folk hero like Henry Ford opined, "History is bunk," historians solemnly entered that into the historical record.

In our time, when a Henry Ford II claims that what

America has uniquely to offer to civilization is the productivity of its corporate industry, who takes notice? No wonder that Ford felt enough pique and frustration to resign from the Ford Foundation recently. Businessmen genuinely feel themselves to be William Graham Sumner's "forgotten men" of this generation.

They often blame the media for this. But for a deeper understanding we must ask: *Why* do the readers of newspapers and magazines, the viewers of TV, take such prurient delight when the indiscretions of Lockheed and Gulf Oil are revealed by the press and networks? Why does the mob smell blood and follow with joy the probings by the SEC and IRS into the doings of the Gulf & Western conglomerate's chieftains? Why do the financial problems of a Bert Lance seem to meet with ill-concealed pleasure rather than sympathy?

Velvet Doghouse

If among customers of the press and the networks there was a reservoir of goodwill and appreciation for the businessman's function, editors would be treating corporations more gently. Editors are themselves businessmen catering to *their* customers' preferences.

I believe businessmen and members of the affluent classes are essentially correct, rather than paranoid, in feeling both unloved and unrespected. I say this taking into account the fact that America is a society in which not much deference is paid to anybody. Generals and congressmen, if we can believe the sociological polls, fare as badly as laywers, judges, professors and accountants. Auden should have labeled ours the Age of Anxious Envy.

Abroad, it was never prestigious to have been "in trade." As de Tocqueville noted, it used to be different here. Business is a displaced elite in America. So it is doubly galling to be newly in the minority.

Businessmen—and there is no need for me to apologize for the sexist version of the word, since the executive suite is almost as undiversified as a monastery—are a minority with the means to fight back. They call in their advertising agents to launch thunderbolts extolling the need for capital formation, the vital nature of profits and the glories of free enterprise.

The National Association of Manufacturers even subsidized a textbook of sound economics, only to have it regarded as an object of sophomoric derision. No matter how many times economists explain that only a few cents of the sales dollar go to profits, the damned public keeps thinking that capital gets the lion's share.

Intellectual Badmouths?

As J. Irwin Miller, longtime head of the successful Cummins Engine Co., pointed out in a recent Indianapolis speech, business's first naïve impulse is to blame its position of low esteem on the socialistic professors. Recognizing that most intellectuals are neither Republicans nor libertarians, I must still agree with Miller that the way to popularity will not be found via using one's economic power to promote "sound" economics and ideology in the schools and colleges. Actually, that which is being taught today in the respectable Harvard Business School differs in no essentials from what students are learning in Siwash and state university.

I must respectfully part company, however, with what I take to be Miller's message: even if businessmen do a better job of delivering the goods, I doubt that they will be accorded an easy ride into the kingdom of heaven. As Schumpeter used to argue, it is so often the *efficiencies* of the market economy that seem to undermine its hold on the people's affections.

George Orwell, a socialist who abhorred totalitarianism and cant, had contempt for those who criticized Kipling's empire builders while sucking the fruits of their patrols. Entrepreneurs must expect a similar fate.

So forswear love. There remains a job to be done. The pay

is good. And perhaps there is cool comfort in the testimony of economic history, which hardly suggests that nationalizing the large corporations and putting in a different set of bureaucrats would do better by the GNP or hasten the reapproach to Eden.

JUDGING CORPORATE HANDOUTS
August 13, 1979

CHRYSLER is in trouble. Ask three economists what to do about that situation and you'll get three answers. Maybe four, if I am one of your sample.

First, there is the hard-boiled consistent advocate of laissez faire. She or he will say: "Let the losers bite the dust. Ours is a profit-and-loss system. If they can't shape up to the market, let them go through the wringers of bankruptcy. The system will be the better for it. Liquidations and closedowns are the healthy catharsis of an effective economic system. If you make an exception this time, next time five claimants will bank on being bailed out of their own risks and follies."

This kind of answer can be given without really thinking about the matter or knowing any facts. Running the system by rule, and not by deliberative decision, means accepting a particular set of understood dogmas and sticking with them through thick or thin.

Bad Endings
The answer you give for Chrysler is the answer you give for Penn Central when it gets into trouble. That same answer applies to Lockheed Aircraft. Or to Franklin National Bank when its deposit liabilities threaten to exceed its remaining assets. Indeed, when the whole banking system is in the kind

of trouble it fell into in 1933, the undiluted logic of "government by rules and not by men" points toward letting nature find its own painful cure, whatever the human and economic cost.

Then there are the pragmatists. Often they bemoan the practice of coddling the poor, of letting those who fail in the struggle for economic subsistence come to the welfare authorities for assistance not matched by any commensurate useful work. But they somehow feel differently about a corporation in trouble. Mind you, they have no wish to exonerate weak management. But, they say, we must think about the workers who will be thrown out of jobs and about the merchants who will thereby lose business in a cumulative chain of lost spending and respending.

If I were Parkinson or Potter writing a handbook for Machiavellian managers, I'd remind them of the old saw "Who steals a handkerchief goes to jail, who steals a county becomes a duke." If you are going bankrupt, be sure you go bankrupt on a big scale.

Westinghouse must have learned from this school. After it rashly contracted to deliver uranium at a price that turned out to be commercially disastrous, the very magnitude of its loss was considered by some to be a mitigating factor. It reminded cynics of the Scot who, on trial for murdering his parents, threw himself on the mercy of the jury on the ground that he was an orphan.

I do not jest. Since antitrust exemptions can be made in case of firms on the verge of failure, one orchestrates a publicity campaign of poor-mouthing oneself in the hope of special privilege. Many staffers inside the Justice Department look on the LTV takeover of Lykes Corp. as a case in point.

My own counsel is to go very slow in weighing the Chrysler petition. Let's ascertain all the key facts first.

The Big Three in the U.S. auto industry have consisted of General Motors, Ford and Chrysler. Henry Ford II, with the help of his U.S. Air Force whiz kids, helped pull Ford Motor Co. out of the chaos it was left in by the aging Henry Ford and his honcho, Harry Bennett.

GM has long been known to be a formidable competitor, a low-cost and innovative producer. The last management team at Chrysler careened from crisis to crisis. No definitive evidence has yet materialized that the new team is essentially better.

Chrysler's commercial paper, to the tune of $1 billion, has lost credit standing. It will have to turn now to commercial banks, at appreciably higher interest rates. Even after selling off foreign assets, the company is strapped for the funds needed to build competitive new small models that meet the energy economies and pollution standards that are the law of the land.

Who Pays the Piper?

Now Chrysler asks for outright tax relief. If that does not materialize—or suffice—we shall no doubt learn of a suitor for its hand in a takeover move. Maybe Volkswagen, even though such a deal has been denied. Maybe one of half a dozen cash-laden oil companies. One of the nimble conglomerates may try to get into the act if the price is right.

I don't oppose all government subsidy in principle. But we must be stringent in any exceptions we make. Actually, going from three to two domestic producers is not so destructive to competition, now that Toyota, Volkswagen, Fiat, Volvo and other foreign makers also compete.

Finally, if Uncle Sam does intervene, Chrysler's management and we stockholders must be made to take our lumps.

KENNEDY'S ANTIMERGER INITIATIVE

September 3, 1979

THE Federal Trade Commission has temporarily blocked Exxon from using more than a billion dollars of its OPEC-sweetened oil profits to buy Reliance, an electric-motor company. Earlier, no one stopped Mobil from using its oil assets to take over Montgomery Ward.

Sen. Edward M. Kennedy has introduced a new bill, S.1246, an amendment to the Clayton Antitrust Act, forbidding the larger oil companies to merge with any business whose assets exceed $100 million. This proposal deserves careful and objective study.

Kennedy is known to be one of the hardest-working senators. He does his homework. That means he and his energetic staff make work for others—including already busy people like me. When introducing his bill, Kennedy asked my evaluation of its economics. He also canvassed expert opinion in the law schools on its optimal wording and scope.

Those Who Care

I cannot complain. Where the public weal is concerned, reciprocity of effort is the rule. When some of us in the National Academy of Sciences learn of a Russian scholar who deserves to be granted the right to leave the U.S.S.R., to whom do we turn for effective relief? To Republican Congresswoman Millicent Fenwick of New Jersey and Democratic Sen. Edward Kennedy of Massachusetts. They try.

My first reaction to the antimerger amendment was cautious. There is a prima facie case that a dynamic society will want funds to flow out of some industries and into others where capital yields more and is more effective.

Three years into World War I, the profits Du Pont made had nowhere to go in the gunpowder industry. So Du Pont put them into General Motors. Swords into plows, we can agree, is a good thing. (But that doesn't mean the Supreme Court erred in later requiring the Du Ponts to divest themselves of direct control of a second empire.)

Against this prima facie case for mobile capital, three telling points must be weighed in this oil instance.

The nation has a need for new domestic oil finds. To lighten the tax on its windfall profits, the industry keeps reminding us of this genuine need. If, on the pretext that the industry will plow the profits back into oil development, the American people go easy on the windfall tax, is it not a violation of the bargain if the companies proceed to diversify out of the energy industry?

It would seem so. Remember, we are not talking about money that is clearly the industry's, to do with whatever it jolly well pleases. The issue of how much the general American people are entitled to share in the scarcity-created energy profits is still moot.

Senator Kennedy is right to insist upon the national interest in this matter. In a sense he is calling the industry's bluff. Taking the industry at its word, Kennedy is ensuring that there be maximum testing of the alleged positive price elasticity of supply of oil.

There is a second tricky aspect of this oil case. Do we really want *all* the oil rents to go back into the oil industry? Why can't profit seekers be the best judge of where capital's yield is highest? Ordinarily, they can. However, as Robert Stobaugh of the Harvard Business School and others have been urging, when the OPEC cartel is charging $22 a barrel for oil it may be good policy for the U.S. to develop alternative energy sources even if their costs are up to $40 a barrel.

Why? Because that way we keep OPEC in check and

prevent it from charging $30 a barrel or more. No private oil company, however large, can be expected to initiate what is a prudent social bargain but a rotten private investment.

Staying Free

Economic science must weigh a third possible merit in the Kennedy proposal. An open society will tolerate bigness when that serves efficiency and is subject to checks and balances. But there is a prima facie case against encouraging imperialistic creation of new oligopoly empires.

Suppose the oil giants proposed to buy a diversified portfolio of *all* the companies on the stock exchanges. That would hurt future oil exploration. But it would not give them hegemony over any domains now competitive. Or suppose they raised their dividends. Or, subject to surveillance by the Internal Revenue Service so that they did not illegitimately convert ordinary income into lightly taxed long-term capital gains, suppose the oil giants bought in their own stock. All these are practices that would have to be argued out in terms of the public interest.

The spectacle of a dozen giants comparable to Du Pont setting off on an acquisition spree raises concern. Let the debate begin.

THE BUSINESSMAN'S SHRINKING PREROGATIVES

Spring, 1972

IT is obvious that in the years ahead, the so-called private corporation will find itself increasingly subjected to external constraints never dreamed of at the Harvard Business School. Not only will the corporation president find he cannot follow policies that will pollute the atmosphere; he will also discover that hundreds of traditional ways of making business decisions will simply no longer be available to him. Society will expand business's responsibilities and take increasing part in deciding how they are to be met.

What will be the new framework within which business decision making will have to operate? How will the new way of life affect growth in national product and distribution of incomes among the social classes?

Confident and detailed forecasting is quite impossible in so cosmic an area as this. The economist who has studied the econometric patterns of past GNP growth can often predict with some assurance that a particular region is on the brink of a vigorous expansion or is nearing an epoch of relative stagnation. The general laws of technology, despite what you read in the Sunday supplements, are conservative and regular and fairly predictable in their unfoldings. Not so the social environment. It takes a seer and a prophet to pinpoint the changes in this sphere. Alas, even a child's rereading of history will show the seers and prophets of the past lacked genuine sorcerer's hats. Neither Karl Marx nor Henry Adams nor Oswald Spengler have been at all near the mark in their prognostications.

Although I shall not rush in where they were brave to tread, I think it is useful to speculate, to let hypotheses well up freely, unrestrained by inhibitory criticisms. The critical testings of experience and analysis will reject and elect among the many possibilities.

Prophet of Doom

Almost 30 years ago, Joseph Schumpeter, in his *Capitalism, Socialism and Democracy,* predicted the shape of things to come after World War II. "Capitalism in an oxygen tent" —that, in a nutshell, was his vision of the timid new world. Such a capitalism, he thought, could linger on for quite a while. But he did not really expect the hospital invalid to perform with the vigor that the youthful capitalism had, in his view, prior to World War I.

Schumpeter was dead wrong. In the two decades since his death, the modern mixed economy has surpassed in performance classical capitalism at its finest hour. The miracle is not that Japan's economy has been growing for two decades at better than 9 per cent per annum in real terms—remarkable as that performance has been. The miracle is that all over the Western world, whether in cynical Austria, effete France, mercurial Italy or complacent America, real growth rates and average living standards have strongly and steadily outperformed the most daring predictions that could have been made by any objective observer of the years between the two world wars.

The developing countries—once called backward countries but which can, in plain truth, be called poor countries —have generally speaking not grown as rapidly economically as the more technologically advanced nations. The widening gap is sad to observe and ominous to contemplate. But it is insufficiently realized that the divergence is not the result of poor performance by the developing nations as compared with either their own pasts or the pasts of the affluent nations at earlier stages of development. Rather it is the mushrooming affluence of the technologically advanced nations that is placing them further out front. Actually, the 1960s saw most of the world's low-income regions grow at rates more rapid than those which generally prevailed in the years of high capitalism, when Queen Victoria reigned in Balmoral Castle and Calvin Coolidge dozed in the White House.

Premature Timing

Was, however, Schumpeter's error merely a case of premature timing? For there are unquestionably parts of the world where material progress has been slow. Witness the miracle of almost negligible economic growth in Latin America. And not even those most sympathetic to the ideals of socialism can find much to cheer about in the lack of economic progress in societies newly freed from colonial rule. What Nkrumah or Nasser or Nehru were able to accomplish under the banner of rational social planning has, in the short run, been disappointing. To the satirist, it is not a case of business in an oxygen tent as much as business in bedlam.

Although I am not an expert on Latin America, I cannot reject the suggestion that the slow growth of Argentina or of Uruguay (the one-time "Switzerland of South America") or of pre-Allende Chile is related to the fact that these societies are neither fish nor fowl, nor good red herring. They place social demands on industry that industry simply cannot effectively meet. Antipathy toward the corporation and the bourgeois way of life has served to hamstring performance. It is nonsense to continue to blame the dictator Perón for a stagnation in the Argentinian economy which has prevailed in the decades since he lost office. But it is not nonsense to infer that the populist imperatives upon which Perón so skillfully played have a pivotal role in explaining the miracle of Argentinian stagnation. There is a dictum attributed to Lenin to the effect that we will ruin the capitalist system by debauching its currency. That is not a very intelligent way to hurt an economic system and advance the day of successful revolution. By contrast, there are few better ways to ruin a modern mixed economy than to insist on 40 to 70 per cent increases in money wage rates within a brief period of time. This, to a degree, has happened time and time again in the unhappy economic history of Latin America.

Shrinking Business Prerogatives

It is thus interesting to note some new forces developing in the wealthier nations. New demands for greater social responsibility are being made of business. At the same time, the principal old demands—ever greater productivity and higher living standards for all—continue to be strongly pressed, perhaps even more so than at any time in the past.

In the face of the rising tide of social concern, some business strengths may be lost. Of course, there will always be sacrifices that are well worth making if on balance the common good is advanced. I am not concerned with the fact that zoning ordinances and taxes on effluence will undoubtedly prevent the corporation of the future from polluting the environment. Of course that will happen. But when it does, it will not be so much a case of losing old legitimate corporate freedoms as being required for the first time to follow good practices. Society and the Promethean business giants will be the better for such fetters.

I am interested, however, in contemplating the restrictions which may be placed on the exercise of previously accepted prerogatives. For example, in the United States, management cannot always shut down an unprofitable textile plant and throw its labor force out of work so that the firm can move to a more congenial environment where net labor costs are lower. In northern Italy, corporations are not always free to trim their labor forces as their efficiency experts would desire. Collective bargaining takes place over the numbers to be employed as well as wage rates, fringe benefits and severance pay. There may be a problem here. It is not that my heart bleeds for the corporation, but that one realizes that consumers and the earners of real wages also have a stake in the avoidance of dead-weight-loss practices.

Society's Power

At any rate, the line between rational concern and paranoia is a fine one. I have no wish to conjure up hobgoblins to terrify the denizens of the executive suite. I shall content myself with one last example of new pressures on corporations.

Ralph Nader is a social force of primary significance. The movement with which his name is associated represents much more than "mere consumerism," although that movement will itself be of increasing importance in the years to come. Naderism involves participatory democracy on the part of the workers and the public interest. You are naïve if you look only at the number of proxy votes the Nader movement is able to mobilize against management. Even if foundations and universities are increasingly persuaded to cast their votes against management, it will be scores of years before opposition votes now 3 and 5 per cent become majority votes of 51 per cent.

The leverage of such movements is not to be found inside the corporate ballot box, but in the minds of men. Once the public comes to believe that what is deemed good by General Motors is no longer good for the public, they will not wait for victory in the voting of shares and proxies. *They will strike directly by legislation.*

Let me illustrate. A group at the Yale Law School recently came up with the ingenious suggestion, presented in an article in the *Yale Law Journal,* that the antitrust division of the Justice Department prevent by legal action the large auto companies from introducing substantial annual or semiannual model changes. This pattern of contrived obsolescence, which Alfred P. Sloane, Jr. innovated to help bring General Motors to its present size and prominence, is said by the Yale reformers to constitute unfair competition and to promote monopolistic imperfection of markets.

At first glance, one might tend to dismiss such proposals as utopian and no real threat to existing corporate hegemony. But often, quite often, criticism prompts some governmental response which can lead to change—even if only through the reaction of an industry to such attention.

I can recall that years of criticism by economists like myself of the monopolistically imposed minimum brokerage rates of the New York Stock Exchange got absolutely nowhere. Yet when the Department of Justice entered the fray with an announcement that it intended to bring antitrust suits against this anomalous practice, it was only a short time until the New York Stock Exchange and the Securities and

Exchange Commission drastically modified the industry's practices.

We must resolve many competing demands. Business is being challenged and society shapes business's ability to respond. Can we tread a path that will avoid the excesses of private greed and narrow-minded management on the one hand and the debilitating destruction of all business prerogatives on the other? We have within our grasp a system that can meet the legitimate demands made upon it now and in the future.

Chapter 4

INCOME AND WEALTH

A general practitioner may have three types of clients. The first may be totally ignorant and incapable of comprehending the basics of how the body operates. The second may be very knowledgeable in his or her own field but innocent with respect to medicine. The third may be a fellow physician in need of an objective independent opinion. As a general practitioner of economics, Samuelson, in this chapter, dispenses advice to the schooled and unschooled.

Samuelson is reluctant to accept the outrageous claims of those who profess to have found the fountain of prosperity. It is impossible in investing to consistently perform better than the system in general. In other words, very few can get in and out of the market at precisely the right time and, hence, maintain a higher rate of return than those who diversify and sit still. Practical finance is a matter of good habits related to thrift, diversification and minimum transactions costs in terms of time, effort and expense.

The emphasis is not on doing well in every single

transaction but rather on maximizing the stock of wealth available to an individual at that time when he or she ceases to be economically productive. However, in times of high unanticipated inflation and low growth, the biggest and best investors do well to minimize the rate of attrition of real wealth. Beyond investment advice, these selections, if read carefully, provide one with valuable lessons in probability and the market system.

Property rights permit individuals in a capitalistic system to own, transfer and realize income from capital goods. The amount of capital goods in a particular society determines, to some extent, economic well-being. Hence, there is much concern in the field of economics about whether the rate of investment in capital goods is sufficient to maintain growth. Similarly, continued replacement and investment in productive resources like machinery, plant and equipment imply that the return to their owners be sufficient. Samuelson deals with these topics in relation to common stocks. Was the return to capital stock low during the seventies because capital was relatively abundant or because the market ignored the high cost of replacement? It may have been appropriate for him to suggest that the expected return, given the political climate, was extremely low. However, Samuelson correctly suggests that government programs designed to stimulate new investment may work, but their primary effect will be to increase the wealth and security of existing owners.

Where a person lives in the world may have more to do with political and economic well-being than personal characteristics such as thrift, diligence or character. Relative economic position within a par-

ticular society could depend to a large extent on being white, male, young and educated. Hence, poverty is not necessarily the absence of virtue. According to Samuelson, poverty should be mitigated and equality of opportunity should be expanded. He attempts to demonstrate that the economic cost of doing so is relatively small. He does not share the fear that moving toward income equalization will encourage the advantaged to take their pay in more devious ways. However, his egalitarianism is carefully limited to income, wealth and opportunity. For example, he makes no arguments for worker-operated firms or against salary differentials per se. Finally, he is concerned that the humane aspects of the New Deal be maintained but recognizes the possibility of bankruptcy if changes are not made in the system. For example, government-guaranteed retirement at 65 may not be necessary or wise given present demographics and improved health.

Maintaining Wealth

COPING
February 10, 1975

WHEN asked what he had done during the French Revolution, the Abbé Sieyès said, "I survived." For members of the middle class, the last few years have been traumatic ones where the security of their lifetime savings is concerned.

The period since the late 1960s has been one of accelerating inflation. Yet, by and large, this has not been a good time for owners of common stocks. This is in contrast to the prior quarter-century, which probably witnessed more rapid, and less variable, capital appreciation than ever before in our history.

Nemesis has played no favorites. Small investors who latched on to hot new issues took a bath in Wall Street. The great institutions—trust departments of banks, mutual funds, life-insurance concerns and corporation pension funds —have also seen their principals shrink, in real purchasing power or even in money terms.

Long-term bonds have been paying ever higher interest rates. But the arrival of each new bond with its higher coupon has meant that each old bond you hold has declined in price. New and young bonds, like all mortals, must in their turn become older and prone to losses in capitalized value.

This is no laughing matter for the bourgeoisie. Never since the Great Depression of the 1930s has there been such a decimation of nest eggs as in recent years. Even the nonadventurous widows who have put their mites into savings accounts and Series E bonds have found that the interest yields they have received are quite inadequate to meet the rises in their cost of subsistence.

Variability of Stocks

One of the occupational diseases of being an economist is that people ask for advice about handling personal finance. Knowing how uncertain is the future, one hesitates to take on such an assignment. But duty forces one on occasion to grapple with these serious and imponderable problems.

Let me review on this occasion some of my own past comments in this column on investment matters.

Most people, history suggests, are not very good at handling their own investments. They don't have the time, the knowledge and the judgment. So good advice to the middle-class person is to hire someone else to do the job and keep the records.

Consider a hypothetical widow with a $100,000 nest egg that she has to preserve in order to live off it.

Suppose her risk tolerance is such that she wishes to put, say, 40 per cent into common stocks. For her, a no-load mutual fund of common stocks still makes good sense, preferably one with a low management fee and low turnover rate of its portfolio. (In the years since I began to write to this effect, no-load funds have gained at the expense of funds that are sold by salesmen who receive a front-end commission, or "load." But the mutual-fund industry as a whole has languished along with the bear market in Wall Street.)

Fixed-Principal Securities

Suppose that, of her remaining $60,000, she wishes to put half into long-term bonds. Keeping track of many different $1,000 bonds, clipping their coupons and preserving tax records is not a chore fit for an amateur. So it would make good sense for her to put this 30 per cent of her principal into a closed-end bond fund, one that pays regular dividends for her to live on. (If she doesn't sleep well, she might divide between three different such funds, primarily for the extra feeling of safety.) To kill two birds with one stone, she might put her whole 70 per cent of long-term investments into a no-load *balanced* mutual fund, which holds bonds and stocks in about a 50-50 ratio.

What about her remaining 30 per cent of liquid holding? In a well-run society, she could put that in the local savings bank and receive the same high rates of return that men of wealth get when they put more than $100,000 into 90-day certificates of deposit (CDs). Ours is not that kind of well-run society, since local banks by law are held down to pay 6 or 7 per cent at the same time that CDs may be paying 8 or 9 or even, on occasion, 12 per cent.

So, aside from a thousand dollars of ready money in the corner bank, she might put the rest into a few of the many new liquid reserve funds that invest in CDs. These have flourished since I first wrote about them. They are safe and convenient, but they do not have a government insurance guarantee.

All in all, this is a no-fuss program. Alas, it is not riskless. But it is, I think, prudent.

INVESTMENT SECRETS
April 5, 1976

COMMON stocks are generally up about 70 per cent since the lows of 1974. The 30-company Dow-Jones index of industrial prices bounces through the magic level of 1,000. Share turnover sets new daily records.

Brokers, naturally, are feeling better. Slowly their individual customers are being drawn back in. Some who had shifted into bonds at those 1974 lows have been asking anxiously whether it is too late to get back into stocks.

Now seems a good time to review the little that has been learned about Wall Street in recent years.

First, whether you can afford only $50,000 to invest or the hundreds of millions of the Mellon Foundation, there is no avoiding *downside risk.* Examine the decade or the quarter-century record of the 100 most respected money managers. As a whole they do not do as well as a feasible portfolio that simply buys and holds virtually all of the Standard & Poor's 500-share index; or as well as a portfolio that simply holds a prorated fraction of all American, Canadian, Japanese and West European stocks in proportion to their outstanding market values.

Of the 100, a few are bound to do better than most. But

the baton of good performance passes from hand to hand so randomly as to lead a trained statistician to the following disappointing hypothesis:

After one corrects portfolio records for volatility and mean return, the best and the worst are only about as good and bad as one would expect to occur by chance alone.

Playing with Money

Hard as it is to beat the comprehensive averages, we all know people who find it easy to do much worse. An M.D., fearful of the times, puts his aged mother-in-law completely in gold, halving her nest egg in 1975. A hard-boiled accountant, knowing no more of hog bellies than any other consumer of bacon and eggs, takes a bath in commodities. A professor of Romance languages, churning 10,000 leveraged dollars in eighteen transactions, wonders how he could have ended up with a loss in the bull-market year of 1975.

The trouble with most of these people is that they *like* the process of investing. They enjoy collecting stocks like postage stamps, entering into their records dividends of $7.50, being able to tell folks at the club how their hot new issue doubled in a fortnight.

The finding that few can beat the averages is not merely a theory of mine. It has been put forth and tested by researchers at the universities of Chicago and Pennsylvania, at Stanford and MIT and elsewhere. It has, of course, been double-checked in the backrooms of Wall Street for weaknesses and rebuttals.

Is the finding really surprising? Is it critical of capitalism and the marketplace? Not at all. It is about what the followers of Adam Smith would hope to be able to claim—that *competition works so efficiently as to discount already in price the best information that skill and resources can mobilize.*

Quiet Prudence

The moral is clear for most readers:

· You must diversify widely.

· You must avoid deadweight loss from commissions involved in turnover and trading.

· Unless you have $20 million, you must utilize *no-load* instruments: either commingled bank trust funds or mutual funds.

Which particular banks or funds? Alas, one is little demonstrably better than another in the long run. A few banks and funds are just beginning to experiment with across-the-board diversification. As yet there exists no convenient $1 billion fund that apes the whole market, requires no load, and that keeps commission turnover and management fees to the feasible minimum. I suspect the future will bring such new and convenient instrumentalities. In the meantime you can do quite well in a few no-load funds of differing philosophy. (These are even good trading vehicles for those under the impression that they can display good timing in going between common stocks and fixed principal assets.)

The prudent way is also the easy way. Someone else holds your certificates and provides a record of your dividends and capital gains for tax-reporting purposes.

This leaves you free to fish, philander or perfect your mousetrap. What you lose is the daydream of that one big killing. What you gain is sleep.

INDEX-FUND INVESTING
August 16, 1976

WHENEVER I write a column about stock-market investing, my mail swells. Although I am not licensed by the SEC to hang out my shingle as a guru of finance, widowers write asking for advice on which stocks to buy.

Not all the letters are admiring. A bad word for gold usually brings in reproof from South Africa and the Rocky Mountains. Revealing the sad truth that front-end loads are hard to justify does not add to one's popularity among stockbrokers. Nor do money managers like to be reminded that their overall record in security selection has been significantly worse than that of a non-managed "index fund," which merely holds virtually all of the stocks that go to make up the Standard & Poor's 500 Composite Stock Price Index.

When I was writing last April's column "Investment Secrets," I knew that the wealthy investor or the corporate pension plan could utilize the Wells Fargo Bank of California, or the American National Bank and Trust Co. of Chicago, or the Batterymarch Financial Management Corp. of Boston to engage in prudent across-the-market index investing. But I had then to report, sadly, that "As yet there exists no convenient . . . fund that apes the whole market, requires no load, and that keeps commission turnover and management fees to the feasible minimum. I suspect the future will bring such new and convenient instrumentalities."

A Better Mousetrap?

Where there is a demand, Nature will find a way. Sooner than I dared expect, my implicit prayer has been answered. There is coming to market, I see from a crisp new prospectus, something called the First Index Investment Trust.

It seems to meet four of my five prudent requirements:

· It is available for the person or family of modest means —with $1,500 to $1 million or more.

· It proposes to match most of the S&P 500, eliminating only the smaller firms and those that might raise certain difficulties for any fiduciary. (Example: if a W.T. Grant is about to go into bankruptcy, those who invest other people's money feel they must shun it.)

· Being essentially unmanaged, its management and total expense charges will be only about two-tenths of 1 per cent of net asset value—perhaps only about a quarter that of the usual mutual fund or bank trust department.

· The commissions frittered away in turnover should be extremely low for such an indexed fund.

· Best of all, such an indexed fund gives that broadest diversification needed to maximize mean return with minimum portfolio variance and volatility.

Caveats

A professor's prayers are rarely answered in full. This is not a no-load fund. Right off the top of your modest nest egg comes 6.01 per cent in the form of a front-end load to cover selling costs. (If you have more than $1 million to invest, the load drops to 1.06 per cent.)

Good ideas, like bad ones, are not bought. Apparently they have to be sold. And that costs money. In my view a front-end load should be incurred—if at all—only by those who intend to hold some minimal fraction of their wealth in common stocks for enough years to amortize the dead-weight initial cost.

If you are under the illusion that you can out-time the market—making a killing on a Carter election victory or defeat, or being able to sell out just before the next recession begins—one of the less diversified no-load funds is your optimum medium.

In buying an index fund, you also give up the illusion that, at some future date, you will be able to boast around the club swimming pool of the tenfold gain you've been able to make in picking stock-market winners. Broad diversification rules out extraordinary losses relative to the whole market; it also, by definition, rules out extraordinary gains.

An index fund is not immune to market risk. If the whole market goes down, your index fund will go down with it.

What each prudent investor must do is to decide what fraction of savings he can afford, in this age of inflation, to keep in equities and in other things. An unmanaged, low-turnover, low-fee index fund is merely an efficient way of holding that part deemed appropriate for equities. As such, it may appeal to the canny.

DEFENSIVE INVESTING

December 20, 1976

CARTER must worry about the nation's economy. You must worry about your own family's assets. Whether your old-age retirement is serene and comfortable, or nasty and brutish, hangs on the outcome of your financial decision making.

Can economics help? Yes, I think it can. Experience has shown that the national economy is too important to be left to non-economists. What is less widely realized is that economics—whose very name traces back to the Greek word for management of the household—is the *practical* subject when it comes to managing assets.

Business schools like Stanford, Wharton, Chicago, MIT and Berkeley are the fountains of hard-boiled wisdom these days. To tune in on the mythology and folklore of impractical finance, the anthropologist has to go to Wall Street, LaSalle Street and State Street. When it comes to the bottom line of measuring how the money managers actually perform with respect to "mean return, corrected for risk," 1976 has driven one more nail in the coffin of those who think the Standard & Poor's index of share prices can be outperformed by the well-paid money managers.

Q and A

Year-end is a good time to answer the questions most put to me.

Q: You have been critical of mutual funds with a selling-commission *load.* Their sales are way down. But how come the *no-load* funds you accept are also down in size?

A: The dice are loaded against managing one's own portfolio. Commissions eat you up. Vital diversification is impossible. The bookkeeping bother is enormous. So mutual or bank funds make sense. The reason mutual funds are now out of favor is that they used to be *sold* to people for the wrong reasons: buyers of cosmetics buy *hope,* not talc; people paid 8 per cent loads in belief of making a market killing.

Q: Are no-loads ideal?

A: Alas, no. They trade too much, wasting your assets. Too often they are spuriously diversified. Management and other fees are unnecessarily high. Still they beat rolling your own. Particularly ones with low fees that almost cover the whole market and keep turnover low.

Q: What's the canny way of buying bonds? Surely, 100 per cent in stocks is rash?

A: Since common stocks have not been a good hedge

against this last decade's inflation, fixed-principal assets should be an important fraction of a well-balanced portfolio: either savings accounts, "money-market" funds, open-end bond or "income" funds, or "balanced" mutual funds.

My omission of Federal government bonds is deliberate. They've been a bad buy for private citizens. At the least, Series E bonds should have a purchasing-power guarantee for limited amounts per family.

Right now savings accounts offer as good an *assured* return as other fixed assets with taxable yields.

Tax-exempt Funds

Q: What do you think of the new open-end municipal funds?

A: The Tax Reform Act of 1976 at long last is closing some loopholes. Gifts made after 1976 will add to one's rate of estate taxation. Heirs will inherit capital-gains tax liability. Even long-term capital gains will be costly to the high earner with considerable assets. Two cheers!

State and local bonds remain as tax shelters. The new open-end municipal funds provide needed diversification along with instant liquidity, minimal bookkeeping and no load. Their management fees are, I think, too high; more ideal would be no-load funds with the zero-management fees of the municipal-bond-unit trusts; but, except in daydreams, you can't have everything.

Q: Which is the best buy?

A: Who can say? Here are the six biggest, in order of present size, with general location and minimum *initial* investment. Load is zero unless otherwise indicated. You should check management and other fees.

1. Fidelity Municipal Fund, Ltd., (Boston). $2,500 minimum.

2. Kemper Municipal Bond Fund, Ltd., (Chicago). $100. 4.75 per cent load.

3. Dreyfus Tax Exempt Bond Fund, Inc., (New York). $2,500.

4. MFS Managed Municipal Bond Trust (Boston). $1,000. 4.75 per cent load.

5. Scudder Managed Municipal Bonds (Boston). $1,000.

6. Federated Tax Free Income Fund (Pittsburgh). $1,000. *Caveat emptor!*

INVESTMENT TRENDS
June 27, 1977

THE securities industry is going through the wringer of keen rate competition. Probably most brokerage firms will not survive.

When the dust settles, society will end up devoting less of its total resources to the buying and selling of securities. The ordinary citizen will have lost some of his old options and gained some new ones.

By and large, the balance of advantage will, I suspect, shift against the individuals who want to manage their own portfolios. Handling the job of mobilizing savings for retirement and future contingencies will instead probably gravitate increasingly to corporate pension plans, to the insurance and banking industries and to Social Security.

Is all this a good or bad thing? The economic system possesses a clear interest in having savings funneled efficiently into alternative investment channels. Before we shed tears over the passing of the old order, we need to investigate whether Main Street and Wall Street are not today doing a more effective job of rationing capital than back in the days of J. Pierpont Morgan, the palmy 1920s or the performance-kick 1960s.

Efficient Markets

Most evidence suggests that particular bonds and stocks are being more rationally priced in 1977 than in 1957 or 1927, to say nothing of 1887. If we could test how typical brokerage-firm customers do, the result would strongly suggest that they'd do better (on a risk-adjusted basis) by simply buying and holding their pro-rata share of the thousands of securities outstanding. The same holds for the big money managers.

The turnover of buying and selling turns out to be for the most part sound and fury, signifying nothing and burning up resources in order-taking, phone charges and billings. That is why so many of the decision makers in Wall Street have, *de facto,* become "closet indexers," jettisoning their disproportionate holdings of IBM, Avon and Kodak in favor of a bit of everything.

It is not that the best and the brightest have thrown in the towel. Rather it is that they now put the strong burden of proof against churning of holdings. So long as experienced investors with the most resources for gathering and analyzing relevant information are prepared to move in when they see mistakes in market pricing, the rest of us cannot do better than embrace the broadest of diversification.

This pill of truth is hard to swallow. Out of my millions of *Newsweek* readers, there are hundreds of thousands who believe they can outperform the Standard & Poor 500-stock index. Otherwise the financial community couldn't pay the rent.

However, I know of no objective evidence to suggest that even a thousand of this group have the information and flair to justify betting on stocks over any extended period. This is the underlying reality one must recognize to understand the shakedown in the investment industry.

Barnum Was Right

Like the cosmetics industry, the securities business is engaged in selling *illusion.* How many dentists are entitled to a serious opinion on the future of soybeans? Surely fewer than play that market.

The hottest thing to hit the equities business in recent years has been the new options market for "puts and calls" (which are contracts giving you the right, at any time in a specified future period, to sell or buy a particular stock at a now-specified price, thereby making a profit if the stock's actual price moves favorably). The various exchanges vie for pieces of this profitable action.

One of my suburban neighbors thinks he can gain 20 per cent annually *buying* call options. Another seeks a good return *selling* options in those *same* stocks. Both can't be right. Probably both are illusioned. My academic colleagues have worked out formulas for pricing options *so they won't be bargains to either buyer or seller.* Experience seems to confirm the formula's realism.

Society does not live by the S&P 500 corporations alone. The economic system still needs to evolve effective ways of appraising and backing smaller risky ventures. My past pleas in this space for financial innovations have been so agreeably answered as to encourage my suggesting a no-load, low-fee mutual fund to merely hold a broad sample of smaller-firm stocks.

HANGING IN THERE

February 13, 1978

MOST of us are going to be poorer later on. It is part of the biological facts of life that we can expect to live on past our period of prime earning power. The rainy day for which people proverbially save is that final retirement stage of life.

The Gettys and Rockefellers, and all those who amass huge fortunes to pass on to their children and grandchildren and to the charitable foundations of their choice, are dramatic exceptions to the general rules of economic life. As MIT's Franco Modigliani has spent his own lifetime in studying, it is *life-cycle saving* that best explains the dynamics of capital formation in the U.S. and in other countries at various stages of economic development.

Although 1977 was a year of fairly vigorous growth for the American economy, the common stocks people held generally declined in value. Pension assets, held by corporations for employees' eventual retirement, suffered from the same general malaise. Those people who earned 6 per cent on their savings accounts were about the only ones who kept up with the increase in the cost of living, but after they paid a quarter of their return in income tax, the real value of their principal actually declined.

Clutching at Straws

Only two kinds of assets held their value. The Social Security payments that most of us have coming when we reach our 60s and 70s have been escalated in accordance with the consumer price index. Despite the periodic rumors of insolvency that get spread, families' first line of defense in the form of Social Security rests securely on the growing earning capacity of the nation, and this provides assurance of a basic minimum for the future.

Also, the values of people's homes continued to grow in most parts of the country. Building costs continue to advance remorselessly, and older homes are buoyed up by the rising prices that have to be charged for new dwellings. Indeed, many a young family has found it necessary to buy a more expensive home than it can afford and only the rise in housing prices has bailed it out from its frenzied overcommitments.

Given the disappointing performance turned in by traditional modes of investment in recent years, people are naturally tempted by some less conventional alternatives. I am frequently asked:

"Can one prudently do better buying diamonds? Oriental rugs? Paintings, sculptures, prints or antiques? Stamps? Farmland, citrus groves, tax-sheltered oil deals? Sun-country condominiums, mountain or shore properties? Gold bars, coins (for example, U.S. eagles, French napoleons, South African krugerrands), gold-mining shares?

"Can one recoup, or at least preserve real value of principal, by buying call options on IBM or GM? Or by buying put options? Or by selling either of such options? Are the odds favorable in soybean futures, pork bellies, silver or copper? Can one provide for old-age needs by taking judicious flyers in foreign-exchange futures (the mark, yen, pound, Swiss franc)?"

No Philosopher's Stone

Careful investigation shows that none of these gambits pays off for the average intelligent amateur. Each new line begins favorably for those who happen to be early birds. And special knowledge and diligence tend to be rewarded as in any form of activity.

Actually, in well-organized competitive markets there is no place to hide when the winds of liquidation are blowing. You are naïve to be taken in by rumors of neighbors who are making killings in London commodity options or in private-mint commemorative issues of coins.

Don't misunderstand: a judicious small position in a closed-end gold fund, or in gold coins bought at low premium, sometimes makes sense; I know a chemist who will die rich because he spends hours studying catalogs and auctions of prints, a field in which he has become expert. But these are not examples easy to imitate. In times adverse to conserving net worth, it is all the more important to hew to investment's golden rules:

Diversify broadly, hold down turnover, keep all fees minimal.

When asked what he had done during the Terror of the French Revolution, the Abbé Sieyès replied, "I survived." Conditions for surviving were never easier than now for those who trouble to become well informed.

COPING SENSIBLY

March 6, 1978

THE small investor can now, for the first time, invest in common stocks and bonds in an efficient and convenient way. I am talking about people who don't have $10 million; who don't want to take *unnecessary* gambles; who operate under no Napoleonic delusions of being able to pick winners that will quadruple their money; who begrudge every minute devoted to keeping tax and personal records, and wish to think about their investments only at New Year's and when preparing their tax returns.

Disinterested experts in finance prescribe for such people as follows:

1. Depending on your tolerance for the irreducible risks involved in owning common stocks, decide what portion of your nest egg you wish to keep in common stocks: 0, 100, 30 or 70 per cent. No one can decide this for you. You must decide at what point you'll sleep best at night, and whether eventually stocks will provide a better inflation hedge than they have done these last dozen years. (Many will settle for 50-50.)

2. For what common stocks you do decide to own, follow the golden rules of prudence:

Diversify broadly, hold down costly turnover, keep all fees (and bookkeeping!) minimal.

3. The same rules (diversification, etc.) apply to your holdings of tax-free and ordinary bonds. If you have taxable income of $20,000 or more, probably the bulk of your bonds should be "municipals"—i.e., state and local issues that escape all federal tax because Congress refuses to close this loophole. Less-affluent people will probably do as well in local savings accounts as in anything else.

Now you know *what* to do. *How* do you do it?

Mutual-Fund Pooling

For most people the best and simplest device is a no-load mutual fund, either of the common-stock, bond-income, money-market variety, or a combination of all three.

There are hundreds of such funds. A couple of dozen of them have the lowest fees and superior diversification practices. I personally resist the temptation to switch to that small fund which happens to have scored the best "performance" record recently.

When at long last I became a grandfather, my gift to young James went into the First Index Investment Trust, which at low expense tries to match the 500 diversified stocks of the Standard & Poor index. True, many funds beat the S&P in 1977; but James has a long life ahead of him and I want to go with the long-run odds. (Needless to say, I could do about as well with the Dreyfus, Fidelity, Scudder, and T. Rowe Price organizations, or a half-dozen other full-line services.)

A Case in Point

For definiteness, here is a sample setup for a 53-year-old engineer earning $30,000 a year. Similar percentages might apply to a widow who just inherited $200,000.

1. Put *half* your net worth into a no-load, low-turnover stock fund like the First Index Investment Trust. Let all dividends and capital gains be automatically reinvested. Draw at your convenience what you want to live on or for vacations. (You will get only a half-dozen simple reports each year; from the year-end slip, you can file your tax return in ten minutes.)

2. Put one-third of your assets in a no-load municipal bond fund (like the Federated Tax-Free Income Fund or Warwick Municipal Bond Fund). You can write checks against this account, using it as a reserve of liquidity. As above, the bookkeeping is minimal. Municipal funds now yield about 5 per cent free of federal tax, and run some risks of capital gains or losses.

3. Keep one-sixth of your portfolio in a local insured bank, to pay small bills and for convenient instant access.

This is a stripped-down version. Your self-employed person's Keogh pension plan, being subject to zero immediate tax, might go to a high-yielding income fund (like the Fidelity Aggressive Income Fund). The risks of holding "junk" bonds can be made tolerable by broad diversification.

Also, those who think they are good at "timing" market swings can switch costlessly from one fund in an organization to another—e.g., reducing First Index holdings in favor of Warwick Municipal, both run by the Vanguard Group. Other variations are possible for opinionated sophisticates.

Most of you, though, will want to stick to basics. Then the finance prof will award you an A for probity, and you can forget about economics.

NO-FUSS CANNY INVESTING

February 4, 1980

MY wife used to listen to Julia Child with high hopes, then put down her pencil, saying, "An omelet is just not worth all that trouble."

This is the way many sensible people feel about the chore of managing their life savings. If the price of prudence is reading *Barron's, Forbes* and the *Institutional Investor,* keeping track of the Commerce Department's leading indicators and figuring out how the raindrops are falling in the soybean counties, then that is just too high a price for a busy biochemist, lawyer or housespouse to pay.

Good Habits

For such people I have good news. There is a way of managing your savings that requires a minimum of work on your part. But you will ask, "Isn't there an easy way and a *right* way? What am I sacrificing by way of safety and mean return when I succumb to the easy way?"

Again, good news. Essentially, nothing imprudent is involved in doing things the simple way—provided you get started with good habits. When I was training my wife to be a widow, I researched the subject at some length. What I learned about the science and art of asset selection confirmed what the late Al Capp once told me about cartooning: "I found that if I spent more than a couple of days a week on my 'Li'l Abner' comic strip, I tended to louse it up."

So it is with your suburban neighbor who calls his broker every day and subscribes to *The London Financial Times.*

His portfolio churns and churns, making more money for the broker than for himself. (I don't have to be reminded that there are exceptions to my generalization: what I am reporting is the *average* success achieved by the active money managers working for the most respected financial organizations.)

Here then is the main recipe for no-fuss canny investing: make great use of no-load mutual funds, preferably those with low expense ratios. Here are some examples:

• Your child is born, and will need to go to college in 1998. Give her now a tax-free gift of $6,000 per year for one or two years. Put the proceeds in a money-market fund—any of the big ones will do—and let the assets accumulate at her low-income-bracket rate. In most states there are minor-custodian acts and you won't need a lawyer; just spend half an hour each year preparing her tax return from the slip of paper the fund sends you. (Query: Is there no better procedure? Answer: Who can tell what will happen in the next two decades? But research by Prof. Zvi Bodie of Boston University, among others, suggests that shortest-term fixed-principal assets do have the *least variance* in *real* purchasing power.)

• You and your spouse together earn $50,000 per year and are taxed accordingly. Instead of keeping your ready cash in a sizable checking or savings account, use one of the tax-exempt money-market funds that let you write checks of more than $500 on your funds. Then pay small bills by bank check, replenishing your funds by writing a large check on the tax-exempt fund. Use such a check to pay your property taxes or finance a trip to Europe.

• You are a widow of 60 left $300,000 in insurance. This must last the twenty-odd years of your life expectancy. I wish there were some annuity you could buy that would guarantee your real purchasing power. But there isn't. All you can do is minimize risk, not escape it.

The Easy Way

The trust department of a local bank can serve you. Or you can match its performance by dividing your principal among three mutual funds. (If they are with the same organization, you can conveniently make switches with a single phone call.) One-third might go into a broadly diversified common-stock fund. Just which fund is not important; what's important is that you not be entirely out of equities in these uncertain times. One-third might go into a bond fund and the final third into a money-market fund, taxable or tax-exempt depending on your tax bracket. (Warning: once you've chosen the path of broad diversification, don't then expect to make a killing with choices that double and triple in value.)

If you do it right, your record keeping will be minimal since the funds' custodian banks will do it all for you. If you study prospectuses, you'll be able to find good funds whose annual expense ratios are well below 1 per cent of asset value.

Do a little research at the beginning. Then relax, knowing you've minimized the irreducible risks and bookkeeping. Besides, you can always change your mind at minimal cost, and start churning your portfolio whenever you feel lucky.

CRACKPOT INVESTING

January 26, 1981

PEOPLE ask me what they should read to protect their savings. It's a hard question. Most of the best sellers on how to invest are likely to do you more harm than good.

That's my view. I base it on decades of personal experience, both as a private investor and as an economist called on to advise nonprofit organizations and forced on occasion to discuss financial methods with friends.

What's one man's opinion against another's? Howard Ruff is glad to pit his hunches against mine. Millions buy his books warning against collapse of the banks, destruction of the dollar by hyperinflation and the breakdown of law and civilization.

Dupes

There are authors aplenty who do well purveying advice like this:

· Sell your stocks and bonds.

· Liquidate bank accounts.

· Buy land, stock a cabin in the woods with food sufficient to outlast a holocaust and keep rifles handy to fend off the shiftless dupes who will try to move in on your prudential turf when the chips are down.

My point is not to exchange fishmonger vituperation with those who differ from the conventional wisdom. Franz Pick, Harry Schultz, Harry Browne, Eliot Janeway, Joe Granville and other well-heeled pundits laugh all the way to the bank thinking it is I who doze in a fool's paradise.

Since economics is not an exact science, they could turn out to be right. But such evidence as there is suggests that you ought not to bet on it.

The essence of science is not personal anecdotes. Science, even inexact science, is *public knowledge,* reproducible for analysis by everyone. For 50 years now, professors at the nation's business schools have been studying the batting averages of chartists and technicians. The goals of security analysts have been compared with subsequent statistical performance by the totality of mutual funds, pension and insurance services and investment counselors.

The findings are uniformly the same. Some do well, some do badly. A few do very well, a few do very badly. Monkeys put to typewriters in the British Museum will, if you wait long enough, reproduce without error the *Encyclopaedia Britannica.* So scientists must apply statistical tests of significance to find whether there's much impressive in the batting average of those few best performers in each epoch.

What is the upshot? The vast preponderance of the evidence suggests that stocks are bought and sold in "efficient markets"—that is, in markets where the checks and balances of many would-be investors result in prices that reflect discountable news and which probabilistically divide the bulls and the bears evenly.

To sum up: there are no easy pickings. Unless you have special sources of information and speedy ways of analyzing the incoming flow of news, you are not able from past patterns of stock prices to achieve excess risk-corrected returns. Those few with exceptional information and ways of successfully interpreting the uncertain imponderables of chance are very few indeed. It's about as hard to spot them as to spot stock bargains. And you'll find that you probably have to pay them full economic rent for their unusual abilities.

Pudding's Proof

So much for stock selection. Even if a Granville's record is mediocre at picking specific stocks, what's the evidence on the ability of the various services to succeed at the game of "timing"? As against merely buying and holding stocks, can you hope to gain from advisory services that tell you for a few hundred dollars annually to get out of the market before a bad year like 1974, and get back in before a good year like 1975?

Here, too, most of the evidence is discouraging. This does not deny that a particular adviser can have a hot run of favorable calls. But south Florida is full of would-be Joe Granvilles, and one of them—like a monkey in the museum —can several times succeed in buying stocks when the Dow-Jones index is at 800 and selling them when it is at 1,000 without astonishing the statisticians.

Merlin the Magician never reveals his proprietary methods. Still, Barnum warns us to weigh what is revealed for plausibility and relevance. On that basis I'd counsel caution and skepticism.

A final warning. You can lose money in anything: gold, real estate, collectibles or a general index of stocks. Diversification is what holds down risk.

LYNCH MONEY-MARKET FUNDS?
April 20, 1981

IN 1939 I invented money-market funds. I asked in the *Quarterly Journal of Economics:* Why not earn interest on the cash we use to buy goods and pay bills? Why not coin land, trees, factories, machines and other assets, using interest-bearing titles to society's assets as our money supply?

I was ahead of my time. But IBM's computer has made my ivory-tower dream come true. Money-market funds run by Dreyfus, Fidelity and Vanguard will each night pay you 14-plus per cent per annum on your funds, and let you write checks on them to pay your big bills. Or, by phone and wire, they'll send your funds to your local bank. At the end of the year, their big-city custodian bank will send you a notice of interest earned on your fund holdings to help you prepare your tax return.

Bankers would like to lynch the inventor of money-market funds. Liquid accounts on Main Street that earn only 5 to 7 per cent are being shifted to New York, Boston and Philadelphia. As a result, local builders are hurting for mortgage money.

Protectionism

When you can't compete with a better mousetrap, you urge your bank and construction lobbyists to persuade Congress to pass a law against those better competitors. If Congress overrules the SEC and accedes to this campaign, money-market funds would be required to keep some sterile reserves with the Federal Reserve. That would lower a little bit the yield the funds can earn for their customers.

What is good public policy in this matter? Let me sketch the fundamentals.

Whether misguided or not, legislation to saddle money-market funds with reserve requirements would only slow down their growth. They do serve an economic purpose in these uncertain times of inflation. They provide more than a convenient form of transaction cash for you and me.

Prof. Eugene Fama of the University of Chicago has shown statistically that the liquid assets that money markets indirectly hold for us in the form of Treasury bills, commercial paper, CDs (negotiable certificates of bank deposits) have turned out to be *a better inflation hedge than common stocks or long-term and medium-term bonds.* When the price index rises, short-term interest rates command an anticipatory inflation premium. When inflation goes to a two-digit rate, yields on 30-day funds rise to a two-digit rate. A perfect hedge? No—but since 1971 funds have been the best game in town.

There is one way Congress could give Main Street bankers a fair shake. Let them match money-market-fund rates on my local bank account. By current law they aren't allowed to compete.

Actually, that would not help local builders much. If my local bank in Cambridge gets the proceeds from my money-market funds, it will have to buy commercial paper, Treasury bills and CDs to match those funds' rates. It cannot tie up my overnight money in 30-year brick and plaster.

Dr. Anthony Downs of the Brookings Institution has argued that housing has become swollen with special government subsidies. I would add that regulatory ceilings on what banks and S&Ls can pay in interest have channeled more resources into house construction than people's tastes justify.

Fruit

Do the funds serve a productive purpose? Avoid a kindergarten mistake. When we send our money to New York, it doesn't stay there. Merely swishing around Wall Street, funds could not generate the real fruit that Fama's data show.

The fruit, in this metaphor, is society's real output, and it is produced, if you will, by economic "trees"—machines, factories and real capital goods. Threshing machines on the prairie, furniture works on Main Street, mines, etc.—such capital assets are the other side of the computer print-outs showing my cash balances.

Since every principal is subject to risks, how can we have safe money based on capital items that rise and fall in value? It is the equity owners, in the hope of profit on their common stocks, who bear the residual risks that remain after they've paid us our interest. The only risk we face is whether tomorrow's interest rate will be low or high, but fortunately, our real return averages out to be remarkably steady.

I see one case for the Fed to require money-market funds to hold reserves:

To anchor the price level, we do need to pin down the *total* of society's money supply. If money-market assets came to be our only money, money-market organizations would be our only banks, needing the reserve controls that banks now face.

TIME TO SELL?
December 11, 1978

AN hour before President Carter announced his new program to save the dollar, I was enjoying my periodic dental checkup. "Now let's turn to serious matters," said my friend in white. "Should I sell out all my common stocks?"

That is not a question to ask a professor of economics. I hope to live with my dentist for a good long time. It is a no-win situation ever to give advice: if it turns out well, people naturally preen themselves on their acumen in accepting the hypothesis you've nominated; if it turns out otherwise, they remember just where they learned it first.

Nonetheless, I overheard myself emitting some cautionary bromides. One does not really sleep better when 100 per cent out of stocks. Those locked-in 9 per cent yields on long-term bonds can look very sour should inflation accelerate. Even though common stocks have turned out to be a rotten hedge against inflation these last dozen years, experience shows that over the long pull . . .

You know how such soothing syrup runs and can yourself fill in the hollows.

The In-and-Out Ploy
The rest of the morning, as I licked my gums, I pondered over what I had done. True, the Dow-Jones averages leaped 30 points that very day in the wake of the President's unanticipated decisiveness. True, I was addressing someone over 21.

But I also harbor a Hippocratic oath: an economist, other things equal, should do no harm; in formulating the odds and stating the main reasons behind them, he should come clean on the uncertainties. Once, when asked for an off-the-record comment on one of the brilliant economists of our time, I said about my friend: "The gods gave him every talent—except the gift of 'maybe.' "

Still, I found myself stubbornly unrepentant. Let me sketch the reasons.

First, I can make a case for selling out now. Stock prices in the past have tended to turn down *before* the economy went into recession. ("The market has forecast nine of the last five recessions," some sage once observed.) A respectable plurality of the good economic forecasters has recently come down on the side of a 1979 recession. Next spring one may well be able to buy those same stocks back at lower prices. In the meantime, a nice quick profit on the reviving bond market may be obtainable.

I can also punch holes in this gambit. It would require nimble timing. Chances are you'd not get back in equities until *after* the balloon had gone up, and then perhaps only at prices even higher than now. Experience reveals few who succeed in playing the in-and-out game. Everyone knows what you know. Why will *you* be lucky Alphonse? Perhaps Wall Street is already discounting the worst that will happen.

Money-Market Astigmatism?

So I'm left with the hard question. *How are American stocks priced relative to their intrinsic values?* Although economists have learned to respect the wisdom and efficiency of the marketplace's checks and balances, on this question they do have an interesting point of view.

A persuasive case can be made that *equities are now cheap from a long-run point of view.* Why? Because the public incorrectly evaluates the effects of inflation on equity values.

The conventional wisdom overdiscounts for the false element in inflationary profits. It underestimates the *implicit* gains in money capital values that accrue when anticipatable inflation is raising the reproduction cost of America's earning assets. It fails to notice the gain that the common stockholder filches from the lending bondholders when they are paid off in melting dollars.

To be sure, there are genuine ways in which fake inflation profits do get overtaxed—as when historic-cost depreciation allowable against tax liability fails to cover replacement-cost depreciation. But my point remains after we have made all such needed corrections.

When we can expect prices to rise 5 per cent a year instead of being stable, it is rational for bond yields to go from 5 per cent to 10—or, to put it another way, for bonds' price-earnings ratios to fall from 20 to 1 to 10 to 1. But it is not rational for inflation to halve the P-E ratio of common stocks. Yet this is what has happened in Wall Street.

In summary, common stocks might be a good hold. Maybe.

CAPITAL SHORTAGE, OR GLUT?

August 26, 1974

TO teach is to affirm." The late Crane Brinton of Harvard, who was himself a great teacher of intellectual history, could not wholeheartedly agree, reminding us that "To teach is also to raise doubt."

So I must raise some important questions. Is it true that capital is now particularly scarce? True that we need less consumer spending and more saving? (After all, it was just one President back who was urging the American people to save an extra 1.5 per cent of their incomes.)

Is it true that the environmentalist lobby is lowering the yield on corporate capital, thereby depleting the funds out of which new capital formation is financed and killing off the incentive for savers to invest in new productive plant and equipment? Are profits minuscule after being corrected to take account of inflationary windfall capital gains on inventories and true replacement costs of plant and equipment being used up? And if so, how does this square with an alleged *scarcity* rather than plethora of capital?

These all are important questions. And we know from the last summit meeting of business economists and businessmen held in the White House by President Nixon that nine out of ten men of the business establishment would answer all these questions with a confident yes.

They may well turn out to be right. But a panel of assistant professors of economics cannot be sure.

Claims

First, we can make a deposition that it would always be nice to have more productive capital. But that is not to say much. 'Twould be nice to have better consumption standards, nice to have (costlessly) more useful public goods and humane government income transfers.

Second, there is this much truth in the capital-scarcity thesis: a number of our basic-materials industries—paper, steel, chemicals, plastics, domestic oil refining—have been on round-the-clock operations even in the current recession. Perhaps this apparent lack of excess capacity would have come as less of a surprise to analysts if the Federal Reserve had revised its inadequate index of capacity earlier.

Third, environmental concern is a legitimate concern. To the degree that it acts like any other useful activity—air-conditioning demand, travel demand, indoor-tennis-court demand—environmental concern will add to capital demand. Far from being merely a net drag on industry, it is also a creator of profit opportunities, as the producers of pumps, catalysts and filter systems know.

So much can be granted to the thesis of capital scarcity.

Counterclaims

Here are points on the other side.

1. If capital is scarce, its yield both before and after taxes *should be up, not down.* The yield is in fact down all over the world, way down. William Nordhaus of Yale has computed the decline in the 1974 Brookings Papers on Economic Activity. After carefully correcting for fictitious inflation gains, he finds that "genuine" after-tax rates of return on capital have fallen to between 5 and 6 per cent in the 1970s. By contrast, they averaged above 8 per cent in the late 1940s, and again in the mid-1960s. Lest you think that it is merely the tax collector at work here, Nordhaus reports a comparable *before-*tax decline in corporate capital yield.

The story is more dramatic in Italy and the U.K. Nor are Germany and Japan immune from this worldwide competing of capital against capital.

2. It is definitely not the case that U.S. families are saving less of their disposable incomes than in recent decades. On the contrary, we are now saving in the 1970s a significantly *larger fraction* of our incomes. Also, corporations seem to plow back savings, in the form of earnings not paid in dividends, much as before. What comes hard these days is new equity capital.

3. In view of the fact that existing assets of U.S. enterprise can be bought at bargain terms, can one wonder that new issues are hard to float? James Tobin, also of Yale, calculates in the July Morgan Guaranty Survey that the ratio of what U.S. assets sell for in Wall Street and what they actually cost

to reproduce is only two-thirds of what it was a decade ago.

Capital scarce? Then why does it sell at such a discount in the free market?

THE UNEASY CASE FOR STOCKS

June 11, 1979

THE U.S. is in a growth recession. That is fact. Whether 1979 will see a genuine recession must still be opinion.

I now think the odds have turned better than even that real gross national product will fall for two or more quarters— the Las Vegas acid test for paying off bets on whether a recession has occurred. President Carter thinks otherwise. He may be right.

Economics is not so exact a science as to be able to settle in advance the fine line between outright and growth recession. But is that critical as you try to preserve your savings and protect your future living standards? Is now the time to dump equities and load up on bonds?

Or should one sit tight at this stage of the cycle, holding short-term bank certificates and money-market funds? A 30-day Treasury bill yields almost 10 per cent a year, which beats what stocks and long-term bonds have been doing for you— even if it still falls short of the 13 per cent a year increase just announced for the consumer price index.

Wall Street Almanac

I sit on boards where just these questions are now being fiercely debated. No one can provide confident answers. But let me review what we know from experience and what stands up to critical analysis.

Hard times for Main Street used to mean bad times for Wall Street. That's why the Dow-Jones averages would turn down first, as traders and investors anxiously peered ahead to anticipate trouble and discount it. As soon as recovery could be seen down the road, common stocks would move up even before production and employment did.

We mustn't exaggerate the market's prescience. Its path shows plenty of false starts and meaningless wiggles. I was guilty of understatement in the aphorism "The stock market has called nine of the last five recessions."

To sum up: past patterns would suggest selling stocks when a sluggish time looms ahead. As interest rates fall naturally and are pushed down by the Federal Reserve policy of leaning against the wind, canny timers catch a nice ride in soaring long-term bond prices. When the worst looks over for business, they nimbly switch back to stocks just in time for their resurgence.

Sounds easy, doesn't it? Why then do so few succeed in playing the timing game? Make no mistake about it: the record for mutual funds and money managers' timing performance shows that many fail for each who succeeds. That's why insurance companies and fiduciaries often forbid by charter the use of discretion and mandate long-run diversification norms between equities and fixed-principal assets.

Think about it. Were it so easy to recognize where we are in the business cycle and profit from its rise and fall, we'd all try to do so. How can every one of us beat out all the others?

Before an identified cycle becomes embalmed in history, the economy is in a perpetual identity crisis. Differences of opinion, Twain said, make horse races. Differences of doubts are what make for 30-million-share days on Wall Street. Yon bull is buying from yon bear; which one proves correct only the IRS will know come next April 15.

At the Starting Gate

The human race is not getting smarter. But we have become more sophisticated and edgy. Often I encounter the following new twist:

"I'm rooting for a recession. As with light beer, less is more. Less inflation will send stocks up. To wait to buy until we can see the whites of the eyes of the next recovery is to risk having the balloon take off without us."

Could be. No use to point out that last time out such reasoning would have cost you a third of your nest egg waiting for others to get the word. This is a time to be different; that's the point.

What makes the case for the bulls more impressive is, I suspect, a quite different point—namely, the widespread suspicion that stocks are grossly undervalued. Precisely because they've been such a lousy inflation hedge these last ten years, they're now rationally a bargain.

Franco Modigliani of MIT and Richard Cohn of the University of Illinois have documented this case in the last *Financial Analysts Journal.* It is a powerful brief. Here is its own short summary: "Because investors capitalize equity [real] earnings at the nominal [inflation-swelled] interest rate, rather than the economically correct real rate, and because they fail to allow for the gain to shareholders accruing from depreciation in the real value of nominal corporate liabilities [as the lender is repaid in melting dollars], they are currently undervaluing the stock market by 50 per cent."

The moral I draw: stay diversified.

WINNERS AND LOSERS
November 24, 1980

AFTER Election Day I asked my day helper how she felt about the outcome.

"I voted for Reagan," she said.

"You must be happy then," I observed fatuously.

"How can I be happy when my sister is about to lose her welfare assistance and my nephew will have to quit his computer course to take a shoeshine job? If their food stamps get cut, I just don't know how they'll get by."

Later that morning outside the bank I ran into a prosperous engineer who had once earned an A from me in an MIT economics course. He apparently had voted for John Anderson and yet he was smiling from ear to ear.

Complexities

When I inquired what there was to cheer about, he explained: "You can't blame me if the country stagnates. I voted against hard money."

"Maybe a dose of fiscal austerity and a credible program of controlled money growth will produce results against inflation," I suggested in my best seminar manner. "Since you studied economics there's a new school of 'rational expectationists' out at the Federal Reserve Bank of Minneapolis. They claim that licking inflation is not all that painful—provided you are determined to do it and people can see that you do mean to last the course."

"Is that how it's been working out in Margaret Thatcher's England?"

"Well, not exactly," I replied. "But the story's not over

there yet. Besides, the monetarists claim that Thatcher hasn't kept a tight enough rein on the money supply."

"What about Chile? Argentina?"

"From an inflation rate of 1,000 per cent per year at its worst, the Chilean monetarists claim to have brought it down to 32 per cent. Not without pain, of course."

"Argentina?"

"The story's not over there. But let me tell you about the successful ending of the 1923 German hyperinflation. And the Austrian and Polish currency restorations."

Alas, my seminar manner had degenerated into my lecture manner and I could see from his glazed eyes that I was telling him more about economics than he cared to know. So I retrieved the situation by asking him what the election was going to mean to him personally. I like to learn economics as well as teach it.

"Since the voters have turned conservative, I might as well reap the benefit," he said. "I used to pay a 91 per cent marginal tax rate 30 years ago and found myself working harder than ever to provide for my old age. Then Eisenhower got my rate down to 77 per cent. Under Nixon my earned income became taxed at only a 50 per cent maximum rate, so now I don't have to work as hard as I used to. Reagan ought to be good for a reduction down to 35 per cent; I'll be able to play golf on Friday as well as Wednesday.

"But that's the least of it. When Ronnie gets my long-term capital-gains tax rate down from 28 per cent to 20 per cent I may spend winters in Florida."

To bring the conversation back under control, I interjected: "But at least with lower capital-gains tax rates you'll save more and take more risks. That'll give the country more and better capital formation, what we need to improve U.S. productivity."

"Professor, you'd better stick to theoretical finance and leave practical matters alone," he advised patronizingly. "You've got it all wrong. Now that the tax on gains is so light, I don't have to take any risks at all. I convert my ordinary investment income into sure-thing long-term capital gains. It's almost like those perpetual-motion machines that Professor Keenan used to lecture us on in thermodynamics. And it's all perfectly legal. I'll have more to spend under Reagan than under Carter, and I won't have to save as much."

Lessons

What had I learned from the above experiences? First, that citizens don't always vote in accordance with what's best for their own pocketbooks.

More important, practical finance confirms what economic theorists ought to have known all along. There are no easy solutions, conservative or liberal.

To expect supply-side miracles in the next few years is naïve. Many of the measures you hope will help to boost productivity will be dissipated, in part by making those of us already rich somewhat richer. And to the degree that those measures do improve productivity, only in the longer run will you be able to detect the improvement.

The Distribution of Income

INEQUALITY
December 17, 1973

THE possibility that a substantial increase in the price of gasoline will hurt the poor is a reminder, if we need one, that income and wealth are quite unequally distributed in a country like ours. It is not true that most people are poor: most families fall in the median and modal income ranges around $12,000; but at today's soaring cost of living and with the natural urge to keep up with the Joneses, that income level will seem poor enough to all but the really poor.

To the extent that a person works harder or to the extent that a person has special needs, some superiority in his income will seem to most people to be justified. But looking at the matter in the abstract, some reduction in the degree of unnecessary inequality will be regarded as a desirable goal by most ethical, religious and philosophical value systems.

Yet when we look at the crude statistics of income and wealth, we find that the last few decades have not much changed the proportions of total income going to the lowest and highest fifths of the population and to the fifths in between. The total of the social pie has grown. But the sharing of the separate pieces is much the same as in 1950. This is an uncomfortable fact that we tend to push out of our minds, perhaps comforting ourselves with the hope that the growth in the shared total will float more and more people out of the abject poverty that has characterized most of mankind in most of its history.

Clashing Views

At the extreme right and the extreme left, this law of conservation of the overall degree of inequality will be regarded without surprise. Vilfredo Pareto, a disillusioned liberal who flirted with Mussolini's Fascism until that too disillusioned him, thought he could formulate a grand social law:

Every society has about the same degree of inequality; there is really very little that governments can do to alter this.

And any Marxist worth his salt will look with amused contempt on the sentimental thesis that a class-dominated society will be willing or even able to share prosperity more widely by peaceful economic evolution.

I belong to the middle group who think that improving minimum standards of living for those at the bottom is a desirable goal. And who think that a gradual reduction in inequality and expansion of equality of opportunity is both desirable and feasible.

But my experience as a student of economics and of history does not permit me to think that the task will be an easy one. Alas, it is not simply a matter of persuading Congress to raise the minimum wage, or of getting the trade unions to ask for a larger wage share at the expense of property return. Indeed, it is hard enough to persuade Congress to modify in any significant degree the gaping loopholes in our progressive income- and death-tax structure.

That Mr. Nixon used such a loophole shocks only the unsophisticated. The shame is on Congress and Administrations that set those loopholes, which aren't by divine decree.

World Trends

Taking the broad view, there is reason to be hopeful. Professor Irving Kravis of the University of Pennsylvania has provided a valuable September 1973 roundup of the known data in the *Annals of the American Academy of Political and Social Science*. Here are some of his findings.

· Inequality in advanced countries tends to be less than in less-developed countries. (Thus, Latin America and Southeast Asia show worse concentrations than does the United States. Denmark, Holland, Israel and countries with more homogeneous populations and with welfare states show more equality than the United States.)

· When a country first takes off into development, there may well be a worsening of inequality. (Thus, the "green revolution" in the Orient may have mostly helped those farmers who have the capital to procure the water and fertilizers that enhance the new hybrid grains' yields.)

· At later stages of growth, as affluence in the European and American sense is approached, inequality may again lessen.

But it will be asked, "Doesn't our rapid growth and affluence depend crucially on inequality?"

In answer, one must note: *The U.S. is no longer at the top in affluence.* Our fractional share in world GNP has been steadily falling. Egalitarian Sweden has now surpassed us in real per capita GNP and probably Switzerland and West Germany have also.

Is our thinking regeared to this momentous fact?

GOLD THROUGH THE GOLDEN DOOR

May 26, 1975

WHAT will be the economic effects of a new Vietnamese migration to the United States? To answer this question, one should try to guess what will be the verdict of a jury of economic historians in the twenty-first century.

Alfred North Whitehead, who spent his final two decades at Harvard, used to praise America to excess. One thing he admired most about us, in comparison with England, was our *variety,* which he attributed to the diversity of origins of this nation of immigrants. Whether or not Mother Nature loves variety, she bestows upon those species that have it her ultimate favor: namely, survival in the Darwinian struggle for existence. From this view, the fact that the Vietnamese are Asians and differ from the run of our citizenry should be an advantage rather than a disadvantage.

Also, the 127,000 would-be immigrants are far from a random sample of the South Vietnamese society—any more than the Cubans in the Miami area are a random sample of pre-Castro Cuban society. Among those now in camps on Guam and the mainland are admittedly some upper-crust lackeys of French, U.S. and indigenous colonial imperialisms. But for the most part, this is a self-selected sample of the vigorous middle and upper-middle classes: trained professionals, entrepreneurs and self-made Establishment leaders. Even to be able to elbow your way onto departing helicopters, like the ability to survive the grim ocean journey in the holds of slave ships, serves as a sieve for energy and resourcefulness.

Importing Human Capital

The analogy that comes to my mind is with that remarkably able stream of refugees from post–World War I Russia, to say nothing of those from Hitler's Europe. Koussevitzky, Timoshenko, Nabokov, Sorokin, Leontief, Kuznets, Stravinsky, Balanchine, Kistiakowsky—the honor list of scholars and artists is a long one. A society that had no need for such people is not so much to be envied as pitied.

One also recalls that the eviction of the Huguenots from France served enormously to enrich England. And also to impoverish France.

I must not fall prey to the fallacy of focusing only on those who come through to the top. Many a Ph.D. ended up driving Paris taxicabs. And so will it be for the Vietnamese. For the most part they will have to begin at the bottom of American society. It is especially hard to come down in the world, as survivors from our ante-bellum South have recorded in verse and song.

For all of Emma Lazarus's fine words about the yearning of huddled masses, typically the newly arrived greenhorns huddled in the sweated slums of our El Dorado. This scenario we see re-enacted today in Puerto Rican Harlem and Mexican-American East Los Angeles.

Credits and Debits

When people move from a low-productivity country to a high one, world real GNP presumably goes up. Those already in the rich country, *taken as a whole* (inclusive of landowners, capital-goods owners and workers of all skills) benefit from the infusion of new labor. So, environmental congestion aside, the U.S. will be the richer in material goods from the importing of Vietnamese, Cuban, Puerto Rican labor—or Irish, German and English.

Switzerland, Germany and France have benefited tremendously from importing "guest" workers from Italy, Yugoslavia, Greece, Spain, Turkey, Algeria and Portugal. Indeed, a Swiss citizen today is rather like the ancient, slave-served Athenians. He probably has a higher real income than the average American. And certainly no Swiss need do the dirty labor that has to be done by somebody in every society: he has a guest to do it, just as Milady on Beacon Hill had a Bridget to do her housework.

Low as seem the wages and living standards of wetbacks in California's Imperial Valley, they are measurably higher than those same groups could earn back home. Those who are hurt by the process are the workers in the receiving country who have pretty much the same skills as the new migrants. They have claims, legitimate claims in this age of redistribution, on the rest of us for compensation out of our enhanced wherewithal.

Why have I said nothing about the fact that we are now in recession, with too few jobs for our own people? Because 35,000 job seekers are negligible in a work force pushing 100 million. Besides, Dr. Burns at the Fed can easily and safely expand credit to take advantage of the extra goods-producing personpower.

UNEMPLOYMENT

September 6, 1976

THE specter that haunts any person of conscience today is the persistence of high rates of unemployment. Last at 7.8 per cent, the rate has been disappointingly slow in melting under the recovery sun.

President Ford and his advisers know that by election eve unemployment is still likely to be above 7 per cent—the rate we used to consider the unthinkable ceiling only three years ago. As I read the Administration's own game plan, when 1979 turns into 1980 we'll still not be back to the 5.5 per cent level of unemployment that prevailed when Ford took office.

The high rate of unemployment, and the desirability of stepping up the pace of the flagging recovery, cannot help but be campaign issues as Carter woos those worried lower-middle-class voters who defected in such large numbers to vote for Eisenhower and Nixon.

Diagnosis and False Cure

Politics aside, how do economists analyze today's chronically higher rates of unemployment?

First, one knows there is a greater element of voluntary choice in today's joblessness than was true in the Depression. Our mixed economy has an elaborate set of welfare measures enabling people to receive some income despite their not finding an acceptable job.

Second, trends of demography are such that more young people and more women are now in the labor force. Both of these groups have always shown a higher propensity to change jobs, to experience a period of unemployment between jobs and between going in and out of the labor force, than adult males of preretirement ages. However, most of the difference between the 4 per cent unemployment levels of the mid-1960s and the recent 7.5 per cent levels cannot be explained away as the inevitable consequence of these demographic changes.

Appalled by the persistence of unemployment, many people write me to suggest we reduce the workweek. Or allow only one breadwinner per family (usually to be a male!). Or that we redistribute incomes to solve what is conceived to be a chronic problem of underconsumption.

One has to reply flatly that there is no merit in these solutions. With everybody made to work short hours, our modern economy would soon again generate stagflation conditions conducive to chronic unemployment. The nub of the problem is *not* that the government lacks the ability to generate enough purchasing power to provide full-time jobs. It has more than enough fiscal and monetary power for that.

Basic Therapy

Why doesn't Congress then do what I've said it *can* do? The reason why a Ford, or even a populist like Carter, doesn't call for a spending program big enough to bring unemployment down to, say, the 4 per cent level is fear that such monetary activism will reactivate inflation.

Economists agree that this is not an idle fear. Where they disagree, and disagree strongly, is on what the traffic will bear: just how low can unemployment be safely brought, and in what time period, before the dogs of inflation are unleashed?

Ford economists give great weight to the fear of inflation. So does the largely Republican-appointed Federal Reserve Board. I think they give excessive weight to this factor. But this is not to say that an honest economist can agree with much of the rhetoric Democratic proponents of the Humphrey-Hawkins bill have produced in Congress.

I hope Carter can find a middle way. Fiscal stimulus (tax reduction and expenditure increase) plus congressional pressure on the Fed for accommodative monetary policy, virtually all economists agree, can step up the flagging pace of the recovery.

That is something, but not enough. Beyond this we need to explore labor-market reforms to make the system less inflation-prone.

Aside from retraining and relocation programs, this should involve opening up better job opportunities to nonwhites, females, youths and the unskilled.

The challenge is to keep the humane system humane. But let us make it operate more like the competitive market, in which the pressure of unused talent holds down the rate of wage inflation. The difficulties in responding successfully to this challenge are enormous, but so would be the social gains.

TAX REFORM

September 27, 1976

WITH glacial slowness, loopholes in the U.S. tax laws are being plugged up. Often, as in the 1976 proposed changes in the federal tax code, it is a question of taking two steps forward and one backward.

Why this drawn-out battle over proper tax legislation? It is because we live in a democracy involving divergent interests. What helps a driller for oil hurts most of the middle- and lower-income classes. Although the number of voters helped is far less than those hurt, the harm done to the latter is so diffused as hardly to be recognizable at time of voting for Congress and the President.

By contrast, one treasured provision in the tax code may

be worth literally millions to particular industries or corporations. It is no wonder that lobbyists are supported to try to influence the course of legislation. The wonder is that there are so few rather than so many Gulf scandals.

The fact that dollars add to a person's effective voting power is an obvious fact. Observers, if anything, exaggerate the importance of such "dollar politics." They thereby give too little attention, I think, to the following facet of human nature: the tendency of those who are not themselves affluent to identify themselves sympathetically with those who are, and thus to favor measures that do help to preserve income and wealth inequalities.

Treating Equals Equally

To put matters bluntly, much of the population, consisting of those most educated and articulate, have a vague fear of tax reform. They identify tax reform with higher taxes for themselves, and by an unknowable amount. The candid view of informed lawyers, such as Stanley Surrey of the Harvard Law School, or of expert economists who have studied tax reform, such as Joseph Pechman of Brookings, is otherwise. Their calculations show that almost all of us stand only to gain from changes in the law that ensure fair treatment of various kinds of incomes.

The whole schedule of income-tax rates could be lower if certain forms of income were not given special treatment. One must pay up to 70 per cent on each dollar of ordinary dividends and interest, and up to 50 per cent on each dollar of salary, because so many dollars of municipal bond interest, of capital gains and of tax-sheltered investments pay little or nothing in the way of taxes.

But, some will argue, "Capitalism breathes through those tax loopholes. Surely, you will jeopardize the high and growing U.S. standard of living if you take seriously the attempt of the tax and Social Security system to mitigate inequalities in opportunity and in condition."

Philosophically, I do not think the argument stands up that a free people, gathering together to set up the rules and laws for a good society, will agree on a social compact that leaves intact the inequality meted out by the market. Instead people subject to the same vicissitudes of life are likely to opt by overwhelming majority to establish a network of graduated or progressive tax rates based upon what is conceived to be ability to pay.

Equality and Progress

My present purpose is not philosophical, but rather to examine pragmatically the relative growth records of those countries that have pursued seriously the problems of mitigating inequality.

The Organization for Economic Cooperation and Development has just published data on income distribution in OECD countries (July 1976). It confirms the suspicion that France has more income inequality than the Netherlands, Sweden or Norway. But what is beginning to cause a stir in French politics is the realization of how very poor are France's poorest. In France, the richest 10 per cent of the nation gets 22 times what the poorest 10 per cent gets; in West Germany, eleven times; in the United States, fifteen times.

Here are the rankings of eleven nations in terms of *after-tax income equality.* Netherlands, Sweden, Norway, U.K., Japan, Canada, Australia, West Germany, U.S., Spain, France.

Compare these actual facts with Rotarian rhetoric on the necessity of inequality for economic progress. If Germany and Japan—to say nothing of Scandinavia and the Netherlands—can achieve vigorous growth and at the same time mitigate inequality, why regard tax reform as bad business?

WELFARE REFORM

August 29, 1977

ENGLAND, Disraeli wrote, was divided into Two Nations, the Privileged and the People—or to put it in plain English, into the rich and the poor. It is still true in 1977 that our society is divided between those in poverty and the rest.

Yet the United States is an affluent nation. Why can we not, by a stroke of the pen, abolish poverty once and for all? That is precisely what some University of Michigan experts fifteen years ago said could be done. Since the group included Wilbur Cohen, Lyndon Johnson's Secretary of HEW, their 1962 words are worth studying:

"The U.S. has arrived at the point where poverty could be abolished easily and simply by the stroke of a pen. To raise every individual and family in the nation now below a subsistence income to the subsistence level would cost about $10 billion a year [perhaps $35 billion in 1977]. This is less than 2 per cent of the gross national product. It is less than 10 per cent of tax revenues. It is about one-fifth [in 1977, one-third] of the cost of national defense."

A bargain, you will say? Rid of poverty once and for all?

Alas, the problem will not go away so easily, I fear. It is true that if Abraham Lincoln had been able to avoid the Civil War by buying out all the slaves at their ante-bellum market prices, we should be billions of dollars ahead, to say nothing of having saved thousands of lives. But that does not mean that a little money will serve to remove the Soviet Union as a threat to our national security, or will solve the problems of cancer, the common cold and energy.

The Greasy Pole

A recent University of Michigan study for the government of 5,000 families shows that for every family actually in poverty there are several others poised on the brink. It confirms what we've long known.

Capitalism is a hotel. Its penthouse suites are always filled, but not necessarily with the same people this decade as last. And its basement dungeons are also jam-packed; but not with the same faces and bodies. While Wilkins Micawber slid into the pit, Uriah Heep was clawing his way out.

Following the same panel of families from 1967 to 1976 revealed how few—20 to 30 per cent—were *all* those years within poverty as officially defined; and how few—less than a quarter—worked their way *permanently* out of that category. What strikes the objective observer is how unrealistic is the usual middle-class view of poverty, as something that shiftless people have brought *voluntarily* on themselves.

What does this comprehensive sample show to be the facts as against the myths? Here is a 1977 summary of the Panel Study of Income Dynamics.

"To date we have found virtually no evidence that . . . such attitudes and behaviors as personal confidence, ambition, achievement, motivation, future orientation, trust in others, planning ahead, economizing, and avoiding risks . . . so often associated with financial success do, in fact, lead to economic improvement."

Instead, to be in poverty is to be old. To be black. To have been uneducated. To be a female head of household. Changes in family composition turn out to be crucial factors.

The Bible says you cannot increase your stature one cubit by thinking on it. Neither can you become white, young, male and financially secure by taking a Dale Carnegie self-improvement course or by resolving to be parsimonious and energetic.

Carter's Proposals

What follows from the finding that the poor are not a permanent small cadre who can be simply put on relief? The moral to be gleaned is that people should be given every incentive to earn income from work, at the same time that the needs they are unable to meet on their own receive humanistic help from the government. The public may be unrealistic on how much the poor can earn by their own efforts. But the public's instinct is correct that the dole is both expensive and destructive of incentives.

Experience makes one skeptical that suitable public- and private-service jobs can be created to save much on transfer payments. Still, the new Carter program will establish the principle that welfare aid is to be adjusted to leave people with an incentive to earn more rather than less. It is yet another attempt to introduce into our chaotic system some variant of the negative income tax. For that, I say hurrah.

ECONOMICS OF DISCRIMINATION

July 10, 1978

REDUCING job discrimination presents fewer policy dilemmas than were involved in last week's Bakke case. Economics shows why.

If a medical school has openings for 100 freshmen, and if 25 nonwhites are admitted, then there are only 75 places left for white applicants. That is a case of what mathematicians and economists call a "zero-sum game." In such a game, every gain of minority or ethnic groups must come at the expense of the rest of the community—the whites, the Establishment group, the charter-member Yankees.

Cooperation or Competition?

Everything that can be said in a zero-sum-game situation of white versus black workers could also be said of foreigners versus immigrants. Benjamin Franklin was one who feared that a flood of new immigrants to America would be at the expense of those who had already settled here. Back at the end of the nineteenth century, Gen. Francis Walker, president of MIT and the most distinguished American economist of his age, held similar views hostile to immigration. When greenhorns take jobs from natives and depress wages for all, Walker believed the native birthrate would drop. The result would be simply a replacement of original Yankee stock by Germans, Irish, Swedes, Jews, Italians, Mexicans and Slavs.

The competition for good jobs between men and women appears in the same stark light to many men who fear for their earnings, perquisites and prestige now that so many women are dedicated to permanent careers in the labor force. Back in the Great Depression, teachers with employed husbands were declared ineligible for employment in many states. "We must spread around the limited total of jobs," it was argued, "and it is unfair that a second female breadwinner should take the bread out of the mouths of families dependent upon a father who cannot find a job."

Upon thoughtful analysis of the nature of the economic system, economists find that it is essentially *not* a zero-sum game. Economists call it "the lump-of-labor fallacy" to believe that in any period—1933 or 1978—there are only so many jobs: it is false philosophy of despair, economists point out, to insist on cutting down on each worker's weekly hours in order to spread out an allegedly limited total of work and of income among as many people as possible.

It is not even the case that the interests of laborers, landowners and owners of capital tools and equipment are in arithmetic opposition. There is no fixed size to the social pie, so that the more that goes to profits and rents, the less will ever be available for wages. Instead, the total of the national output is produced by the *cooperation* of the factors of production: original natural resources and produced capital goods, human endowments as modified by training and education.

When a country gains new manpower from the excess of births over deaths or from immigration and increased female participation, its same land and complement of capital assets can produce a larger social pie. Most of this increment goes to the new supply of workers: employers do not give workers anything out of altruism; the worker earns his keep.

Good Tidings

Important consequences follow from these basic economic principles. The problem put to the Supreme Court—how to allocate a fixed total of desirable prizes among more people than there are prizes—is not the problem we face in seeking racial justice.

With each productive input largely earning its own keep, both men and an enhanced supply of women can hope to perform good paying jobs. Neither the "poor whites" nor other groups in the community have to fear particularly that out of *their* economic hides will have to come any advance in well-being achieved by black Americans, native Indian Americans, Americans of Mexican descent or other minority groups.

This is an essentially cheerful finding. It is subject to one qualification. The law of diminishing returns does tell us that when you crowd more laborers on a fixed total of land and capital goods, there can be some pulling down of the wage rate previously enjoyed by the smaller complement of workers. Fortunately, our best econometric studies show this to be a small effect.

SOCIAL SECURITY: A-OK

April 14, 1975

As the age of 40 nears, a thoroughgoing health checkup is in order. Our Social Security system for old-age-retirement pensions, started in 1937 under FDR, has been going for 38 years. Fears have been expressed that it is becoming actuarially unsound; and, much worse, that at some time in the future, it will become bankrupt and be unable to pay the pensions so desperately needed and which people have earned the right to expect.

We have just had two independent audits. One is by the thirteen-person Social Security Advisory Council, consisting of representatives of the general public, labor, management, and the self-employed. Chaired by W. Allen Wallis, chancellor of the University of Rochester, this includes a fair example of Establishment leaders and is, if anything, weighted on the conservative side.

The other is by the Panel on Social Security Financing, appointed by 1974 Senate resolution and charged with giving ". . . an expert, independent analysis of the actuarial status of the social-security system." Chaired by William C. L. Hsiao of the Harvard School of Public Health, who is both an actuary and an economist, it includes three other actuaries and two other economists. If the actuaries have reputations for excellence and fair-mindedness in their profession matching that of the economists in my profession, the Hsiao panel inspires confidence and serves as a valuable second opinion to supplement the Wallis council's checkup on Social Security health.

Clean Bill of Health

The clinical findings are favorable. The patient is sound with a life expectancy that can be measured in the centuries. Both authorities agree.

To be sure, there are some minor defects in need of attention, so to speak, like a mole that might become serious if not attended to. Retired participants have their pensions indexed, to protect them from inflation. The formula is a proper one. But the way that earners who are not yet retired have their stipends computed is defective and could result after years of inflation in an inequitable and burdensome benefit cost. Just as there are alternative ways of treating an undesirable mole, so there are alternative ways of correcting the arithmetic of preretirement indexing: both groups recommend immediate attention to this matter.

The basic problem facing the Social Security system is that its financing must take account of present declining birth rates, increasing years of life expectancy in retirement, productivity trends in the economy and plausible ranges of average inflation. Using the most reasonable guesses on these trends, one finds that the now-scheduled timing of tax changes and benefits will by the end of the 1980s threaten to deplete the so-called trust fund set up for Social Security. There is nothing new about this finding, which has been familiar to experts for years. However, the Hsaio panel estimates, which seem more realistic than those of the Wallis council, suggest that in 50 years the cost of the program, relative to total payrolls, will double to 20 per cent from the present 10 per cent. This is a sharp revision of previous official projections.

Needed Improvements

What ought to be done to restore the system to the pink of health? For the present, nothing *has* to be done: but both groups believe that it would be well to plan *now* to augment revenues.

Remarkable indeed is the general recommendation of the Wallis council, subject to some dissents but still commanding a majority of this nonradical group, that *some recourse be made to general tax revenues of the Treasury rather than continue to rely exclusively on payroll taxing of prospective recipients.* This is a bold stand that, on reflection, I endorse. What is important is the principle. What is less crucial is the specific recommendation of the council that it be the hospital-insurance part of the Medicare program that be put on the general taxpayers' shoulders.

The present system is neither fish nor fowl, but it *is* good red herring. Unlike private insurance, this is a case of social insurance in which the premiums levied on workers do not suffice to finance future benefits fully. But still there is adherence to the principle that benefits are to be related to earnings; and every earner is given the feeling that the benefits received are deserved by right.

Continued good health requires continued changes. Eventually we shall have comprehensive health insurance. And before that, I pray, a fairer deal for women.

FINANCING PENSIONS

April 4, 1978

I T is, sadly, an old story that union pension funds are not always handled wisely and honestly. Frank Fitzsimmons of the Teamsters union is being criticized today for many of the same things that his predecessors, Jimmy Hoffa and Dave Beck, had to be criticized for in their time.

It is, sadly, also an old story that many corporate pension

funds have not always been handled optimally. Quite aside from outright fraud and breach of faith, companies used to go out of business leaving behind them unhonored commitments to workers who face a tough period of retirement with no pension income other than their bare minimum of Social Security.

When I hear complaints about the new regulations under ERISA (Employee Retirement Income Security Act), I remember abuses in the old system. And, now that the first hysteria has died down, we no longer hear of many cases where employers have been persuaded to omit pension plans for fear of the red tape involved.

There is no excuse in this age for scandalous mishandling of pension funds. Good and prudent management—they are the same thing in an uncertain world where no one can *guarantee* lucky investment results but where intelligent procedures can be agreed on—are available to organizations that want them. Just last week, for example, several New York City pension funds reformed their portfolio practices by converting a portion of their assets to "index" funds.

Old Ways

Pension management was not always so easy. Historically, trade unions came to grief in this area for reasons quite beyond their control.

Craft unions often began in the nineteenth century as beneficial cooperatives. Living workers were assessed to pay burial expenses and minimal survivors' benefits for workers who died or reached retirement. Actuarial funding of this obligation seemed out of the question; yet it did not matter so long as the trade and the union continued to grow. But when the time came that industry did not need new glass blowers, or when new workers deserted the old beneficial associations precisely to avoid their accrued obligations, these voluntary systems broke down in bankruptcy.

When lecturing at a small Roman Catholic college, I

found that many of the monastic orders are facing a similar crisis today. A nun who is a Ph.D. in economics told me that her old-age support is in doubt now that her order cannot recruit new members. "Why not go under Social Security?" I asked naïvely. Her reply was sad: "That would require a million dollars in catch-up; and we just don't have the money."

Modern Pitfalls

I ought to add that our Social Security system is also *an actuarially unfunded* system. It would be disastrous to let people opt to go in and out of the system at will. Fortunately, there is no danger of that. Still, there is no obligation for this generation to have children at the same rate as did previous generations. Therefore, when those born during the baby-boom period of the '50s reach retirement age in the next century, their stipends will be felt as more of a burden by the thinner ranks of the then working population.

Two other perils dog union pension funds. First, there is always someone—an employer, a beleaguered city treasurer, your friendly congressman dreaming of "worker capitalism" or the local bargaining agent concerned that a factory not go out of business—who is advocating that the pension moneys be invested in the workers' own industry, firm or city. Sometimes, it works out fine. Not rarely, this violation of the principle of sound diversification of risk proved costly to older workers. ERISA properly set limits on such practices.

Second, union leaders of goodwill are tempted to put the money entrusted to them into good causes: ghetto housing projects, capital-development banks, environmental protection. The motives are good. But it is hard enough to preserve and enhance capital when you are single-mindedly pursuing that end. It is doubly hard to serve both God and Mammon.

What are the percepts of good management? Practical experience and theoretical economics agree on a few simple fundamentals.

Diversification of ownership of both stocks and bonds, with minimal turnover rates and loan-expense rations—these are the golden rules.

Anyone can do it. So why not insist that it be done?

AN UNLUCKY GENERATION

October 10, 1977

DEMOCRACY has its own peculiar modes of behavior. Congress will fritter a year arguing fruitlessly about energy. Then, in an afternoon, while the rest of the country is watching a ball game, it will abolish the rule for presumed automatic retirement at 65, a measure with grave consequences for years to come.

My generation stands to benefit. To us who hath shall be given; from them that hath not shall be taken away.

It is the age group around 30 that deserves our pity. For it is the swollen cohort, product of the postwar baby boom in which my Doris Day generation went gaga over playing house in the suburbs and proceeded to have three, four and five children.

The infants of the Class of 1947 found kindergartens too small for their numbers. And that was to be their fate all through school. For them, competition to get into colleges was fierce.

The unkindest cut of all awaited them when the time came to enter the labor market. There were two reasons:

Competing Job Seekers

1. Their sheer weight of numbers required them to compete with each other for relative pittances in pay. Social Security wage data show how relatively depressed have been their wage earnings, compared with my generation's and with what youths used to earn in relative wages.

2. Eschewing the Doris Day image in favor of that of Mary Tyler Moore, more women began to compete for lifetime jobs in the labor force, interrupted only briefly to bear and care for one or two children. One effect, to bring the underlying population trend below the replacement level, is fairly obvious. Hardly less obvious is the fact that, just when women are most insistent to terminate discriminatory differences in pay and career opportunity, employers can play off against them their own numerous sisters.

When Italians fill low-status jobs in Switzerland and Mexicans do the dirty work in California and Texas, it is not the salaries of the middle-class elite that suffer. To the contrary, a charter-member Swiss lives the good life of the ancient free citizen of Athens who was supported by an infrastructure of slave labor.

One can see in the Social Security data that parents of the late-1940s babies have been doing relatively well. Particularly for white males, automatic improvements in pay and status accrue just from seniority of age. Now, thanks to Congress, a typical MIT or Yale professor may have the option of working an extra five years at top pay.

Since the rate of growth of school populations has dropped, how can usurpation of these best jobs help but narrow the opportunities of the young? If several years are added to a tenure span that previously averaged some 30 years, at least 10 per cent fewer people can hope to get such slots in each generation of the new steady state. In the first five years ahead, replacement openings drop virtually to zero!

A Double Whammy

Is all this unfair? As some sage observed: Who said that life is fair? Besides, if we parents have exploited our children, why can't those children hope in the fullness of time to get their own back at the expense of *their* children?

It won't work out that way. Because the Mary Tyler Moore generation will have so few children, the really big shock will come when they reach their late 60s. Their standard of life during years of old-age retirement, whether financed by Social Security or voluntary pension arrangements, will have to come out of whatever is then produced by the skimpy ranks of my generation's grandchildren!

To verify this, I have consulted an up-to-date projection of the future U.S. population from the Harvard Center for Population Studies. In 1975, each person over 65 had about six people in the working-year ages of 15 to 64 to support her or him. That multiple will shrink. By the year 2025, it will have shrunk to only four such workers.

The lesson is not to set rigid age limits to spread out limited job opportunity. If modern medical science bestows more years of good health and if we want to work and earn, the system should be run so that exercising this discretion does not ruin someone else's opportunities. More flexibility in wage rates—less for the very young and old—would be a step in the right direction.

SOCIAL SECURITY TAXING

April 17, 1978

CONGRESS last year raised payroll taxes, thinking that necessary to put Social Security on a solvent financial basis. Now there is a strong move to roll back some of the increase in order to lessen the burden on business and workers.

What are the merits and demerits of the many proposals for reform now being discussed? Will the system go bust? What role should the concept of "actuarial soundness" play in the domain of "social insurance"? Should general tax revenues play any role?

Begin with fundamentals. The basic economic problem has little to do with whether we maintain a reserve fund that holds government securities whose interest and principal can be drawn on in future years to finance promised benefits.

The basic problem is that the system will be supporting many more older people, requiring pension support, disability compensation and medical care, by the turn of the century. The question is how many or few workers of prime age—20 to 70—there will be to support the older ones with compulsory contributions from earnings.

Looking at the problem in this way shows that those of us who are now middle-aged have little to fear. Our generation produced the baby boom of 1940–60. When the time comes for us to retire, there will be many taxable workers among our daughters and sons. The tax rate to finance all this, whether on payrolls or out of general income taxes on corporations and persons, should be supportable unless the system goes hog-wild in inefficiency and profligate benefits.

Trouble Ahead

The rub will come for the generation of the baby boom. If it had continued in our ways, marrying early and having more than the couple of children needed for mere population replacement, then the Ponzi process of exponential increase could repeat itself in the fashion of a chain-letter scheme in its early phase.

That possibility is, however, no longer relevant. Since 1957, at least, the trend in demography has veered toward a sharply lower birth rate.

People are marrying later. More women are working permanently outside the home. Targets for ultimate family size are being scaled down. As more and more wives put off throughout their twenties having a first baby, more couples will end up below their actual targets.

So, looking ahead into the twenty-first century, we see a heavier burden of the old on the working young.

Is there not, however, a ray of hope in the 1977 upturn in births? Just as fads send skirt hemlines up and down, don't swings in fashion operate in the realm of human fertility?

Most population experts I've talked to are skeptical that the 1977 rise represents a significant and lasting rebound. They point out that most of the gain merely reflects the swelling number of people in their twenties and thirties, a temporary swelling inherited from the past baby boom. True, there is a genuine increase in fertility, probably centered among wives who long put off having children and now think it is their last chance. But, whatever the motivations, we are still below the replacement level and a significant rebound above it does not seem indicated by the trends.

Preparing Now

The current debate hardly touches these fundamentals, which are controversial in their own right. More than next year's business is at stake.

If future generations must plan on a lower ratio of producers to older dependents, should we raise taxes now to get the body politic accustomed to bearing higher taxes? On first thought, that seems to smack of my jumping rope now to help my grandchildren be in better condition for the prizefights they will be facing later.

On reflection, economists realize that this 1978 generation could help the 2018 generation by consuming less today, in order that more resources go now into building the capital formation that will give 2018 more and better factories and equipment, and the higher labor productivity out of which to support the 2018 aged.

To connect this up with Social Security taxes, suppose we bear higher taxes now (whether on payrolls or incomes is immaterial). If that reduces demand enough to let the Federal Reserve lower interest rates by whatever is needed to draw into capital formation all the resources released from the consumption trades, we have in principle prepared in this generation to help the next generation.

ECONOMICS OF OLD AGE

March 30, 1981

THIS month the *New England Journal of Medicine* made us give up coffee for the sake of our pancreas. Earlier we learned that the process that takes the caffeine out of coffee may leave carcinogens in its place. As an economist concerned with the economics of Social Security, I have been pondering last July's article by Dr. James F. Fries of the Stanford Medical Center. It is entitled "Aging, Natural Death and the Compression of Morbidity." Fries intends to give us cheer. His thesis is dramatic. I paraphrase it as follows.

One-Hoss Shays

Life, Hobbes said, used to be short and brutish. Life, Fries argues, is in no danger of becoming inhumanely long. Science can't keep us going long after 85: our cells are programed to self-destruct at the same maximal ages as in times past.

Those myths of chaps in the Caucasus and Andes who live on and on in their second century are myths based on scanty birth-registration data. Where records are kept that scientists can respect, the oldest person now alive is only 114.

From the standpoint of an actuary concerned about Social Security burdens, that's the good news. Also good news is Fries's second finding.

Even if 85 represents the cutoff point to the normal human life span, more and more people are reaching it. And they do so in increasingly good health.

"Father enjoyed an active life for 85 years and died in his sleep (or after a brief terminal illness)." That will be the common story when humans attain the "rectangular actuarial life tables" that Fries foresees.

What does a rectangular life table mean? Suppose all the millions born in 1981 lived to the year 2066, and all then died on their eighty-fifth birthdays. The curve showing how many out of 100 survived to each age would be a horizontal line up to age 85; then it would drop down to zero, like the side of a box or rectangle. This, of course, is the extreme case, one we're moving toward.

Remember the marvelous one-hoss shay of Oliver Wendell Holmes's poem? It was so balanced in all its parts that after exactly 100 years all fell to dust at the same time. Polls show that is how we all want to die: suddenly, without warning, and while in a state of autumnal grace.

As I have stated the Fries thesis, it has a reassuring truth for economics. We shall not become Methuselahs, living on indefinitely as a burden to society and with no comfort to ourselves.

But M.D.'s can whistle in the dark reaching for an optimistic diagnosis that the cold facts may not sustain. Even as the actuarial life table of survival probabilities is becoming more nearly rectangular, the penultimate years of expensive and gloomy life are increasing, not decreasing.

Make your own rounds of nearby nursing homes to verify this sober fact. With antibiotics, antihypertensive, intravenous and other emergency procedures, people—some of them very unhappy people by their own accounts—are kept living on into their late eighties and nineties. When actuaries put a microscope on the way that the force of mortality—the risk of dying each day—changes at 85 and after, they find no magic point of discontinuous acceleration. The paradigm of

Holmes's one-hoss shay is merely an overdramatic metaphor.

Too-Early Retirement

Enough of my second opinions. Fries has taught us an important moral.

It makes no sense to encourage or force people to retire at 65 or earlier.

It makes even less sense in the case of women. Statistically speaking, a 70-year-old woman is further from death than her 67-year-old brother. Her hand is steadier, her brain is clearer. And, actuaries warn us, she faces more years of dependency before she dies.

I remember a German novelist who treated people as being of the same age not if they were born at the same time but if they were going to die at the same time. That is the view we should take in framing a rational system of lifetime programing and Social Security.

It is a scandal that public and private pension plans are encouraging early retirement. Often an oldster can keep but 35 cents of each new dollar earned. Why work?

Virtually all men used to be in the labor force at ages such as 55 and 60. Now the census shows an appreciable fraction already retired at those ages.

Let Congress take notice of Fries's findings. And, septuagenarian Ronald Reagan, realize that the bell tolls for thee—as it does for all of us.

Chapter Five

CLUES TO ECONOMIC PROSPERITY AT HOME AND ABROAD

*A*S far as international economics is concerned, *Samuelson is an orthodox neoclassical economist. The succession from Adam Smith's theory of comparative advantage remains intact. In a previous section, Samuelson recommends that the government not support an ailing Chrysler Corporation, but he is willing to discuss the terms if the democratic process decides to intervene. He is adamantly opposed to tariff protection. This is not inconsistency. What the market metes out may be adjusted for internally. However, the unvarnished truth about domestic vis-à-vis international productivity must be faced.*

Samuelson outlines reasons for a floating exchange rate system. First, a floating rate has allowed the U.S. economy, since 1971, to adjust with minimum grief to changing world conditions and rising oil prices. Second, it permits a country to establish appropriate domestic policy without concern for the balance of payments. If imports exceed exports, the dollar will devalue, making foreign goods less attractive to U.S. citizens and at the same time making U.S. goods more attractive to foreigners. Third, the forces of the supply and demand for the U.S. dollar are best able to determine the "appropriate" exchange rate consistent with national objectives. Finally, Samuelson dismisses the argument that the value of the dollar should be maintained because the dollar is the key reserve currency in the free world. Samuelson indicates that political power and a strong currency have never been necessarily associated.

Hard work and thrift, values that are culturally transmitted, are the keys to economic growth. Samuelson indicates that a society may choose at its own risk to ignore other values in order to achieve economic growth. He doubts that better-formulated property rights and/or government incentives leading to unrestrained individualism will necessarily lead to or maintain prosperity. On the other hand, given widespread alienation, populist democracy could destroy economic growth.

In this chapter, one sees Samuelson from three vantage points. First, as a scientist of the market and politics, he knows that on average long-term consumption levels cannot be kept higher than productivity. In the political realm, he knows about the fragile consensus of politicians and interest groups. Second, as an adviser to governments and households, he practices prudence and pragmatism in choosing alternatives, as he preoccupies himself with long-term survival and well-being. Fi-

nally, he observes *the social and intellectual milieu, the institutions, and the changing fortunes of the wealth of nations.*

Free Trade

STEEL STATISM
February 26, 1968

THE steel industry is mounting a strong campaign for protective quotas against competitive imports from abroad. Last year they were asking Congress for "temporary tariffs." But since they know in their heart of hearts that there is nothing "temporary" about their need for protection from competition, and since once you have asked the state to intervene in your favor you have already given up the principle of believing in free enterprise, the steel industry has now joined textiles, glass and oil in lobbying for quotas to set quantitative curbs on imports.

Let me state the industry's case. Then appraise it.

Claim and Counterclaim

1. Steel imports from Europe and Japan have been growing at an accelerated rate. Our exports, which used to be among the highest in the world, are shrinking rapidly.

2. According to the American Iron and Steel Institute—the spokesman for the industry—these trends will continue into the future. By 1975 imports will take 20 rather than 12 per cent of the total market. These additional imports will displace some 60,000 steelworkers.

3. The basic reason for "invasion" of our markets by imports is this: although America is the world's most efficient producer of steel in terms of total man-hours required—as

reckoned in the steel mill and in the factories that make steel-making equipment—our efficiency is still not as much greater than efficiency abroad as are the money wages that American industries have to pay *in comparison with* money wages abroad. U.S. Steel, according to Roger Blough, must pay about $40 a day to attract workers from other American industries; Japanese steel companies need pay only the equivalent of $10 a day to get help. Our mills are more efficient, but not four times as efficient. And they cannot be made so.

4. For national defense and security, our domestic industry deserves protection. To quote Mr. Blough, "Can we, for example, be assured of the strong industrial base in steel we need for modern defense if one-quarter or more of the steel we require were imported from countries lying uncomfortably close to the Soviet Union or China?"

5. There is world overcapacity in steel. Steel is dumped here at lower costs than sold at home. No other country lets free trade prevail in steel. Why should we?

6. A quota, limiting steel imports to the percentage they had in the last three years (about 10 per cent) would improve our future balance of payments, and heaven knows it needs improving.

Here is the economists' reply.

We gain most in international trade when we buy goods made with labor *lower paid* than our own. When an industry does not have an efficiency exceeding foreign efficiency by the average proportion that our money wages exceed foreign wages, we lack "comparative advantage" in that industry. And we gain in American living standards by letting that industry shrink.

By its own admission, steel lacks comparative advantage. Just as U.S. Steel buys power whenever it cannot produce it as cheaply, the U.S. should buy its steel in least-cost markets. This way our products made of steel can be most numerous and our real standard of living be highest.

If the steel lobby said, "Give us quotas and they will cut

into profitable American exports *elsewhere* by an equivalent number of billions of dollars," no literate congressman would listen to their pleas for protection. (Naturally I exclude congressmen from Gary and Pittsburgh.)

Verdict for Dismissal

America still has a surplus of exports over imports amounting to billions of dollars per year. This demonstrates that other industries do have the comparative advantage steel lacks. True, our cold-war offshore needs and our foreign-aid desires are so large—particularly when coupled with the wish of our corporations to make direct investment abroad—that our private export surplus is too small for our needs. Tariffs, quotas and direct controls can temporarily bridge the gap. But neither in the short nor long run does steel have a special case for protection. And let us remember that a quota is the most malignant form of protection, much worse than a tariff.

When the time comes that steel must stand in line with the merchant marine for subsidy in terms of national defense, it will be hard to distinguish it from a nationalized industry. That time is not remotely near.

THREAT OF NEW TARIFFS

August 11, 1980

THE germ of protectionism lies dormant, ever-present in American political life. The same can be said of political life abroad. France, Japan, the other advanced nations, as well as developing countries in Africa, Asia and Latin America, are constantly tempted to legislate tariffs against imports. Or to impose numerical quotas. Or, outside the formal bounds of explicit legislation, to set up bureaucratic obstacles to trade and to follow commercial practices that discriminate against goods produced by foreigners.

Nations struggle in the modern period against their own baser natures. We all pay lip service to free trade. National leaders hold summit meetings to proclaim fresh rounds of tariff reductions and quota reductions. GATT, the General Agreement on Tariffs and Trade, represents an official collective effort to move toward freer international trade, with a bureaucracy located in Geneva dedicated to promoting this noble cause.

Free Trade?

The remarkable thing is how unfettered international commerce has generally been in this last half of the twentieth century. The volume of trade has grown at an even faster rate than real world product. And that is saying much, since there has never been so rapid and sustained a pattern of real world growth as in the decades of the 1950s and the 1960s. In comparison with the mercantilistic age that preceded Adam Smith and the between-the-wars decades of the 1920s and 1930s, international trade has been virtually free.

Economists, who are supposed to be a contentious bunch, have generally agreed that the community at large stands to gain in material standard of living from specialization and exchange according to the various nations' comparative advantage. This is one textbook theory that on the whole seems to have been vindicated by the actual experience of economic history.

You will have to look hard for cases in which a nation has succeeded in raising its level of productivity and real income by building walls against foreign imports. On the other hand, there are numerous examples of rapid development by countries that are import- and export-minded: Britain in the nineteenth century, Germany and Japan after they freed themselves from feudalism and entered the industrial age. A study for the National Bureau of Economic Research, by Jagdish Bhagwati of MIT and Columbia and Anne O. Krueger of the University of Minnesota, has inferred from the available evidence that economic development tends to be more successful under a regimen of export promotion than one of import protection.

South Korea, Taiwan, Hong Kong and Singapore have been so successful in this process of export growth that they are sometimes referred to as the "gang of four." The index of manufacturing production soars in those places, and also in Malaysia and the Philippines. The other side of the coin is languishing manufacturing production and employment in Western Europe, North America and the advanced countries generally. The United States is, of course, not immune to competition in manufacturing, even though statistics of Switzerland and West Germany show that we've done relatively better since the peak of 1973 than those nations have.

Steel-industry leaders have been clamoring for protection ever since the 1950s. The inroads made by Japanese and German automobile companies have converted Detroit executives from card-carrying free-traders to lobbyists for protection of their market. Douglas Fraser, the head of the United Auto Workers, has finally and predictably thrown in the towel on the philosophy of free trade.

Holding Firm

The current recession increases the political clout of the protectionists. There are no other jobs immediately available to workers who lose their jobs because of competing imports.

Is there now an economic case to be made for protection? Can our trend of deteriorating real incomes be reversed by judicious quotas?

No. Once we decide we don't want the recession that Washington has deliberately created, we know the tools of tax cutting and credit easing that can bring it to an end.

Rather than rely on tariffs to create American jobs, economists favor letting the dollar float downward to make our goods competitive.

What government cannot do is guarantee jobs for all at real wage levels higher than our productivity can justify.

Exchange Rates

GOLD
July 8, 1974

THE time is coming when Congress and the President will permit Americans again to hold gold legally. From the standpoint of economics—jobs, incomes, interest rates, inflation, lifetime savings—gold has not the slightest importance.

Freud and Keynes could agree on one thing though. Gold has an almost mythical fascination for the human psyche. College sophomores quiver in indignation over the rape of their rights that took place before they were born, when FDR pushed through—and the High Court upheld—a law striking down the right to hold gold.

The gold standard, as a way of determining automatically the supply of money and price levels all over the world, is dead forever. It was a far from perfect system at best. It worked adequately for only a few decades before World War I, when wages and prices were flexible downward and upward.

Up or Down?

What will allowing Americans to hold gold mean? Will it lead to a great upsurge in the price of gold? To gold at $300 per ounce, about double the present free-market price and many times the now-dead *official* International Monetary Fund price of $42.22 per ounce?

Maybe a new set of customers for gold would, other things equal, tend to raise its market price. But at about the same time, there is likely to be a new supply of gold thrown on the market by official treasuries—either acting in concert or, like Italy today, trying desperately to meet their oil debts by hocking any liquid assets at hand. That would tend to depress the price of gold.

Moreover, there is an old adage on Wall Street: "Buy on rumor; sell on the news." Speculators all over the world know how the winds are blowing in Washington. And many have been discounting in advance the coming legalization of gold ownership on the part of U.S. citizens. So the run-up in prices that the gold bugs have been hoping for may be short-lived or may even never occur.

Who cares? South Africa cares. It is the biggest gold producer, and its mining output constitutes one of its principal export earnings.

The Soviet Union cares. It is the second-biggest miner of gold. Last year, its sales of gold at more than $100 an ounce did help feed its people and finance imports of the technical goods needed for its long-term industrial development.

Beyond them, gold is unimportant. Thus, for Canada and the western United States, to say that gold is peanuts would be to magnify its importance. After all, peanuts are by no means an insignificant crop.

Gold hoarders also care. Most are in the game for the hope of making capital gains. Yet for every two who in these last couple of years have profits to show in coins, bullion or in South African mine shares there are ten who have not yet recouped the losses in yield and price taken over the last decade in gold speculations.

Coin dealers have a stake in the game. I have never understood how anyone with the intelligence to practice medicine could have the stupidity to overpay, by 14 per cent or more, to buy thousands of dollars worth of silver bullion from dealers who advertise in the financial press. At almost no commission charge they could get their silver bullion or coins from the organized futures exchanges in New York and Chicago. But there is no fool like a frightened and avaricious fool. And it is not just doctors who fritter away their money. Some top bankers have recently made the headlines as prime suckers in modern versions of the old Ponzi swindle!

Government Folly

Anyone in a free country has a right to lose his own money. But there is no need, in a well-run country, for government to enter into the frenzy. I hope that members of the IMF will not be led, by a desire to enhance and preserve the liquidating value of their official gold hoards, to create a new demand for gold in the form of an official guarantee to support its price within the range of recent market quotations.

Make no mistake about it. If the IMF adopts an official price of gold in the range of, say, $140–$160 an ounce, that will not end the gold speculation and contrive a new equilibrium state. The gold bugs will most likely bid gold to a premium above any official price. And then they'll point to the premium as evidence that a higher official price is needed.

Governments should, for once, prove Barnum was wrong in saying there's a sucker born every minute.

GOLD AND THE DOLLAR
October 31, 1977

EACH month the news comes that the U.S. is importing more than it is exporting. There is no end in sight. Experts expect the 1978 deficit in our current balance of payments to be similarly large. Is it time now to prop up the dollar, fret about vague scenarios for international disaster, join the gold bugs?

The sinking dollar has other effects. To the discomfort of the Japanese, the yen floats upward relative to the dollar. Toyotas and Hondas tend to become more expensive relative to Fords and Chevrolets. It even begins to make sense to buy an American-built car.

Switzerland beckons in time of financial stress as a haven for nervous money. The inflow raises the price of the Swiss franc: traditional Swiss watches have long since become too expensive for many to buy, and real Swiss GNP has been hard hit.

The West German mark and the French franc have been strong. Miracle of miracles, the British pound has moved upward under the sunshine of North Sea oil and the reflux of speculative balances. U.K. net reserves have risen all the way to zero, an astounding improvement.

Turbid Crosscurrents

U.S. inflation rates are lower than most and the dollar is not the weakest currency around. The Canadian dollar is weaker still. And no wonder. Galbraithian price-wage controls don't succeed in controlling the inflation there. Quebec threatens to secede. The investment climate in Canada is regarded by foot-loose capitalists as among the least friendly around. Strikes proliferate.

The Swedish miracle may have run its course. The remarkable productivity gains that used to offset whopping wage increases have finally come to an end. The Swedish market share in world exports has fallen. In desperation, the successor to the Labor government broke away from the snake grip of the mark and devalued the krona by 10 per cent overnight.

These international events have ignited the fears of men of property. When in doubt, old men's fancies turn to thoughts of gold. Younger men, operating on the "greater fool" theory, take a flyer in gold futures, hoping to cash in on the rise. For a time the whole operation becomes a self-fulfilling prophecy. Those nimblest in getting off the tiger first might end up ahead.

From the peak price of $200 per ounce on Dec. 31, 1974, the day when gold became a legal holding for Americans, gold's price dropped away to almost a half by the fall of 1976. Since that trough, the price recovered slowly. Recently, it has taken off, surpassing $160 an ounce.

The gold bugs are back in business. They can scratch up the ante for half-page ads. An upcoming convention on gold in New Orleans will be like old home week, a gathering of the clan.

What should the informed and concerned citizen and statesman make of all this? How will prosperity and unemployment be affected? What should Wall Street be watching for?

What Matters

To help think about these important questions, let me first clear the deck of unimportant issues. Gold is one such. Whether its price soars, whether South Africa's political scene turns unstable—these are vital matters only to someone sweating out a bull position in gold.

Adam Smith and Charles de Gaulle are dead. No knowledgeable observer would bet on the world's going back to the gold standard, or even to the modified parities of the Bretton Woods era. Gyrations in gold's price are today *symptoms* of happenings in finance, not causes.

Secretary of the Treasury Michael Blumenthal is correct, if overfrank, in tolerating downward floating of the dollar. Our recovery exceeds those of Germany and Japan. U.S. and world harvests are fairly bountiful, and we price energy so as to use up Mideastern reserves rather than our own. Economic law therefore supports appreciation of the mark and yen.

When Germany and Japan wake up, as they are likely to do now that their societies are paying a terrible price for their slack economies, our export balance will improve. A futile attempt to puff up the dollar will merely squander reserves, increase steelworker unemployment and put off the approach to equilibrium.

We should ration prudently our limited capacity for worrying. Let us save our worrying for better causes than the floatings of the dollar.

DOLLAR ESSENTIALS

January 23, 1978

THERE is a widespread impression that the dollar is in trouble, and that this weakness of our exchange rate betokens something very rotten—not in Denmark, but here in the U.S.

Although widespread impressions can be very wrong, sometimes they do turn out to be right. Therefore, I should like to review in depth the case for reasonable men to worry about weakness in our floating dollar.

Should we be doing something about this weakness? Intervene massively to support the dollar by selling the mark, yen, pound and other foreign currencies?

Should Arthur Burns's successor at the Fed, G. William Miller, go all out in a crusade against inflation? Stop resisting rises in interest rates? And even engineer some further rises? Should the Carter people scale down their growth targets for 1978?

Have we been wrong in urging upon Germany and Japan actions to invigorate their recoveries? Rather, should it be we who ought to be heeding urgings to run the U.S. economy in the German mode of sluggishness? Does prevention of runaway inflation and preservation of U.S. prosperity depend on this about-face?

Recognizing (1) that the U.S. has special responsibilities in the free world and (2) that the dollar is a *key currency* for international transactions and for holding, should we be ready to sacrifice, if necessary, some economic well-being in order to help the world order?

History's Lessons

I believe that careful analysis of the facts and likelihoods will justify a negative rather than a positive answer to each of these provocative questions. Here are the reasons:

First, the policy of "clean floating" ("benign" or "malign" neglect by government) is not a Democratic policy nor a Jimmy Carter or Michael Blumenthal innovation. It is the policy originated and insisted upon by Richard Nixon's Secretary of Treasury, George Shultz. It is also the policy favored by 80 out of 100 economic scholars, ranging from Milton Friedman to Walter Heller. Experience over the last two years with fluctuating exchange rates has not caused them to recant in favor of rate pegging.

Second, it is a naïve misreading of history to equate "national greatness" with a "strong currency." When Churchill in 1925 put the pound at the pre-1914 parity, he did not restore Britannia's rule; instead he put another nail in its coffin, as far as relative real GNP was concerned. When France clung to gold in the years preceding 1939, both its economy and society paid a horrible price. And for what? For nothing that historians have ever been able to discover.

Third, as the last few weeks have confirmed, merely having Carter announce that America would intervene, and having the Fed do so, cannot dispose of the problem. Our imports over the next few years may well exceed our exports by more than foreigners will be wanting to invest here, even when there is no threat of dollar depreciation. If so, it is a King Canute stupidity to try to peg the dollar at an unrealistic height.

Present Dangers

The gnomes of Europe are not so naïve as to be unaware of this. Now they are unveiling the next step that all along they have wanted of the U.S.—namely, that we impose the higher interest rates, the anti-inflation slowdown policies and all the measures that countries crucified on the historic gold standard were supposed to take to "defend their currency." What tyrannies and stupidities have been committed in the name of that cause!

President Carter has been trying to reap some benefit from the general panic associated with the dollar's weakness. To get the electorate to do something soon about our profligate use of energy, he is saying, in effect:

"Do you want a better stock market? A stronger dollar? Lower prices for world staples? Do you want to avert a money crunch brought about by desperate Federal Reserve measures to defend the dollar? Then pass my energy program." Fair enough, if the gambit works. But let's not succumb to our own hysteria.

To bankers, I say, have some confidence in the free market.

To the Fed, counterspeculate to support the dollar only when that will earn rather than cost you money. To the country, I say, there is no need to engineer a recession just to achieve the vainglory of a pegged dollar parity.

IN DEFENSE OF FLOATING

March 27, 1978

ONE of the world's leading economists recently penned these sad words: "Why do I so often want to cry at what public figures, the press, and television commentators say about economic affairs?"

I suggest that the abysmal ignorance that Robert Solow complained of reaches its height—or depth—in connection with the so-called dollar crisis. Here is some evidence:

President Jimmy Carter opined in a press conference recently that, after giving the matter some study, he could assure the world that the dollar's drop had been overdone.

What does a President know about how to appraise fundamental equilibrium values? President Herbert Hoover asserted that the 1929 crash had pushed stocks down to below their intrinsic worth. He believed what he was saying, just as every President since 1940 has been sincere in urging people to put their savings in so rash a form as U.S. Savings Bonds.

To be sure, Mr. Carter has strong reinforcements. Chairman David Rockefeller of the Chase bank has asserted that U.S. policy actions must be taken to offset effectively the psychological forces of speculation that have made the dollar float downward. Robert V. Roosa, of Brown Brothers, Harriman but formerly Under Secretary of Treasury in charge of foreign finance, like Dr. Rockefeller, has excellent training in economics. Dr. Roosa hailed the January announcement of America's intervention to stabilize the dollar as a move to save us and the world from the perils of "a disorderly encounter of a new kind."

An Open Case

Most journalists write as if it were established that the regimen of free floating has been something of a disaster, except for speculators. I can assure the reader that a poll of the juries of experts in the analysis of international trade will elicit few verdicts that the system would be better off today if the dollar had somehow been pegged at last year's higher parity vis-à-vis the Deutsche mark, yen or Swiss franc.

So what is all the wailing about? Had Chancellor Schmidt and Prime Minister Fukuda been given their way by President Carter and Treasury Secretary Michael Blumenthal, the U.S. interventions to stabilize the dollar would have left us tens of billions poorer today and we'd be having a 1978 crisis of sharp parity readjustments.

To back up our dubious interventions, the Fed would have had to clamp down on the money supply, numbing the forces of recovery in building and private investment. Production would presumably be lower than it now is. (Although profits would be lower, some Wall Streeters think that share prices would get a lift from any strengthening of the dollar.)

And there would be another consequence of any intervention to dirty up the float of the dollar: the unemployment rate might now be moving to 7 rather than to 6 per cent.

Cui Bono?

And for what purpose would these costs of restriction have been incurred? To have achieved a better control over inflation? Studies by Prof. Rudiger Dornbusch of MIT estimate that the price level today would be less than 1 per cent below actual levels; perhaps by 1980 there would be another 1 per cent abatement in the price index. This is not an appetizing choice for voters.

Would the Germans and Swiss be better off if we listened to their advice? Let's think the matter through.

Curtailing U.S. imports might be all the anemic world recovery needs to bring it to a halt. Canada, Mexico and the other developing countries would be hardest hit. Western Europe would not escape the blow.

It is not my position that governments should never intervene in foreign-exchange markets. Liberty and personal freedoms do not expire when floats get dirty. In practice, most interventions are stupid attempts to defend the indefensible, setups for canny speculators.

My point is that *the case is not clear that the dollar has become fundamentally undervalued.* And, as any chart will show, exchange markets have been *less* disorderly and volatile this year than they were in 1973.

If Germany and Japan grow faster, if a U.S. energy program limits our oil imports, the dollar may later float upward. That would be no proof that it is now unduly low.

Please, more thinking and fact-finding, less hand wringing.

INTERNATIONAL FINANCE

October 2, 1978

Lord Keynes used to say there are two opinions in economics, *public* opinion and *inside* opinion.

Being an old Etonian and intellectual snob from Cambridge University, Keynes naturally had a low appraisal of uninformed general opinion in comparison with the views and knowledge of the inner circle of government officials, Establishment bankers and economic experts.

Today it is different. Inside opinion is split on the state of the dollar. Poll bankers and foreign-government officials. I think you will learn their views resemble the following:

1. The decline in the dollar exchange rate relative to the German mark, the Japanese yen and the Swiss franc is a disaster.

2. President Carter, Treasury Secretary Michael Blumenthal and Under Secretary of State Richard N. Cooper must bear the blame for unwillingness to intervene to support the dollar. The needed stitch in time was not provided. The U.S. should still do what it failed to do earlier, even though the recommended intervention will now be more costly.

3. The background cause of the dollar's weakness is America's profligate fiscal and monetary policy. The post-1975 recovery, on which we pride ourselves, has been too much of a good thing; it betokens a disregard for the problem of inflation, with ominous consequences still to come. Congressional vacillation on energy only compounds the felonies.

Economists' Vision

By contrast, take a poll of 5,000 U.S. economists gathered at a convention. Or better, sample views of the 1,000 who specialize in international finance and macroeconomics. Three-quarters would hold the following quite different opinions (and, I believe, a similar poll of economists in Western Europe would produce a bare majority who would also concur):

1. If the dollar floats downward (or upward, for that matter), that is a good or bad thing depending upon whether it represents a movement *toward* or *away from* equilibrium.

2. The great advantage of getting away from the shackles of pegged exchange rates, à la the old Bretton Woods regime or the limping gold standard, is that it permits each country to pursue its own economic objectives. Thus, if the Germans insist on fighting inflation at the cost of short-run stagnation, that is their privilege under flexible exchange rates. Then, as U.S. output grows relative to theirs, the mark should rise and the dollar fall. If Japan's low costs let it develop a huge export surplus, the proper cure is for the dollar to fall until our import surplus is brought down to a tolerable level.

3. There is still need for economic discipline. A nation should tax and spend publicly only that fraction of its GNP that it deems philosophically worthwhile, on a democratic cost-benefit analysis of the importance of burden sharing and meeting social needs as against private dispositions of market incomes. It must still decide on how to determine short-term compromises between the goals of price stability and employment opportunity. The point is that these basic decisions become primarily *domestic* matters once a flexible exchange-rate regime gives each country its maximum freedom and autonomy—a freedom to enjoy or to abuse.

Current Policy

The annual meeting of the International Monetary Fund and World Bank, now taking place in Washington, is a forum in which the above contrasting views will be debated both publicly and in the hotel corridors. Somehow a unified insiders' consensus will have to emerge.

There are yet few signs that the U.S. trade deficit is on its way toward being permanently reversed. I must therefore warn against the tempting assumption that the dollar has already dropped so much that it can be safely assumed now to be an undervalued currency. Agnosticism is still in order. One must counsel Carter against premature agreement to peg the dollar by massive interventions and binding guarantees.

Chairman G. William Miller of the Federal Reserve Board is aware that the U.S. recovery could turn into a 1979 mini-recession. I trust that he and his Fed colleagues will not yield to Continental bankers' demands that we deliberately court a recession to fight inflation and defend existing dollar parities. Such stop-go policy invites populist reaction later as the 1980 election looms near.

WHO NEEDS A 'NEW ORDER'?

October 13, 1980

LAST week's joint annual meeting of the International Monetary Fund and World Bank in Washington was rated above the average for such affairs. But once again the hopes of those who seek desperately for "a new international order" came to nought.

We are used to disappointments in today's imperfect world. But should an economist regret that nothing resulted in the way of fundamental reform of the post–Bretton Woods system of international finance? I think not, and in saying this, I believe I speak for the vast majority of American economists regardless of political persuasion.

Before discussing the issues, let me salute the eloquent valedictory address of Robert S. McNamara, who is about to step down as head of the World Bank after thirteen years of service. His emphasis on an activist policy in attacking global poverty touched even that hard-boiled audience of bankers and financiers, and clearly overshadowed President Carter's lackluster speech that followed.

Gold

Early in the Presidential campaign, candidate Reagan was known to have some interest in putting America back on the gold standard. It was rumored that Prof. Arthur Laffer was one of Reagan's advisers. Aside from originating the "Laffer curve," which provides the economic rationale for the Kemp-Roth tax cuts and promises that these will result in so much business activity that no revenue will be lost, Professor Laffer is known to favor fixed exchange rates based on gold. He has been a public critic of the Nixon policies of floating exchange rates first engineered by former Treasury Secretary George Shultz, Laffer's old mentor.

The rise in the price of gold in mid-September was fed by rumors. One was the report that some important Mideast OPEC powers would be putting pressure on the IMF to give gold a more prominent role in the international monetary system—and that, if the IMF balked, those OPEC powers would unilaterally add to their own gold reserves. So far no such thing has happened.

It must be a further disappointment to the gold bulls that Ronald Reagan is perceived to be moving toward Alan Greenspan and George Shultz as economic advisers and away from such purveyors of supply-side snake oil as Arthur Laffer. Gold's price has dropped below its recent high despite the unsettled Iraq-Iran conflict. Its very gyrations in the futures markets belie the notion that monetary stability can be found in that direction.

Since there are absolutely no signs that the world is about to go back to the *disciplines* of the pre-1914 gold standard, the whole notion of a new international order is more a slogan than a definite concept. To the developing nations it means commodity-cartel arrangements to improve their terms of trade vis-à-vis the advanced countries. That is hardly what the French and other supporters of stable exchange rates have in mind.

Pipe Dreams

I think the only real issue is between the present regime of floating exchange rates and the alternative regime of strong government interventions to minimize exchange-rate fluctuations. In short, the choice is between the present system and the old Bretton Woods system that collapsed in 1971.

To decide on such a choice, we need to call on economic principle and historical experience. In my interpretation, both argue strongly against the wisdom or feasibility of pegged rates.

The gold standard, it should be recalled, had a short life. In every crisis it broke down.

That's ancient history. What about the more recent evidence?

The Bretton Woods system was doomed, incapable of being saved and not worth saving. From 1959 on, the dollar had become hopelessly overvalued, a sitting pigeon for cool speculators. When the house of cards finally collapsed, it was a welcome relief.

The present system is not chaos. It works. Thank providence that in an era that has included an eightfold increase in the real price of OPEC oil, with its implied recycling of hundreds of billions of dollars of international reserves, we have had exchange-rate flexibility.

No one need know how the mark, yen and dollar should be valued when next fall's IMF–World Bank meeting comes around. That is a blessing, since in fact no one does.

WHAT'S HAPPENING TO THE AFFLUENT STATE?
September, 1971

THIRTY years ago, when the Carnegie Foundation wished to commission a study on the race problem in America, it picked Gunnar Myrdal from Sweden precisely for the reason that he was unencumbered by previous knowledge of the subject. By this criterion, I am well qualified to speculate on the future of Scandinavian society, for mine is only a superficial acquaintance with the deep currents of modern life in those countries.

A knowledge of current trends in American society may, perhaps, make up in part for this deficiency. For I have long insisted that much of what is called the "Americanization of Europe" is merely a reflection of the fact that we reached affluence earliest, and what one nation will want to do at a high level of income turns out to be very much like what another nation will come to want to do in the same circumstance. Finally, it was an advantage to de Tocqueville that he came to America with the eye of a stranger. By contrast with his European preconceptions, he could discern the new features of the developing American society.

In 1950, Sweden was a middle-class society. That old and somewhat misleading expression "the middle way" was intended to describe the Scandivanian blend between capitalism and socialism, but the pun on the word "middle" is suggestive in its class connotation. Not only had the aristocracy come to count for nothing, except on the shrinking society pages, but in addition most of the working class had, in effect, moved up into the middle classes. In this, Sweden was approaching the state that had long prevailed in America, where almost everyone tells Dr. Gallup that he belongs to the middle class. This pattern contrasts, I think, with that in England, where Disraeli's "two nations" still has a reality today. Accent and school background combine with a genuine feeling on the part of the working classes that it is unamiable for an able young chap to go to night school and better himself and be upwardly mobile, in a way that seems odd to any American observer.

Although both America and Sweden were until recently middle-class, I think it fair to say that in Sweden to be middle-class meant to be a member of the bourgeoisie. To be bourgeois, perhaps, means more than to be in a certain income bracket and percentile of the income distribution. It means to have the customs and unconscious preconceptions of the kind of family written about in Thomas Mann's autobiographical novel *Buddenbrooks*. The characters one views on the stage of Ibsen and Strindberg represent that class in its tensions, guilts and hypocrisies; in a larger sense, the great age of the nineteenth-century novel outside of Russia, from Jane Austen to George Eliot, Stendahl to Balzac and Flaubert, reflect the *mores* of that society. To understand the distinction between the bourgeoisie and the mere middle classes, the American example is instructive. Ours has long been a plutocracy. Where money counts, entrance into the elite is quick and turnover is high. The example, which I take from my wife's family, of a genteel spinster who lives frugally on an inheritance so that it can be passed on intact, would be a commonplace in Europe, but within America a rarity outside New England or the Old South.

Acids of Modern Life

When I describe Sweden as having been a bourgeoisie in 1950, this dating is emphasized to pinpoint the fact that the acids of modern life have been undermining the bone and cartilage of the bourgeois *Weltanschauung.* A visitor to Stockholm is struck by this process. More than in any other Scandinavian country, he expects to encounter in Sweden formality of manners—the bow, the handshake, the *skal,* the speech of welcome and of thanks for the food, the flowers and candy and thanks for the hostess. Only in Japan does he meet so elaborate an etiquette. But, and this is my point, at each five-year interval the visitor notes a further decay in the protocol, or at least in the seriousness with which it is obeyed. During the last Nobel week in Stockholm, I heard not a single speech of welcome in which my host did not excuse himself in words such as these: "Earlier at this point it would have been customary for me to make a speech, but that is no longer necessary." Nevertheless, plainly contradicting himself, he would proceed to extend a cordial welcome.

This decline of the bourgeoisie, which one sees going on all over the world, seems to me to be ultimately traceable to two related causes. First, there is affluence itself. When a Belgian of my acquaintance came out of a Nazi occupational prison and vowed to have ten children, his father was aghast: "You are dissipating the thrift of more than a century in one generation." In an affluent society thrift is no longer a necessity to keep from falling into the abyss of poverty.

The second cause contributing to the erosion of middle-class values seems to be higher education. The song after World War I went, "How're yer gonna keep 'em down on the farm, after they've seen Paree?" And how, I ask, can you keep them happy making and selling soap in Cincinnati or Gothenburg after they've been to Yale or Uppsala?

Take only the ancient questions of Swedish neutrality. Twenty years ago that had a clear and palpable meaning. A country which last saw war in the Napoleonic epoch was reluctant to become embroiled even in good causes. How different things are now. Nor, I believe, is this merely a reflection of the revulsion occasioned by the Vietnam war, bad as that war is. In an earlier age, sensitive consciences would also have disapproved strongly of the British campaigns against the Boers or Hitler's acts against minorities. But disapproval would have been a matter of private conscience and not been permitted to become an issue of national politics.

The generation gap highlights these changes. Youth culture tends to foreshadow general culture, not merely because young people grow up, but also because people when young have less of a vested interest in previous patterns of society. Let me illustrate the changes that seem to be going on by a personal anecdote. Last December, the publisher of the Swedish translation of my economics textbook gave a nice lunch for me. I asked him, "Why did you bother to prepare a Swedish translation? All educated Swedes know English." He replied, "Our students are losing their English. They are better than early generations when it comes to the speaking vocabulary needed to travel abroad. But where grammar and subtler vocabulary are involved, there is a falling off in their mastery of the language because they are no longer drilled at school in the way they used to be."

I found this incredible, yet when I asked around for corroboration, I was assured that this was indeed so and that the very translation of a basic text like mine would contribute further to the process. Still, I could not feel satisfied with the answers until one person gave me the clue to the puzzle. "Actually, no one likes to study for exams in a text outside his native language. I didn't like it in my time, nor did my father before me. But, today, what students don't want to do, they don't have to do."

The Berkeley Disease

The Berkeley disease, which is the Cambridge or Paris or Buenos Aires disease, travels everywhere. Anyone who remembers the respectful, but silent, members of a Scandinavian economics seminar must welcome the change. But without question, all this is undermining to the established way of doing things. Nor is the end in sight. Although many of those who participate in the new forms of youth culture when they are 23 will, by the time they are 33, fit into the suburban mold of business and professional life, it is naïve to think that the next generation of middle-aged people can ever be the same as their fathers and grandfathers.

When acid eats in, where will the process end? What will remain? I do not think there is any way of predicting the answers. As the Russians are learning, once you permit a loosening of the structure of society, there is no telling how far it will go. The post-Victorians long since learned this same lesson.

The present age, it seems to me, is quite comparable to that of the early nineteenth century. Edmund Burke deplored the passing of the feudal order. To Jeremy Bentham and the other utilitarians, no custom in England was sacrosanct. Why, they asked, does yon woman hang for stealing a handkerchief when this countess can with impunity enclose the common lands of a whole region? The established modes of law and life could not stand up under such a scrutiny.

Today, the same fundamental questioning is under way. It is not merely that people ask, why is U.S. Steel permitted to pollute the Great Lakes? External effects that go beyond the corporation itself have always been open to regulation and zoning. Now, the *Yale Law Review* can seriously propose that General Motors no longer be permitted to introduce annual style changes in its automobiles, even though such practices are conducive to its long-run profit and similar policies are available to its few large rivals. Literally nothing is sacrosanct. Any day Ralph Nader may come knocking at your door. Not only does he bring the force of public opinion to bear against the corporation for doing what corporations have traditionally felt was at their own discretion. The force of law follows hard upon the heels of public opinion. The public needs the protection of an ombudsman; the harried chairman of the board is learning that he needs on his personal staff a representative of the new culture to give him advance warning of the direction from which the next tornado may blow.

Special Significance

If I am at all near the mark in these speculations, they may have a special significance for Scandinavian society. The United States is so affluent, so endowed with varied natural resources, that our rate of material progress can taper off without revolutionary consequences. We shall merely advance a little slower toward even greater affluence.

Perhaps the same will be true of Sweden. Continuing to grow no less slowly than her peer, the United States, she may find her lead being reduced in comparison with Japan or Italy or West Germany. She can comfort herself with the consideration that they, too, in their turn, will begin to succumb to the blandishments of affluence. But perhaps this complacent prospect does not truly apply to a small country, not blessed with a wide spectrum of natural resources, whose material pre-eminence was attributable to her ingenuity and puritan-ethic diligence.

After my last visit to Sweden, I wrote in *Newsweek* and elsewhere that there was something of a miracle involved in the Swedish welfare state. It was almost too good to be true to find a society in which egalitarianism in legislation coexisted with zealous productivity, piece rates and other incentive mechanisms. Minute regulation of business life by a strong state coexisted with jealous preservation of personal liberties, civil rights and democratic checks and balances on government by an alert electorate.

Events since then, such as the strikes and revolts of the professional and white-collar classes, suggest that it may indeed have been too good to be true, and that in the future the Scandinavian consensus will wear thin. Whether that will be good or bad for Sweden I am unable to say. But I know it will be a sad thing for the world which looks toward the Scandinavian pattern. I think of a sensitive critic of the present order like Prof. Joan Robinson of Cambridge University. Alienated from her own society, too-long hopeful that the Stalinist bureaucracies of Eastern Europe would soften, Mrs. Robinson has turned her eyes toward China and North Korea. In all of her many writings, I do not recall any evaluation of the Scandinavian alternative, an alternative that is ever-present in the minds of American economists of my generation.

The word "socialism" means nothing to them. Nasser and Nkrumah labeled socialism on their banners; but good intentions concerning planning do not bring chickens into every pot. If the balancing act by which Sweden is able to generate rapid technological advance within a framework of social redistribution gives out, what abyss lies below? The shadow on the wall for all of us, I fear, is not the totalitarian revolution of a Lenin or Mao. It is not a relapse into the laissez faire of Queen Victoria or President Coolidge. Argentina, I dare to suggest, is the pattern which no modern man may face without crossing himself and saying, "There but for the Grace of God . . ."

In 1945, no competent economist could have predicted that countries like Argentina or Chile would fail to grow mightily in the next quarter of a century. With temperate climates, they stood at the takeoff point for rapid advance. Yet, even before correction for burgeoning population numbers, their rate of real GNP growth has been almost negligible. How was this miracle contrived? The time has long passed when we can continue to blame Argentinian stagnation on Perón. Uruguay, the one-time Switzerland of Latin America, had no dictator. Yet it managed to escape economic growth.

Why? I suspect the answer has to be found in populist democracy. If in the time of England's Industrial Revolution men had had the political power to try to rectify within a generation the unconscionable inequities of life, in which a privileged few live well off the sweat of the multitude, it is doubtful that the industrial revolution could ever have continued. The outcome would not have been a rational, planned economy with a Professor Tinbergen or Frisch at the helm. The outcome would have been legislated increases in money wages of as much as 40 per cent per year. The outcome might well have been pretty much like that we have seen in those Latin American countries which have reached the brink of economic development while, so to speak, fully or overly developed in the political sphere.

The Schumpeter Prophecy

Rome was not built in a day. Rome did not decline in a day. I see no realistic danger that Sweden or Canada or the United States will this year, or in the next decade, revert to the stagnation of Latin America. But it may well be that the wise social observer, 30 years from now looking back toward our time, will have discerned the beginning of the process I describe. Thirty years ago, my old teacher Joseph Schumpeter, in his *Socialism, Capitalism and Democracy*, predicted that the very successes of the mixed economy would produce alienation in its young. He was wrong in his timing, so very wrong. But who can walk the streets of Princeton or Stockholm or Toronto and deny his prescience?

JAPAN REVISITED

November 15, 1971

VISITING Japan for the first time in a dozen years is an overpowering experience, particularly at this time of crisis in Japanese-American relations.

To paraphrase Lincoln Steffens, "I have seen the *past.* And it worked!" The miracle of Japan's growth needs no retelling. The mills of the gods grind exceeding fast when they grind at 10 per cent interest.

Japan is now the No. 3 economy of the world. Undoubtedly she will pass the Soviet Union in this century. By 2000 her per capita GNP may outstrip ours just as we outstripped Britain, the 1800 champ.

What we call the NEP, the Japanese call the "Nixon shock." Business surveys show a swing to fear of recession more violent than I have ever seen before.

Such despair, I think excessive. Once the yen has been appreciated 15 per cent vis-à-vis the dollar, Japan's more efficient exporters will be able to hold their share of world markets. That is, they'll be able to compete *if* given a fair chance and not made special targets of import quotas.

A Coolidge World

Being in Japan led me back to my childhood world of the 1920s. Here is a democracy where the trains run on time; a society where *the people* run on time—run, not walk.

Japanese and German citizens, led to disastrous military defeats by leaders seeking glory, came out of the war sick of the state and politics. An able young Japanese no longer dreams of going into the foreign service or army. Like the

Yale graduates of 1925 he wants to cultivate his garden, that is, make his pile. His wife wants the three C's—car, color TV, air conditioning. And she is getting them. Even the peasants are prosperous. It shows what providence and 10 per cent growth can do for a poor country!

Perhaps Keynes was right when he said that it is better for a man to tyrannize over his pocketbook than tyrannize over his neighbor. A man from Mars—make it Venus—who knew no history of wars or bigotry, might well rank Germany and Japan as the two most *decent* societies of the postwar world.

The question is, can the rest of the world afford Japanese growth? And can the Japanese afford to grow in this next decade according to the pattern they have maintained in the past?

Let me begin with Japan's problem.

> *Ill fares the land,*
> *to hastening ills a prey*
> *Where wealth accumulates,*
> *and men decay.*

Tokyo is a mess. Only the Japanese could live in it. New Yorkers would bring it to a big bang in a month. The world's largest city, it may be the most polluted and congested.

And this is only typical of the neglect in social-overhead capital that has been going on for a generation. Man does not live by transistor radios alone. A government more interested in roads for trucks than sidewalks for people is not meeting its accruing social costs.

I must not exaggerate. Life expectancy—a test of whether prosperity reaches down to all strata of society—has improved dramatically and soon will surpass our mediocre record.

The White Peril

Still, Japan is no longer a poor Asian country. She can afford the housing she has neglected. The Nixon shock can prove a blessing if it makes her now turn inward.

Actually, Japan has little choice. According to the OECD, she is slated to grow 160 per cent in the 1970s, as against less than 60 per cent for us and the Europeans. To keep to an export-oriented boom, in which she maintains her exports at 9 per cent of the GNP, Japan's exports would have to grow three times as fast as those of the rest of us.

Is it really feasible for her to aspire to so great a further penetration of world markets, now that she is already such a significant fraction of total trade?

There is the further factor that Japanese are not given the fair share they deserve. We veer from contempt of Japanese as capable only of making shoddy Christmas-tree ornaments, to thinking of them as supermen whose costs and precision Americans and Europeans could never compete with. Ugly racism has to be fought, in the economic as well as political and social spheres.

Another time I must return to the unspeakable voluntary and mandatory quotas that President Nixon's team—notably Secretary Stans and his Assistant Secretary—are trying to impose on textiles, steel, autos and TVs. Aimed at the Japanese, the knife cuts our own throats too.

TWO SUCCESS STORIES
March 9, 1981

ONE studies pathology to learn lessons useful for good health. There is no shortage of cases that involve economic failure: Great Britain, before and after Thatcher; the Great

Leap Backward under Chairman Mao during the Cultural Revolution; closer to home, the trend toward higher inflation and higher unemployment.

One may also learn about good health by leaving the sick wards and observing attested examples of successful living. I don't say we should believe every recipe for a long life given by garrulous octogenarians. A skeptical respect for testable fact is all the more important when we are weighing claims for success.

Where does one observe economic success? Japan comes to mind. To admit the truth, Americans envy the Japanese for their ingenuity, drive, cleverness and thrift. No need to add here to what is already threatening to become myth.

Austria and Norway are less-known cases. They offer special interest at this time when Americans are weighing whether to follow President Reagan's desire to return to market capitalism.

Austria

After World War I, when the Hapsburg empire was split up, little Austria seemed a basket case. Allegedly, it was eating into its capital. Class warfare was paving the way for home-grown Fascism and the ultimate takeover by the Nazis.

Since World War II it has been quite another story. A government that is nominally Social Democratic, but which operates conservatively, has held power under Chancellor Bruno Kreisky. Year after year, even in the 1970s, real per capita GNP rises. A trip to Vienna confirms that unemployment and inflation remain minimal.

Why this success? I dismiss as facetious the explanation given me by one high official: "Austria has done so well because we exported all our economists to England and the United States."

Living in the shadow of the Soviet bloc, as Finland could

also testify in connection with its own excellent GNP progress of recent years, Austrian factions play down their differences. Thomas Carlyle would insist that we should also not underestimate the unifying role of Bruno Kreisky as an astute and well-loved leader.

Hard work and thrift are thus given scope to create their slow miracles. Although not a member of the Common Market, Austria enjoys the full advantage of trade with West Germany and the free world, at the same time that it exchanges with its Communist neighbors.

Norway

To be born a Norwegian is to inherit a life expectancy of more than 75 years, child health care and education, job opportunity in the prime years and retirement income at a standard of living close to that of your working years. Poverty, as we know it in the Bronx or West Virginia, is virtually abolished.

At the same time Norwegians can speak their mind: you can curse abortion, caricature the Prime Minister, join the Communist Party and still keep your university chair or government job. Besides, prime skiing is twenty minutes outside Oslo.

To be fair, I must acknowledge that the Norwegian society is a remarkably homogeneous one. If its population were as diverse as ours, its veneer of tolerance and consensus would be severely tested.

But what about North Sea oil? You can't speak of Norwegian affluence and progress without giving oil a pivotal role. And there is more oil still to be found.

Norwegian Challenges

What counts is how a society uses its opportunities. Britain has much North Sea oil. So far that has given it a strong pound. And it is said to provide breathing space. Breathing space for what? For Margaret Thatcher's fairy wand to re-create the incentives of the Manchester marketplace of 1850 and the supply-side miracles entailed thereby?

Or, as in the case of Dutch North Sea gas, will the Norwegian royalties go to underwrite expanded government welfare programs? Can they learn from Saudi Arabia and Iran, who let oil create gold-rush-style inflations at home—with instant millionaires and erosion of social stability?

Norwegians now debate these issues. David Stockman and Jack Kemp might counsel the Norwegian Government to get out of the oil business; to give each citizen ownership certificates in the oil finds, and let the market work out the result. The Norwegian people might then hate themselves when they wake up in the morning with a headache, but what's freedom for?

I doubt this view will sell in Oslo.